AUSTRALIAN
WOMEN
PILOTS

KATHY MEXTED is a writer, photographer and editor. Inspired by her father, she learnt to fly in 1991, before she became a writer. Now she writes more than she flies, though her eyes and mind are usually turned skywards. She grew up in Finley, New South Wales, and currently lives with her family on 40 hectares in central Victoria. This is her first book.

Praise for *Australian Women Pilots*

'I grew up in the same town as Kathy and woke to the same agricultural aeroplanes flying overhead. It was a definitive sound that led me to a lifelong fascination with aeroplanes. Kathy was the only female pilot I knew. Likewise, when I moved to Melbourne and we formed Spiderbait, I was the only female bass player I knew. My role models were Kim Deal and Suzi Quatro, but my all-time favourite was Tina Weymouth from Talking Heads. Like most of these pilots, I also inhabited a man's world, was often away from home, working mostly with men, and figuring out how I fitted into it all. In my 30-year music career I've had many girls approach me to tell me that they picked up a bass after seeing me play. It is important to have role models and I hope that by reading this book, young women will see what they can be.'

Janet English, bass guitarist with Spiderbait

'When Kathy asked me to read and review her book Australian Women Pilots I was immediately interested. I am not one to get on a bandwagon about sexism and discrimination, but I have heard people discuss the merits of singling out women pilots versus pilots in general. To those people, I explain that I have attended a number of Australian Women Pilots' Association functions, been the guest speaker at a number of them, and am also very proud of the women pilots I employ and have trained in the military. When asked why I celebrate the achievements of women rather than just pilots, it is because women pilots have been a minority group through the 20th century. Minority groups need to be celebrated, and written about, and encouraged to grow, so they can grow out of the 'minority' status. Otherwise, there is the risk they will fade away into history as the 'once there was' group, without the passion being passed from generation to generation to continue to build, or never be given opportunities that they are more than capable of handling.

Kathy's book is a tribute to those women pilots who trailblazed their way into our history books but are rarely talked about. Everyone can rattle off famous aviators in Australia, though most of them are male pilots. That is fine, as the majority were in fact male pilots due to the reasons already mentioned. But there are a lot of courageous stories of women battling against the odds, battling against discrimination, battling against nature to achieve dreams beyond what was considered achievable. From Kathy's own stories of growing up flying with her father, learning the love of aviation and gaining her own licence, to the much talked about Nancy Bird Walton, Lyn Gray and Georgia Maxwell just to name a few, dreaming and courage is always at the forefront.

I hope you enjoy reading these stories, and supporting the growing number of women pilots within our country, as much as I do. Pass this book onto a young woman, who has a dream, and inspire her to take action in whatever direction she chooses … who knows where she can end up.'

Matt Hall, former RAAF Fighter Combat (Top Gun) Instructor and 2019 Red Bull Air Race World Champion

To Mum and Aunty June
The best of friends
Who cheered us on
How I wish you were here for this

To Dad
Who because he loved flying
I could be what I could see

To Denis
They always said
'Whoever he marries will have to like aeroplanes'
Thanks for choosing me

To the beautiful young women we are raising
Kate, my wonderful travel companion
Never lose that spark
Amelia, your perseverance and quiet determination inspire us
You will make a great pilot if that's where you continue

And to our No 1 son, Harrison
You set your goal and
got your wings today
We are so proud of your integrity and dedication

AUSTRALIAN WOMEN PILOTS

AMAZING TRUE STORIES OF WOMEN IN THE AIR

KATHY MEXTED

NEWSOUTH

A NewSouth book

Published by
NewSouth Publishing
University of New South Wales Press Ltd
University of New South Wales
Sydney NSW 2052
AUSTRALIA
newsouthpublishing.com

© Kathy Mexted
First published 2020

10 9 8 7 6 5 4 3 2 1

This book is copyright. Apart from any fair dealing for the purpose of private study, research, criticism or review, as permitted under the *Copyright Act*, no part of this book may be reproduced by any process without written permission. Inquiries should be addressed to the publisher.

A catalogue record for this book is available from the National Library of Australia

ISBN: 9781742236971 (paperback)
9781742245065 (ebook)
9781742249582 (ePDF)

Internal design Josephine Pajor-Markus
Cover design Nada Backovic
Cover images Nancy Bird in a Gipsy Moth wearing her leather flying helmet, goggles and fur-lined gloves, Kingsford Smith Flying School, 1933 (State Library of NSW, photographer unknown); Mardi Gething in 1943 in one of the many military aircraft she flew as a ferry pilot while in the Air Transport Auxiliary (Mardi Gething, personal photograph collection); Georgia Maxwell on the wing of an AT-802 firebomber (*The Daily Telegraph*, Nicola Gibson)

All reasonable efforts were taken to obtain permission to use copyright material reproduced in this book, but in some cases copyright could not be traced. The author welcomes information in this regard.

CONTENTS

INTRODUCTION		ix
1	**NANCY BIRD WALTON:** A young pioneer	1
2	**MARDI GETHING:** World War II ATA ferry pilot	27
3	**PATRICIA TOOLE:** Down in the New Guinea jungle	43
4	**GABY KENNARD:** Around the world solo	70
5	**MARION McCALL:** Dawn to Dusk with the bishop	98
6	**LYN GRAY:** Ferry pilot with a wet footprint	123
7	**DEBORAH LAWRIE (WARDLEY):** In court with Ansett	147
8	**GEORGIA MAXWELL:** Aerial application and firebombing	177
9	**NICOLE FORRESTER:** From Akubra to flight helmet	201
10	**ESTHER VELDSTRA:** Pilot for the Royal Flying Doctor Service	220
SOURCES		242
A NOTE ON THE ILLUSTRATIONS		247
ACKNOWLEDGEMENTS		249

INTRODUCTION

It was a perfect spring day in 1978 and, being the fifth of eight kids, it was a rare privilege to be alone with Dad. I was 16 and we were heading east above the road to Berrigan from our home at Finley (population 2300), in the southern Riverina of New South Wales. Sitting side by side in his much-loved Piper Archer VH-MAU, a four-seat American aluminium aeroplane, there was comfort in our silence. He, a farmer and auctioneer, studied his neighbours' paddocks gliding by either side of the Riverina Highway and the Mulwala Canal, around 1500 feet below us.

The plane was brand new and Dad loved flying it as much as his five mates who co-owned it. They called themselves The Finley Flying Group, and the white aeroplane together with its corrugated iron hangar were their sole assets.

The Archer sat proud and central on the dirt floor of the hangar that bore a welcoming FINLEY in large red letters on its roof, like a salve for lost souls. The southern wall had black marks and a shining repair patch where a visitor's refuelling mishap had sent exploding drums of avgas sky high, lighting the place up like cracker night.

The sliding doors were hard to drag and their rattle echoed loudly in the silence. Once cracked open, a single shaft of light illuminated the red and gold stripes of the aeroplane and woke up the red-back spiders. I'd like to say that they scurried, but they clung to the corrugations, in the dark recesses near where my flat palms pushed the doors open. They were still there when my nervous fingers curled around the edges to haul the doors closed, dragging them back across the gritty tracks, later in the day. The last job after every flight was to bolt the doors, then sign the book and hide the key.

Screeching cockatoos perched high in the sugar gums bookended the days and occasionally a rogue sheep escaped the neighbour's paddock to wander up the runway. I always feared disturbing a snake in the dry grass, or worse, somewhere in the aeroplane.

It was a different life out there. It was usually quiet. Nowhere else in town had a windsock, nor required a fuel drain – the residual of which was carefully poured onto the capeweeds and bindi-eyes in a futile attempt to kill them.

As Dad rested his hands on his knees, I wondered what forces were keeping us in the air so straight and level. Did he realise he'd let go of the controls? I figured then that flying was either incredibly technical to be able to do that, or that it wasn't as hard as I'd imagined. Maybe I should know how to take over, just in case … It seemed irresponsible not to at least learn something. I studied the instrument panel with a new curiosity and checked our attitude against the flat, green and yellow chequered horizon.

When he came back into the moment, I asked about the inner workings of MAU. Surprisingly, he let me steer and as I leant forward, gripped by the task, we ascended, descended and banked as I tried to hold course for Berrigan. Out the side of his mouth, Dad commented, 'You're hangin' on pretty tight there.'

The next thing he said, after a while, was a surprise. 'You seem to be enjoying that [thoughtful silence]. If you'd like to learn to fly, I'll pay for it.' It was totally unexpected. I could ride a galloping horse without trepidation, but had a healthy fear of the unknown with aeroplanes. Out on the farm I was still trying to differentiate second gear from reverse in Dalgety's three-speed column-shift company car.

Soon after this, however, I went for a ride with an aerial application pilot (a crop duster or ag pilot). He put the Piper Pawnee through its paces and I thought this was the most fun you could ever

INTRODUCTION

have. Instead of being sick I was beaming and he reckoned I should be an ag pilot. 'There is another female aggy,' he said tauntingly. It was just a thought.

I'd only ever heard of two women pilots. The first and most formidable was our svelte school librarian/girls monitor, Mrs Edwards. We never discussed flying; just the woefully inadequate length of our Year 11 girls' school uniforms. But I knew she had a licence.

The other was the aspiring Ansett pilot, Deborah Lawrie (Wardley), who was a regular on the nightly news. They were giving her a hell of a time and, until the successful outcome of her court case, it seemed that women weren't welcome at the controls. Not without a fight, anyway. This only made Mrs Edwards all the more mysterious.

The careers advice given out at the local high school was an A4 sheet of paper with a long and mostly foreign list of job titles. We were told to tick the ones we liked the look of. I saw Pilot and thought, pffft. Whoever gets to do that? Later though, that one quiet comment from my father and the unorthodox introduction from the ag pilot were positive motivation.

By the time Deborah Wardley finally won her case against Ansett in 1980 I had left school, moved to Melbourne and was now responsible for my own endeavours.

Societal attitudes changed significantly between 1978 and 1990 and so had my own. When I returned to Finley in 1990, more mature after a couple of career changes and ten years away, four of them overseas, I finally packed my insecurities and a rather lean cheque book and fronted Williams Aviation at the nearby Tocumwal Airport.

John Williams, as calm an instructor as you could hope for, welcomed me warmly, acknowledged the connection with Dad and proceeded to teach me, $110 at a time, how to fly over the country that I knew at close range. From falling off my bike, falling off my horse and wrestling with lambs on the farm, that dirt was in and under my skin. And now I wanted to fly above it at 120 knots.

I'm not sure if it was enthusiasm or funds that had shifted with Dad, but he graciously allowed me to pay for the whole thing myself, though he loaned me the last $1000 I needed to hastily finish navigation training so I could move away to be with Denis, my now husband. After Dad passed away, I found my tally card, showing that the $1000 had been repaid in odd amounts with paycheques I earned at $10 per hour with dishpan hands in a guesthouse sink.

The most memorable part of learning to fly is when a pilot flies solo for the first time. It is a theme that is repeated throughout the stories in this book.

I decided that I'd just have enough lessons to see if I could go solo. John Williams said, 'If you go solo, you may as well get your licence because you'll have done the hardest bit by then.'

The solo flight came around in 13 short hours when the junior instructor got out of the plane saying: 'Taxi back to the threshold of Runway 36. Do one circuit and then stop. Then come back and get me. Don't forget to come back and get me; it's a long walk home.'

I looked north, along the almighty great white lines that ran up the centre of the bitumen runway. A grass glider strip ran parallel on my left. There was not a puff of wind and the instructor was a speck in the distance.

Tocumwal was a short-lived base for bomber and paratrooper training during World War II. After the military's departure, Tocumwal was left with a fabulous airfield on which a pair of kilometre-long, sealed cross-runways still cut the quadrants of the compass, and on the end of which I now sat in an idling two-seat Cessna 152.

How many hundreds of pilots had gone from this strip before me in bombers, gliders and powered planes? My own father in a Victa Airtourer 20 years earlier.

As if I was saying a prayer, I chanted off the pre-departure checklist, nervously wiped my palms on my thighs and took a deep breath. I gave a radio call, 'All traffic Tocumwal, Bravo Tango Foxtrot

INTRODUCTION

rolling runway 36 for a circuit,' then pushed the throttle forward, gaining speed and steering with my feet to stay on the oversized white centreline. The plane felt noticeably lighter without the instructor beside me. It was so liberating! Halfway through the take-off roll, as the airspeed indicator wound up through 50 knots, I noticed movement from my one o'clock position. A mob of kangaroos came bounding out of the paddock and across the runway in front of me. The little Cessna's nose bounced, wanting to fly, and that seemed like the perfect moment to lift off on my first solo flight. With one other woman – Annie Duff – I received my wings that year alongside 25 men.

A year later I landed 140 kilometres away in Albury on my first solo navigation flight. From the terminal, I called Mum on the public phone. She'd promised to wait for the call and when I excitedly told her, 'I'm here! I did it!' she laughed and said, 'That's great, Kath. Now see if you can get yourself home.'

I completed my navigation training on Thursday 5 November 1992. I flew 300 kilometres, from Tocumwal to Moorabbin in suburban Melbourne, across to Essendon then over Flemington racecourse, looking down on Oaks Day and the masses of people on the ground. I knew they'd be spilling champagne and walking home with their shoes in their hands. I smiled down at them and thought, 'I don't reckon you're having as much fun as I am today.'

I turned right over the Westgate Bridge, then made my way to St Arnaud, a quiet isolated airport beyond Bendigo. I landed there and shut down the aeroplane. After bouncing around in the heat with radio static squawking all the way, I hopped out and went for a walk. There were sheep! I sat down and laughed. This was all such an adventure that few could fully understand. About 20 years later, my sister Fran also learnt to fly, in the same aeroplane with the same instructor. She excitedly messaged me one night: 'You never told me this was so much fun!'

AUSTRALIAN WOMEN PILOTS

TWO DAYS AFTER MY LAST NAV FLIGHT, WILLIAMS AVIATION celebrated their ten-year anniversary and Wings Night, and John called together all the female pilots for a photo. There were nine of us present. Not quite one for every year of operation. The ratio was one or two per cent of all licence holders in Australia and the photo was remarkable enough to make the local paper. Women pilots today represent about five per cent of licence holders, as the RAAF and the airlines seek to redress the gender imbalance while training organisations actively include women in their marketing.

Around that time too, I bought a book by legendary aviator Nancy Bird Walton. The title was derived from a conversation she had had in 1936 with a customer who needed a flight. When Nancy came onto the phone, the customer exclaimed, 'My god, it's a woman!'; hence the name of her book. That's how I learnt about the Australian Women Pilots Association (AWPA).

I became a member of the AWPA in 1992 for a few years, helping with their Fear of Flying clinics in Sydney and Melbourne, where my nursing and flying experience came together nicely. I then re-joined the Association in 2016 because I was required to do a work presentation at their Annual Conference.

When 88-year-old Patricia Toole spoke at that conference about her time in New Guinea, working as a charter pilot for Gibbes Sepik Airways, I put down my glass, picked up my camera and moved to the front of the room for one of the most riveting speeches I've ever heard. The crowd cheered and stood in appreciation when she finished.

I had been thinking about putting stories together for this book for some time and was compiling a list of women to approach. Now I knew I wanted to tell Pat's story. Back at our table, I asked her if I could profile her. She was delighted and we started immediately; however, I looked forward to a lengthy engagement at her home in Brisbane three weeks later. Unfortunately, Pat passed away a week

INTRODUCTION

before I got there, and I was unusually sad to have this new friendship cut so short.

Many of us present at that conference commented that we'd been talking about Pat non-stop afterwards, and it was in that mood that I sat down to try to do justice to her story. One family member said with surprise that they'd never quite seen 'the story' in Pat's story until it was presented to them thus.

I then set about finding more women to profile; not to make any grand statements about equality or heroics (although those themes recur), but rather to shine a light on some of these wonderful Australian stories that are unknown or forgotten. I followed a rough timeline, showing a shift in attitudes and opportunities and a spread of experiences, personalities and geography.

There are, of course, many women worthy of mention and we should acknowledge the first woman in Australia to fly: Florence Taylor, an architect, who hopped in her husband's glider on a Sydney beach and took to the air in 1909. There was no licensing at that time and so the credit for the first licensed Australian woman goes to Hilda Hope McMaugh who gained her qualification in the UK in 1919 but was unable to use it back home because it was illegal for women to fly. So it was not until eight years later that a 49-year-old widowed mother of three flew into the record books as the first Australian woman to hold an Australian pilot licence. Millicent Bryant was licensed on 23 March 1927. Those who came after her proved their stoicism and faced some opposition from the men around them.

By 1929, Phyllis Arnott, of the famous biscuit family, was the first woman granted a B licence (commercial pilot licence) in Australia. Phyllis was financially independent. She didn't need to work and never used the privilege the B licence afforded her. A few years later that honour went to Nancy Bird, who actually did need the cash to pay off her aeroplanes. Nancy was the eleventh woman to receive a

B licence, but the first one to actually use it. It's a fine point that was endlessly clarified by Nancy and by her supporters ever since.

At the time of writing, the Civil Aviation Safety Authority tells me there are 31 696 licensed Australian pilots, of which 1957 are women. There are 13 241 commercial pilots. Learning to fly did not lead me to chase a commercial flying career, though had I not married, I might have. But it did give me a faith in my own abilities and opened a big new world. From the air, rainbows are not always seen simply as an arch. One day I saw a half rainbow on its side, like a capital C. One day my sister Fran saw a whole rainbow – a full circle. Once Aminta Hennessy saw a full rainbow and flew through it. We wouldn't have seen them if we'd stayed on the ground.

I want this book to inspire you to try new things and to know these stories of Australian women stepping up to the plate. And maybe if somebody offers you the controls of whatever it is, you will take the chance to grab them with both hands and hang on tight.

Thanks for reading. I hope you enjoy these stories.

1

NANCY BIRD WALTON

A YOUNG PIONEER

*Once a girl has obtained her flying licence …
she has won her wings, and no piece of paper,
current or expired, can take that away from her.*

(Nancy Bird Walton)

A newspaper article promised 'crazy flying and aeronautics' at the Wingham Air Pageant and Nancy Bird wanted a slice of it. The refreshment tent ladies were so flat out serving tea and scones to the hungry masses they wouldn't have had time to notice young Nancy's unruly auburn curls bob through the crowd and approach the well-known air show and endurance pilot Reg Annabel. Excitedly, Nancy handed over a week's wages – £1 – to pay for her first ever joy ride, and it was in Reg's sleek new open cockpit Gipsy Moth biplane. The beautiful timber and canvas craft was the sport plane of its day. Reg had just circumnavigated Australia and was now flying the Moth around on the airshow circuit.

This was September 1930 and teenage Nancy already knew she wanted to fly. Having left school when she was just 13, she went to work for her father and uncle at their store in Mount George, on the mid-north coast of New South Wales, where they also had the local cream contract. Meanwhile, her mother stayed down in Manly so the other five children could finish school.

Travelling 30 kilometres east from Mount George to Wingham, Nancy had been full of excitement as she jostled with the rattling cream cans on her dad's truck. She was three weeks shy of her fifteenth birthday and that night she lay awake dreaming of a bright future – one that most definitely involved flying.

Australian aviation was 20 years old at that time and there were only 60 aeroplanes flying in Australia. Air travel was just coming within reach for the general public. Returned Great War pilots (the few that had survived) continued to fly around the country, doing their best to eke out a living while doing what they loved. Flying.

But none of that concerned Nancy as she smoothed a supple leather flying helmet over her small head and a pair of bug-eyed goggles across her eyes to defend against insects and grass seeds blowing up from the floor after start-up. At only 157 centimetres tall, the helmet and goggles were possibly the only visible part of her from outside the aircraft.

From the pilot's seat behind her, Reg let the Gipsy Moth accelerate across the grass until it gained enough speed to roar, bouncing over the ground faster than the cream truck ever could. Deafened by engine noise, the wind whipped around their heads as they sped away, leaving a turbulent blast of spring debris in their wake.

The colourful gathering below quickly shrank to an indistinguishable mass on the edge of the large circular racecourse. The land flattened out to look like a map and Nancy's world, once so certain, was now surreal as altitude brought an entirely new perspective.

Back on the ground again, she upended her purse and immediately booked a second joy flight. This time she paid an extra 30 shillings for the pilot to do aerobatics – a couple of loops, a spin and some stall turns.

Not knowing what to expect, most passengers on a joy flight like this subconsciously reach for their chest to clutch the seatbelt for reassurance. About six minutes into the air, Reg would have levelled out at 3000 feet to perform the first loop. Purring along at 80 knots, he would have poled forward. The engine would roar and a view of the ground would fill the front windshield. It can feel like a death dive, but to Nancy it was wildly exciting. But then, applying full power, Reg would have gently levered the stick back and climbed in an arc.

As Nancy's stomach was pushed low towards her pelvis, her brain would have pushed back against her skull while the horizon disappeared below the nose of the plane. Staring at the spinning propeller and wide-open sky, only the centrifugal force would have held her in place. As Reg pushed the joystick forward slightly, in a heart-stopping moment, the world would be upside down and her stomach would now be up against her ribs. Body light on the seat, the ground would have slid into view like a roller blind from above Nancy's head as they came out the bottom of the loop and back level and ready for the second one.

Nancy was absolutely thrilled with the aerobatics. Her flying career as one of Australia's most recognisable woman pilots had just begun. Or it would. As soon as she was old enough.

AS A FIRST STEP, NANCY EQUIPPED HERSELF WITH A COPY OF Swoffer's *Learning to Fly* (first published in 1929), a dark blue book that fits neatly into the hand. Its 150 pages of text and diagrams detail the basics of flying.

The first page explains the impossibility of learning something as hands-on as flying a plane by reading about it from a book. Nothing's changed there in 80 years. But just reading the book was motivating enough for Nancy to return to Wingham in June 1933 when Charles Kingsford Smith took a rest from his record-breaking flights to come barnstorming with his flying circus.

Back then, pilots, usually in groups, often took their fragile canvas, timber and wire flying machines around the countryside, performing stunts and giving joy rides for money. The groups were called a flying circus and the popup events were known as barnstorming (an American term) because pilots would land beside the barn, which then became the venue. The spectators usually stood safely near a barn as the aeroplanes whirled overhead.

Sir Charles Edward Kingsford Smith MC AFC (1897–1935), often called Smithy, was the most famous man in Australia at the time, revered for his wartime prowess and his record-breaking flights, most notably crossing the Pacific Ocean with co-pilot and business partner Charles Ulm. They flew an incredible 11 000 kilometres in three hops of 27, 34 and 20 hours each, navigating to vital pinpoint locations in the vast Pacific Ocean. Having landed in Brisbane, 300 000 people turned out at Sydney to greet them when they arrived there. But now, five years and several records later, Smithy had parted ways with Ulm and was setting up his own aviation business at Mascot in Sydney. Kingsford Smith Aviation included flight training and maintenance.

Determined by nature and convinced she would learn to fly, in the intervening three years Nancy had purchased a leather flying jacket, a helmet and some goggles. Barnstorming at Wingham, Smithy's team watched her approach across the field in this get-up and wondered where on earth she'd come from. The stars aligned though when, with all the assurance of youth, Nancy informed Smithy of her intention to learn to fly.

Of course, he invited her to his new flying school because he was polite and she was sweet, and students bring money and Smithy needed it. He probably assumed she wouldn't show. But when the famous Charles Kingsford Smith invites you to learn to fly with him, it would be a great lost opportunity not to appear. Nancy had already decided she would become a pilot and so the timing was right.

Nine weeks later, as her seventeenth birthday approached, Nancy was ready to go and informed her father accordingly. Whether from fear or frustration, her father exploded in a fit of emotion. It did nothing to slow down his daughter.

In her three and a half years at the store, Nancy had almost saved the £200 needed for a pilot licence. Much of it was from her £1 weekly wage and it was topped up from an insurance policy her father had taken out, which matured when she turned 16. Nancy went home to her mother at Manly and for each flying lesson undertook the lengthy trip from Manly to the airfield over at Mascot. This involved a tram and a ferry and ultimately a long walk.

Smithy took Nancy for her first one or two flying lessons (there's conflicting reports and I was unable to locate her logbook) and while he was a brilliant pilot, his time was better spent building the business and pursuing more record-breaking ventures.

In *Born to Fly,* Nancy says Smithy told her, 'You know Nancy, I don't approve of women in aviation, it's not the right place for them.' However, they became good friends and he often collected her from the city, along with his office manager, and gave them a lift out to the airfield.

There was a lot to be gained just by being in his realm, and the connections she made at his hangar served her well. After her initial lessons, Smithy came and went on other, more serious ventures. Being such a natural pilot, he didn't understand the time it takes for most newcomers to learn and so he handed her over to a more patient instructor – Pat Hall, for whom she also had the utmost respect.

The following two years passed with Nancy installed either in the aeroplane learning to fly, beside the engineers in the hangar or sitting out on the grass under the buzzing aeroplanes watching, breathing in the whole spectacle and making friends. She revelled in the atmosphere, the place, the excitement of being part of the elite group of people involved with aviation. But when it came time to go it alone, she baulked.

When Pat Hall offered her the chance to do her first solo, something every student relishes and dreads in equal parts, Nancy refused to go. Had she waited and wanted it for too long? It is an instructor's job to assess the student and Hall certainly wouldn't have sent her if he didn't think she could do it.

Nancy got home and realised what she'd done, then spent a sleepless night berating herself. Shortly afterwards, however, she got back in the plane and successfully flew it around the circuit alone. Within six weeks of beginning her flying lessons, she had her A licence, which meant she could fly the aeroplane but only within sight of the airfield.

As she tried to figure out how to fit in with the men, the diminutive novice pilot later defied the norm and dispensed with frocks in favour of custom-made knickerbockers that enabled her to more easily scramble in and out of cockpits. This was an awkward and delicate exercise, which involved straddling the side wall, then lifting the right leg high and squeezing awkwardly down into the seat. There were precious few women around the small airfield, and when she gained her B (commercial) licence, Nancy was the youngest woman in the British Commonwealth to do so. By 1935 she was the eleventh Australian woman to gain a B licence. No-one could dispute her dedication to the task as she rolled up her sleeves in the hangar and undertook the engineering component, which would enable her to manage some of her own repairs and to fly for payment.

There was another woman who already had a couple of years flying experience and she and Nancy quickly became friends. Twenty-one-year-old Peg McKillop, like most other female pilots then, had a substantial private income and simply flew for fun. This put her and Nancy on completely different footings as Nancy knew that she would have to fly for income if she was to pursue her dream, so the relationship might have foundered there.

But, while Nancy's father had been none too thrilled about her departure from Mount George and subsequent career choice, he could see that she was doing well with her flying and he had a change of heart. He and a relative offered Nancy £400 and a business plan was hatched.

Nancy bought a salvaged Gipsy Moth aeroplane on the cheap and had it rebuilt. It was from the estate of Reg Annabel, the man who introduced her to flying. The daredevil pioneering aviator had performed many feats in his career, not the least of which was flying under the Sydney Harbour Bridge – a manoeuvre that was then swiftly prohibited by the authorities.

Applied boldly near the nose of the freshly silver painted Moth was its new name, *Vincere*, which means 'To Conquer' and she had that as her goal. To conquer both the air and the constant warnings she received about the lack of flying opportunities available to women. The purchase and rebuild took all of her £400.

AUSTRALIAN WOMEN PILOTS

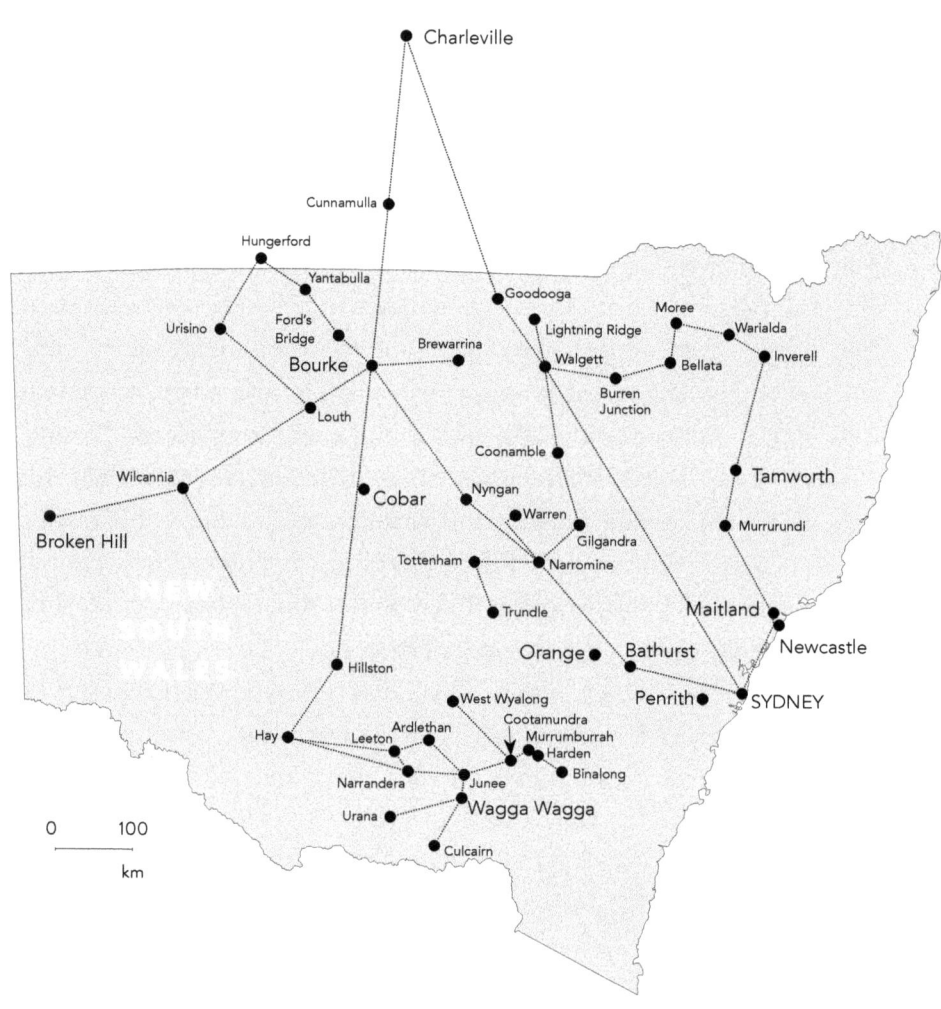

Routes of Nancy Bird Walton's barnstorming and clinic rounds

And so, operating on a wing and a prayer, 'Big Bird' (Peg's nickname, because she was tall) and 'Little Bird' (Nancy's, because she wasn't) set course in early 1935 for Tamworth – their first port of call on an eight-week barnstorming tour in NSW, during which the only thing greater than society's resistance to female pilots was the determination of the women in the plane.

They departed Sydney in the cool of autumn, with Nancy straining against the seat cushion, squinting through her goggles against the ocean's glint as she scanned the coast for Newcastle, 115 kilometres to the north.

Using only a compass for direction, a watch, and a ruler to measure distance on a rudimentary road map, Nancy had to constantly calculate her time and distance to assess her airspeed, in order to figure out her landing options. The Gipsy Moth could only manage two hours plus 45 minutes of mandatory reserve. At a speed of 80 knots, she could fly about 260 kilometres in nil wind.

The next day, from Newcastle at sea level, Nancy and Peg pushed the flimsy little canvas and timber aeroplane to its limit of 80 knots, climbing for about ten minutes until they reached 5000 feet, the lowest safe altitude for that flight as they tackled the mountains of the Great Dividing Range, which peaks at 4600 feet (1400 metres) to the west of Newcastle, before flattening out towards Tamworth on the other side. In the Moth's open cockpit, they consulted their flapping maps, with Nancy shouting through a Gosport (speaking) tube over to Peg in the front, discussing their course and anticipating their arrival in an aircraft for which brakes were not yet invented.

They arrived safely in Tamworth and were overjoyed when they got their first paying passenger. In doing so, Nancy became the first woman to operate an aircraft commercially in Australia. But rather than thinking about the record books, Nancy had a more immediate concern: paying the bills. She needed to sell those joy flights to keep herself and Peg operational. A Gipsy Moth has two seats and so a pilot could take just one passenger at a time.

The money they earned was enough to pay for the fuel and repairs, but the whole venture was really made viable because of Peg's extensive contact list of property owners and friends who hosted them as they made their way around the district.

The barnstorming course was plotted against a calendar of agricultural shows and race meetings. This assured a ready crowd when they landed in paddocks next door. It was a clever strategy devised by Nancy but not always supported by the various committees who watched their annual event lose its lustre as the crowd's eyes (and spending) turned skyward.

As her career gained traction, the public life of Nancy Bird also took flight. It didn't take long for the media to cotton on to her endeavours and *Woman* magazine paid a small retainer in return for its name to be painted from one side of the underwing right across to the other in large black capital letters so it was clearly visible from the ground. It was possibly the earliest example of advertising on an aircraft. Nancy also wrote a regular column for the magazine. Her daring adventures made great reading in the Depression era, when housewives could only dream of such freedom and excitement.

There was certainly plenty of freedom in the wide blue yonder but sometimes the excitement got fairly confronting. It's hard to appreciate today that these women flew into a town or property and then looked for a paddock, road, racetrack or claypan to land on; flying an aeroplane with minimal power and no brakes. Aerodromes didn't appear in great numbers until the 1960s and so pilots would have to assess their landing options from the air when they arrived. If they landed without hitting a stump, fence or ditch, or sinking into a bog, then it was a good day. And if they returned to the airport the next morning to find their lightweight aircraft had managed to stay upright and tied down rather than being upturned by a strong wind, then that was a good day too.

As Nancy and Peg took in the dozen or so stops on their first tour, some 1100 kilometres from Mascot to Tamworth, Moree, Burren Junction, Walgett, Narromine and back to Mascot, they shared bedrooms, meals and the flying. It was close living, with a luggage compartment measuring just 70 cm long, 60 cm wide and 30 cm high at the highest point – hardly bigger than a picnic basket, or a few shoeboxes – which also had to accommodate tie-down ropes and other essentials. So, it was a carefully selected few items that each packed into a tiny bag. Any smaller essentials were carried within Peg's puffy flight suit.

It was during this trip that Peg met her future husband, also a pilot, when the women landed on his property, Malaraway Station, just south of Moree, NSW. While Peg would remember that flight fondly (as the destination became her future home), Nancy's experience was less glowing. The rough landing blew out the old tyres on the Gipsy Moth and in that moment, the meagre profits were blown as well.

Further along the track, it was a fortuitous meeting in Narromine that changed the course of the barnstorming business. Local entrepreneur Tom Perry, well known for his vision and generosity, took a fatherly interest in Nancy's exploits and offered to underwrite a loan for her to buy a better aeroplane. It only took one more splutter from the Gipsy Moth's about-to-expire engine and Nancy's decision was made. She needed something more reliable, but it created a conundrum.

Should she go more heavily into debt in the hope of successfully creating a business to service its loan? Scratching for cash from joy flights and managing on a marginal income to buy fuel the next day is a precarious plan at best. When Peg returned home to Orange for a spell at the end of the three-month tour, Nancy flew *Vincere* up to Dubbo for a month. Southern Air Lines was just then being established there and Tom Perry had invested £10 000 in the business. He installed Nancy as his public relations person. Her job was to promote aviation to a sceptical public and try to garner interest in it as a viable means of transport. It was a tough sell against the well-established and efficient railway, but the flip side was that Nancy, still considering Perry's offer of a loan, was in the right place at the right time for what came next.

Reverend Stanley Drummond, the Methodist minister at Wilcannia, happened to be in town and invited her to Bourke three months later to fly the outback nursing sister on her rounds. It was the break Nancy needed and the 'trial' led to the work she would ultimately be remembered for.

In the meantime, in August 1935, Nancy and Peg began their second barnstorming tour, over the same route as before. They broke their itinerary in September to join a host of other aviators up in Narromine for the regular air pageant held there. It was a chance to reconnect with flying friends over a fun and exciting weekend. Nancy and Peg won a large silver trophy, which, it was suggested, would do well to be filled with champagne at the pub. But the ever-sensible Tom Perry pulled the party back a notch, noting the unsuitability of such a deed on a Sunday.

The other prize-winner from the event was an Englishman who invited Nancy to co-pilot with him on a UK–Australia air race. She was also tossing up whether to join the record-setters by flying herself from Japan to Australia. The reality though, was that she would wake in fright at the thought of flying over water. And money, the great leveller of dreams, prohibited both ventures. Ultimately, the winner was the Far West Children's Health Scheme, which benefitted enormously when Nancy chose to take up the Reverend's offer.

At the end of the second barnstorming tour, in October 1935, the women pinned up their hair, strapped down their leather helmets and flew north from Hillston to Bourke. They made their way from the Bogan to the Darling Rivers over great stretches of timbered country that provided very few navigational references, or options for a forced landing. This gave way to the black soil country around Bourke where they landed in a glorious sunset. It was an exciting welcome and

Nancy eagerly anticipated the trial run for Reverend Drummond's clinic rounds. Nancy turned 20 the following week, which she spent in company with the perpetually strained clinic nurse, Sister Webb.

If life during the Great War and then a long stint in the outback weren't challenging enough, the poor nursing sister now had to climb into the forward seat of *Vincere*, cocooned by emergency rations and a cumbersome set of baby scales.

For Nancy's part, she was now not only a pilot but a nursing assistant. While Sister Webb attended to mothers and infants at the pub in Louth, the first stop of their clinic tour, Nancy distributed books and comics to the older children. It was so exciting to have an aeroplane land at Louth that the school gave the kids half a day off to go out and have a look at it.

Then came the test, a 75-minute flight north-west to Urisino Station over some lost and lonely country; the 'Never-Never'. In the fading afternoon light, they searched for the Bourke–Wanaaring Road, which on the grossly inadequate road map was just a thin line that followed the telegraph wire. Beyond these two landmarks – the road and the telegraph wire – lay the endless outback, the edge of civilisation, from which it would be almost impossible to establish a position report. With Sister Webb, rather than Peg, now occupying the other seat, Nancy was on her own in unfamiliar and challenging country.

Despite the challenges, they did arrive at Urisino Station, from where the women undertook a one-day, 290-kilometre round car trip so that Sister Webb could minister to 40 children; it was a journey she made every six weeks. Nancy took in the rough corrugated iron shacks set on barren ground and was awed by the strength and conviction of the women who stuck it out there.

In this remote country, 200 kilometres out the back of Bourke, Nancy left the throttle open and was almost run over when she swung the prop and *Vincere* kicked into life and rolled away. In a Laurel and Hardy–like scene, she chased the aeroplane, jumped up, reached inside the cockpit and pulled back the throttle to stop the aircraft embedding itself in trees. This wouldn't have happened had there been a second pilot to manage the usual start-up procedure.

The next challenge was getting from Hungerford to Yantabulla. The road kept disappearing under sand drifts that continually swamped it. But arriving in Yantabulla, Nancy's navigational woes paled against the plight of the policeman's wife.

Sick to death of bread, salted meat and black tea, the policeman's wife reckoned it was immoral to station a mother and her children out here at the back of nowhere. There wasn't enough fresh food to make a decent meal for the kids. With much fellow feeling for this poor woman, Nancy and Sister Webb handed over their fresh fruit. As a cinematic backdrop, a canvas water bag hung from the verandah post, impotent against an unrelenting drought wind on a 43°C day.

The travellers dug even deeper then and gifted one of their most precious possessions, their iced emergency water brought from Urisino. It would have been their only saviour if they'd broken down out there, but it was a calculated risk, for the women were almost home and the young family was desperate. Feeling so grateful for the fruit and water, the policeman's wife probably felt like jumping in the aeroplane with them as Nancy and Sister Webb disappeared in a cloud of dust and made for Bourke.

That was Nancy's introduction to the life she was beginning. It was enough to convince her to write to Mr Perry and accept his offer. She would replace *Vincere* with something bigger, more comfortable and more reliable.

Nancy and Peg were ready to head back to Sydney and did so just as the drought broke. Their flying was always heavily dictated by weather; however, they flew home to Sydney in moderate to heavy rain, which pelted them incessantly in the open cockpit.

As if *Vincere* knew its days were numbered, it saved the best for last. On a charter flight over a Sydney polo field, the engine drew its final breath, which resulted in a silent descent into Mascot. Regardless of what her jackaroo passenger thought about the forced landing, Nancy was sad to part with the Gipsy Moth. *Vincere* had given Peg and Nancy a lot of fun and enabled Nancy's start in aviation.

Nancy sold the Gipsy Moth and invested in a shiny modern Leopard Moth, VH-UUG. Its enclosed cabin, three leather seats and cooling and heating abilities were absolute luxury. The new monoplane would be like trading a farm ute with no suspension for the latest model air-conditioned sedan with leather seats and power steering. It had been a huge year for Nancy, from buying *Vincere*, followed by two barnstorming tours and finally heading off with a commercial contract in a new aeroplane.

In mid-November 1935, after only a couple of hours cross-training on the Leopard Moth, it was time for Nancy to walk the line – one she'd painted for herself. She intended to fly from Sydney, traverse the Blue Mountains and across to the far west of the state. The de Havilland sales reps waved her off; however, the engineers were convinced that the beautiful new craft would not survive the expedition in the hands of its inexperienced owner. At the time, Nancy had little choice if she wanted to be a working pilot. She was never going to be employed ahead of a man, and there were still plenty of them looking for work. In buying her own aeroplane, she bought herself a job and the opportunity to fly for a living. She now had to make it work.

The sturdier Leopard Moth cruised at 120 knots across the Blue Mountains, smoother and faster than the fragile old *Vincere* ever travelled. It was a lonely ride without Peg, made worse by the news that her friend and hero Charles Kingsford Smith was missing off the Burmese coast.

Arriving in Bourke alone and with limited funds, the generosity of another working woman, Mrs Fitzgerald, the hotel proprietor, helped her out. Mrs Fitzgerald took Nancy under her wing and offered her full board for £2 per week. The hotel was home for the next nine months.

Reverend Drummond's parish extended far beyond the railway's end, over lonely isolated country. Out there, an appallingly large number of children lacked government or medical assistance to combat the prevalence of trachoma, a bacterial infection that is still a leading cause of childhood blindness. Bourke was the location of Australian ophthalmologist Fred Hollows' work 30 years later and he is now buried in the local cemetery.

Drummond hoped to get grossly disadvantaged children to Sydney where they could be treated properly and where they could stay until fully recovered. This was a different role to the Royal Flying Doctor Service (RFDS), which had been operating out of Cloncurry in Queensland, 1600 kilometres north, for the past eight years. RFDS had established a broader network the previous year, with a NSW base at Broken Hill, 800 kilometres south of Bourke. Nancy was not connected with either of these, geographically or professionally.

Reverend Drummond wanted Nancy to fly Sister Webb on her regular rounds out of Bourke. At times Nancy carried critically ill patients to a hospital but that was the exception rather than the norm – distinct from the RFDS, which flies a doctor out for more detailed work. Sister Webb was more like a mothercraft nurse doing a regular round to check on the mothers and children. For Nancy, this work would be infinitely more satisfying than touting for joy flights on a barnstorming trip.

The clinic rounds contract was run with the help of a government subsidy of £100 for a six-month trial as a retainer and a guarantee of the same again to be on standby and to ensure this work took priority over everything else. The aeroplane had cost £1700 and its hangar £70. The contract was Nancy's only certainty, but it fell far short of what she needed. To survive the six months, between the aero-medical work Nancy was available for charters, usually taking stock buyers and station owners between properties.

The nervous Sister Webb was coaxed back into the aeroplane on the assurance that the Leopard would be vastly more comfortable than the Gipsy, but the summer heat and resulting turbulence did little to reduce her distaste for flight. By Christmas, a permanent clinic was established in Bourke, staffed by Sister Margot Silver, which left Sister Webb to live out her days on more agreeable earthly adventures that didn't involve flying.

Nancy embarked on a regular clinic round from Bourke to Louth – Urisino – Hungerford – Yantabulla – Ford's Bridge – and back to Bourke. It was a loop of about 200 kilometres that arced out west of Bourke. The motoring maps from the men at the local garage weren't very accurate and so a positive position fix often meant landing at a station to ask directions. Without obvious landmarks like rivers and mountains, Nancy was reduced to navigating along the Overland Telegraph line, a single wire on a single line of posts with a clearing either side, and just about the right width to safely land alongside if required. Without radio, the only way to call for help was to scale a post and cut the telegraph wire, then spend a day or two on emergency rations while waiting for a telegraph linesman to show up looking for the fault that the pilot had just created. It was a rudimentary fall-back, but at least it brought hope of rescue within a few days. Thankfully, Nancy never had an accident or emergency.

As she settled into this starkly unknown territory, the maps slowly mattered less and the featureless uninhabited dry country that had at first been confronting became familiar. But it was the fear of a fatality in those wide expanses that made her shudder years later, thinking about what might have been if things hadn't gone to plan. It would have been a lonely demise, as often nobody knew where she was or what her movements were. Drawing on the story of a lost and delirious Aboriginal tracker found 'swimming' in the sand by

Urisino Station workers, Nancy always carried a survival pack of water, barley sugar, raisins and chocolate. If this could happen to an experienced tracker who knew the country intimately, how much more easily might a newcomer become lost and disoriented?

Charter work was coveted and to fulfil her mandate, she flew one day in thick sleety rain to Narromine. On the 320 kilometre trip, she flew just above the railway line, as she knew there were no hills en route and it was her only visual clue and navigation aid. The only problem was finding another aircraft coming the other way, doing the same thing, but such was the risk in the early days of aviation. Nancy later regretted her naivety in doing that flight. It was one of the tales in her rich collection: farmers giving dodgy instructions that included looking for sheep dung as a marker, flying ill patients, landing on inadequate ground and breaking down.

There was more hair-raising flying at the end of 1936 when Nancy took a reprieve from the outback and entered an air pageant from Brisbane to Adelaide via Sydney and Melbourne. Relishing the reunion with other pilots – Lores Bonney, Freda Thompson, Ivy Pearce and May Bradford – Nancy went on to win and claim the Ladies Trophy by one minute. Much of the trip was scooting along, sandwiched between the railway and the low-hanging cloud. The overall race winner was Reg Ansett, who later established Ansett Airlines.

Just as Kingsford Smith had found, Nancy struggled to convince the government to sponsor her pioneering work. Her contract with the Far West Children's Health Scheme ceased at the end of 1936. It had lasted just one year. Railway carriages returned as mobile clinics and the nurses went back to motor vehicles for their outback rounds. The Scheme still operates with its original intent; however, after Nancy's time aeroplanes never again featured in regular patient care.

Nancy was now without a job, but still greatly in debt and so she shifted 450 kilometres north to the larger centre of Charleville, Queensland, in the vain hope that the government would utilise her in aerial ambulance work. It seems astonishing now that she could be turned away when she was prepared to fulfil a need, using her own aircraft and having already gained outback experience.

She was glad to be back in a larger town though, after the remoteness of Bourke. She loved the contact with civilisation in Charleville: a hangar, skilled engineers and the pilots based there with the fledgling Qantas were all important in maintaining her momentum, which was starting to flag.

Other Australian women pilots, Nancy's contemporaries, mostly flew on the coin of their wealthy families and achieved great notoriety. In 1934 Freda Thompson flew herself from England to Australia, financially supported by her family, and by 1936 Lores Bonney had already circumnavigated Australia, flown to England and was preparing to fly to South Africa – all paid for by her husband. Even Peg had departed the scene and gone to England. Colin Kelman followed soon after and as a married couple they flew themselves back to Australia.

In stark contrast to the cashed-up high profile 'aviatrix' of the time, it was expense that forced Nancy, a lone single 21-year-old to again relocate – this time to Cunnamulla on the Warrego River in south-west Queensland.

Cunnamulla was smaller than Charleville but the welcome was huge and Mrs Davis, the publican, provided a rent-free room at the pub. Nancy's existing client base, established during the barnstorming tours, was pleased to see her back in town. So was the mayor who, seeing what both the NSW and Queensland governments refused, went to great lengths to support her by offering his shire engineer for aircraft maintenance.

The district valued her services. The Department of Civil Aviation informally gave leeway for Nancy to operate in a less-than-ideal regulatory situation as her aircraft rarely had the necessary weekly safety certificate for flight. In Smithy's hangar, Nancy had received basic aircraft maintenance training but for the more complex tasks she required the services of a professional, the nearest thing being the shire engineer.

Now in her third year of operation, by early 1937 Nancy was quite well known and well regarded. She had no trouble rejecting the romantic overtures of the wealthy graziers of Narromine, and even less rejecting the self-professed bashful bachelor who reached out from Victoria. His was one of many fan letters she received around that time, and it finished 'PS: I am at present learning to fly'. While this was surely flattering, she'd have been infinitely more interested if he were learning to be an engineer. A photo in *My God! It's a Woman*, of Nancy in a frock and pith helmet sitting sullenly on the Leopard Moth's wheel is captioned: 'Desperation – I had engine trouble and the nearest ground engineer was more than two hundred miles away. I would have married the first one to come my way.'

Struggling to see the romance in the debt, engine troubles and fatigue; managing her business without a mentor; flying without insurance; and living as an unsupported single woman finally took its toll. Nancy's seemingly limitless enthusiasm succumbed to the realities of one so young going it alone. The hurdles were too high and she became unwell.

Her initial six-month stint in the outback had stretched to two years and it was Reverend John Flynn, having established the RFDS a decade prior, who took Nancy aside for a fatherly word. Life in the outback was just too tough for a woman in her situation, he said. Famed aviator PG Taylor, who she knew from Kingsford Smith's sphere, echoed the sentiment, and a few years later there were the harsh words of Defence Minister Harold Thorby. He had expressed the belief that women were biologically unsuitable to be pilots – Kiwi Jean Batten and Englishwoman Amy Johnson being notable exceptions. There was no consideration given here that, despite her youth and tiny stature, Nancy had been successfully operating as a commercial pilot running her own business. She was well known in Australia and to be excluded from the ranks of the 'notable exceptions' was a direct blow.

Nancy's creeping anxiety finally peaked when she was flying from Sydney to Goodooga on the Queensland border and she encountered menacing low cloud over the Blue Mountains. In *Born to Fly* she says:

> … as we got nearer to the mountains I could see there wasn't much room between them and the clouds. Suddenly what I had been feeling for months came to a head – everything inside me revolted against those clouds and those mountains and it was almost as though the machine stood on its tail rather than go into it. So I turned back and landed again at Mascot … In my heart I knew I could have got through if I wanted to … I didn't ever want to fly again … I suppose I had really had a sort of controlled nervous breakdown. I didn't recognise it as that – I really didn't feel anything except a very strong desire not to fly again in that dreadful western turbulence.

Anybody who has spent a few summer days in the west will know exactly what she was talking about. The 42-degree days out there might cool down to 36 degrees at dawn, but then it heats right up again. It is relentless.

There is never shame in baulking at bad weather; in fact that decision is and was applauded. There is an aviation saying: 'It's better to be on the ground wishing you were flying than to be flying and wishing you were on the ground. Even eagles stay in their tree when the weather is no good.' Nancy put the aeroplane in the hangar and went home, dejectedly, to her mother's house in Manly. She meant it when she said she didn't want to fly again. She sold the lot and walked away from flying with exactly the same amount of cash she'd gone in with. Four hundred pounds. It was March 1938 and she was

23 years old. Nancy didn't return to the outback for many years, but she maintained a fondness for the place and the people who inhabited it.

Nancy needn't have felt so bad though; she had disproven the naysayers and supported herself in commercial aviation for three years. By leaving the dangers of it behind, she became one of the few who lived to tell the tales. She was so well known by then that it was deemed necessary for her to issue a press release stating that she was done with flying. In reality though, she wasn't done with aviation.

Nancy used her £400 to undertake an overseas research tour at the invitation of Dutch airline KLM. She now saw a future not as a pilot but perhaps in some sort of ground service around catering or administration, and collected ideas and information for a Sydney exhibition. From Europe she travelled to America and on the ship crossing the Pacific met her husband to be, Charles Walton. In December 1939, amid news of looming war, major newspapers ran a small item stating that Miss Bird was married in a small private ceremony in Sydney. Reverend Flynn officiated.

The new bride soon undertook work with the Women's Auxiliary Australian Air Force and says she was invited to England to fly with the Air Transport Auxiliary but was unable to accept due to a wartime ban on women travelling. A second obstacle was the fact that she was married, and in *Born to Fly* comments that her husband and his family had firm views that a wife's place was by her husband's side.

Despite having her wings clipped, Nancy clung to her aviation connections for the rest of her life. Her contemporaries either died or retired from public life but Nancy continued to stand up for the causes she believed in, such as supporting Arthur Butler in establishing the NSW Air Ambulance during the 1960s and putting a toe into the political arena. However, it is her role as the founder of the Australian Women Pilots' Association (AWPA) for which she is most revered.

During her flying career, as a young woman with few connections, Nancy struggled to meet the high cost of flying. Most women pilots had funding from family or other external sources. She believed that an association would promote camaraderie and support for women pilots.

In a small white envelope postmarked 29 August 1949, Senja Havard (now Robey) received an invitation on Nancy's personal stationery. The stiff white pre-printed card invited Senja to a meeting at Mascot. About eight Sydney women gathered in the timber aero club building that stood where the international terminal car park is now. Against the chink of cup upon saucer, Nancy proposed the formation of the AWPA. In 2016, Senja, aged 90, recalled that anything Nancy proposed was seen as a good idea. And this was definitely a good idea. A year later, on 16 September 1950, at the inaugural meeting at Sydney's Bankstown airport, 35 women became founding members. Nancy was president from 1950–55 and from 1959–60.

The Association still aims to encourage and support women interested in aviation and while flying, to create networking opportunities. In a 1965 article for the AWPA magazine *Airnews*, Nancy wrote:

> Once a girl has obtained her flying licence, we are of the opinion that like the boys in the Air Force she has won her wings, and no piece of paper, current or expired can take that away from her.

AWPA brought many women back into the fold and, being around aeroplanes again, many decided to return to flying. For Nancy, it eventually didn't sit well that she was a 'Penguin President'. Penguins don't fly. With a student licence, Nancy decided that she'd be happy to fly with her good friend Maie Casey, wife of the Australian Governor-General, Richard Casey. Maie, or whoever else

Nancy could hop in with, would do the flying and Nancy was a well-qualified co-pilot.

In 1958 after a 20 year absence, Nancy renewed her licence and was delighted to be given her original licence number. She became the first non-American woman to win a trophy in the All Women's Transcontinental Air Race across America in 1958. This event is more commonly referred to as the Powder Puff Derby.

Her close friend and champion balloon pilot, Jenny Houghton, recalls Nancy's quiet determination. On a 1986 trip to India to speak at an international women's flying convention held at the Taj Palace, Nancy arrived at Delhi airport to find her luggage had been misplaced. When airport authorities deemed it gone for good, she stood her ground and gently informed them that she was meeting the Indian prime minister in precisely two hours and didn't intend to do it in her travelling clothes.

Other members of AWPA who knew Nancy well recall her turning up at their homes with moral support and practical help during some of their trying personal challenges. Her own home was always open to women pilots.

Of all the great pioneering aviators that she had known and worked with, Nancy was one of the few who survived into old age. In Sydney, she was accessible and thrived as an aviation ambassador. She loved getting out, enjoying both the attention and the socialising.

Over time, Nancy distributed her memorabilia to the Australian War Memorial and the National Library in Canberra, and to the Mitchell Library and the Powerhouse Museum in Sydney. She has a road, an airport terminal, a control tower, a Royal Aeronautical Society lecture, an Australian Women Pilots' Association Award, a NSW Air Ambulance King Air aircraft and a NSW Rural Fire Service DC-10 fire tanker named after her. The National Trust declared her a National Living Treasure and she was awarded an Order of the British Empire, an Order of Australia, an Order of St John and an

Honorary Bachelor of Engineering. Her book, *My God! It's a Woman* went into space with Australian astronaut Andy Thomas. He and his astronaut wife returned the (space-travelled) book to her when Andy was speaking to aviation students by special invitation in the Great Hall of Sydney University. Nancy was an invited guest. Importantly, the new $5.3 billion Western Sydney Airport at Badgery's Creek will officially become the Western Sydney International (Nancy-Bird Walton) Airport.

While Nancy's legacy seems disproportionate to her actual flying achievements, it isn't just the power of publicity that makes her a household name. As long-time family friend and fellow aviator Dick Smith confirmed, what Nancy did in the 1930s, alone in those conditions and in the face of male prejudice, was remarkable. And standing firmly atop her pioneer pedestal, Nancy used her greatest skill, public relations, to set up the rest of her life. She was available in Sydney for speaking engagements or other opportunities and she used her connections to make things happen. She had also seen the evolution of aviation from rudimentary biplanes through to the most sophisticated Airbus and when delivering a speech, could recall those transitions with good humour and clarity.

In September 2008 Captain Elyse Fordham gently splintered a bottle of champagne across the hull of Qantas's first Airbus A380, VH-OQA, christening it the *Nancy-Bird Walton*. Sporting her trademark triple strand of pearls, the 93-year-old guest of honour sat through Qantas CEO Geoff Dixon's two-minute speech where he applauded her courage, resilience and optimism. She then stood at the podium to make her own speech.

'Fortunately, I couldn't hear all that. I'm sure it was exaggerated,' she said matter-of-factly to a chorus of laughter. 'Qantas announced that they'd name this magnificent aircraft after me on my ninetieth birthday three years ago. I made it my business to stay alive for today's ceremony and I've made it … I've made it!' she said animatedly.

Three months later, the same Airbus did a low and slow pass over Nancy's funeral at St Andrew's Cathedral in George Street, Sydney. Inside, her granddaughter Anna Holman spoke of 'Our Mum, our Nan, our friend, our Nancy, a dearly loved member of our family … who led us with the grace of a glider and the determination of a jet fighter.'

Interspersed among the crowd were pink outfits, accessorised with strings of pearls, Nancy's favourite combination, worn by AWPA members. They continue to benefit from the organisation that was then 58 years old. Its senior commercial airline and RAAF members now enjoy comfort in the cockpit beyond the wildest imaginings of the young Nancy Bird, who had to ask the station workers to remove a fence so she could take off from an isolated barren paddock in the outback. Nancy would have loved their life, but she was too far ahead of her time.

2

MARDI GETHING
WORLD WAR II ATA FERRY PILOT

Just as the Battle of Britain is the accomplishment and achievement of the RAF, likewise it can be declared that the ATA sustained and supported them in the battle.

(Lord Beaverbrook at the 1945 ceremony that
disbanded the Air Transport Auxiliary)

They say you don't just fly a Spitfire, you wear it, and hovering around 151 centimetres (or 5 feet) tall, Australian pilot Margaret 'Mardi' Gething and her booster cushion slipped comfortably into the narrow cockpit where everything was in arm's reach.

The Spitfire, a single-engine single-seat fighter aircraft – the pride of Britain – was designed by a brilliant team of men as a weapon of war. And though it was men who flew and fought in the Spitfire during World War II, there was a small band of women in a male-dominated role during that time who ferried the aircraft from the production line to the airfields from which the fighters were launched for battle. Twenty-two-year-old Mardi was one of these formidable women.

Mardi had a B (commercial) licence and 194 flying hours when she joined Britain's Air Transport Auxiliary (ATA) in 1942. She quickly found herself ferrying many types of aeroplanes around wartime Britain and flew the Spitfire more than any other. Its finely balanced control systems made it a dream to fly.

In her two years as an ATA ferry pilot, Mardi flew almost 600 hours in 26 different aircraft types. Her logbook is a who's who of classic World War II fighter aircraft, including the Hurricane, Tempest, Typhoon, Mustang and Blenheim bomber. And to the envy of every star-struck aviation enthusiast hanging over the fence, 233 flights were in the British hero, the cutting-edge Spitfire. To put this in context, a modern-day military enthusiast might feel the same way about an F-35.

MARDI WAS BORN IN MELBOURNE IN DECEMBER 1920, AROUND the time her next eldest sibling was finishing primary school. Her highly respected father, Sir Herbert Gepp, was an analytical chemist and metallurgist, and a public servant. He was a self-made man whose wealth, and the high regard in which he was held, were at odds with his humble beginnings.

MARDI GETHING

Mardi enjoyed the benefits of being the 'baby' of the family, sliding along in the wake of her three sisters and brother. As a 13-year-old, that meant grabbing hold of her sisters' coat-tails and begging to be allowed along for a joy flight at Essendon airport. It paid off.

As they took to the skies above Essendon, the wind roared through the flying wires of the plane and around Mardi's face in the open cockpit. She was so taken with the thrill of it all, she held a flapping handkerchief high above her head and jubilantly released it into the turbulent air.

Too young to start flying lessons, she indulged her teenage equestrian love and also competed as a school girl champion diver. Her interest in aeroplanes resurfaced when Sir Herbert and Lady Gepp prepared to fly to the outback in the famous Kingsford Smith *Southern Cross*.

In early 1939, as an 18-year-old new graduate from Merton Hall at Melbourne Girls Grammar School, Mardi pushed aside any concerns about Europe's political instability and boarded the luxurious SS *Orford*, bound for England. With her 31-year-old sister Kathleen as a chaperone, adventure beckoned.

The 18 000-tonne steamer had timber furniture and linen tablecloths in the dining room, glass doors and detailed patterned rugs in the writing room, and potted palms and cane chairs on the wide timber deck. A grand stairway with brass trim helped to bind the whole lot together. This fine ship had been at the opening of the Sydney Harbour Bridge and was one of the first in the Parade of Ships to pass under the recently completed bridge. It would now power along at 18 knots, rolling across the ocean through sunny days and dreamy twinkling nights. Mardi relished the journey and her first taste of adult freedom.

Conversations on board included other people's adventures. RAF Squadron Leader Richard Kellett and his navigator/relief pilot

Flight Lieutenant Richard Gething brought adventurous tales right to the dinner table on the six-week sea crossing. They were returning to England having just established a long-distance record for their country on a flight from Egypt to Australia. The men's high mood on board the ship, celebrating their success, brought Mardi again into conversations about flying.

Upon their return to England, King George VI awarded the two men (and others) the Air Force Cross for what *Aeroplane* magazine reported as a risky undertaking of the highest skill, endurance and achievement. It was an admirable achievement, especially for Richard Gething, who was only 27 years old. He was a friendly man who enjoyed a chat and he and his companion were great company for the Australian travellers.

MARDI ARRIVED IN ENGLAND TO ENJOY A 'SEASON'; A PRESentation at court (young women could be 'presented' to the reigning monarch) followed by a summer of socialising. While they were on a preliminary ski trip to Switzerland, the BBC radio dramatically announced that the Germans had violated the Munich Agreement by invading Czechoslovakia. War in Europe was imminent. The announcer offered platitudes to try to ease public alarm, but the message was as clear in Melbourne as it was in Europe. The Gepps were no more placated than anybody else. They cabled their daughters, asking them to return to England.

With time on her hands back in England, Mardi changed tack. Why not do something useful – like learn to fly? When she asked them to fund her lessons, her parents had many questions.

In a letter to the family 65 years later, Nancy Bird Walton, who had met the Gepp family through their connections with Charles Kingsford Smith, recalled a conversation with Sir Herbert, who asked whether it was a good idea for Mardi to learn to fly. There's no prize for guessing what Nancy's reply was and so plans took a complete 180-degree turn then, with the funds set aside for Mardi's 'season' now diverted to a flying fund.

At Thanet Aero Club near Ramsgate in Kent, Mardi enthusiastically took to the air in a Hornet Moth. Each morning she walked several kilometres to the airfield. In just under seven flying hours, she was able to fly solo. It's an event that only another pilot can truly understand and, from his nearby base, Richard came over to Ramsgate aerodrome to congratulate the new pilot.

With her A (private) licence completed, Mardi was eager to continue to her B (commercial) licence and to her utter surprise, her parents agreed. That summer, while the London Season advanced into full Quickstep without her, Mardi immersed herself in flying, with the occasional long weekend in Cheshire as a guest of the Gething family.

This period of grace wasn't to last very long though, because, as the threat of war loomed, their parents secured a passage to North America for Mardi and Kathleen to continue on their round-the-world journey. During a few snatched days with the Gethings, the phone rang to recall Richard to immediate duty with the RAF. Within a week the sisters had arrived in Nova Scotia; Germany had invaded Poland; and Britain had declared war.

Sir Herbert kept a concerned eye on his daughters as they travelled around and he now cabled and suggested Mardi finish her flight training in Oakland, California. She gladly spent ten days at the Boeing School of Aeronautics, learning to be a flying instructor. She was the only woman on the course, but this did not hinder her results. She and Kathleen then finished their yearlong round-the-world trip by sailing on the last leg for Australia.

Arriving home just in time for her nineteenth birthday at Christmas 1939, Mardi was then old enough to qualify for her B licence. She had plans to use it, perhaps for instructing others or to organise a flying nurses corps to help with the war effort.

No sooner had she arrived in Australia, than Richard arrived in Canada. He was posted to the Empire Air Training Scheme, specialising in navigation to train Commonwealth pilots. In early March he proposed via phone. On 24 March 1940, *The Age* reported a late afternoon party at Waveney, the Gepps' home in suburban Armadale, where 150 guests assembled to wish Mardi well. The following day she and her mother, Lady Jessie Gepp, left for San Francisco, then Toronto, Canada where the Australian high commissioner walked Mardi down the aisle, and she married Richard Gething.

Later that year, during their time in Canada, London and much of Coventry was being flattened by the Blitz and recovering from the Battle of Britain. The whole of England was living on rations and under the constant fear that war brings. By comparison, Canadian life rolled along much as it always had, albeit with training aeroplanes flying overhead and a Red Cross that was ready but not required. The streets had a smattering of military uniforms, many of whom were the recently trained RAF pilots. They filed through the flight training, then boarded ships and headed back to active service.

At the end of 1941 Richard was posted back to the Air Ministry in London. Before leaving Canada, however, Mardi did some currency training with a one-hour dual check flight in a Tiger Moth, hoping that with a current licence she may be able to use it. She wasted no time in making herself available and, within a week of being back in London, had completed her flight test with the Air Transport Auxiliary (ATA). This was a civilian organisation of pilots who transported military aircraft from the aircraft factories to the airfields, thereby freeing up the military pilots for combat and other duties.

Mardi felt sure she'd be employed with the ATA as she already had 194 hours experience and had passed the medical. The sticking point though, was her height. She was at least a hand's span too short for the ATA and the recruiters held fast. It was extremely frustrating.

The ATA was based at White Waltham, west of London, just beyond today's Heathrow Airport and Windsor Castle. It had been going for four years and when the need for ferry pilots eclipsed the need for them to be tall, Mardi got her break. In August 1942, she became one of about 60 women working for them.

By the time she left, there were about 100 women. Over the period of the war, around 166 women came and went; some staying for as little as a few weeks and some for the whole war. They were outnumbered by men by around seven to one.

Organised by Pauline Gower, a determined pilot with some political clout, it didn't take long for the women to prove their worth and progress from flying the smallest simple aircraft to flying all types of heavier and more complex machines. It is easy to write with a simple tap on the keyboard – all types of aircraft – but this was a mammoth undertaking for any pilot. The ATA pilots had to be adaptable, flying many types of craft, with often no prior knowledge, let alone training, on that type. By contrast, the combat pilots were endorsed on one particular type and flew only that type of aeroplane.

On 12 August 1942, the same day Churchill arrived in Moscow to meet Stalin, Mardi arrived in Luton (north of London) for two weeks of ground school. It was a brave new world: Morse Code, Navigation, Emergency Drills and so on. Initial drills had everybody on their feet, throwing on overalls and helmets, gathering up their maps, plotting a course and reporting ready for duty. From September to November of 1942, Mardi and one other woman trained on large Hawker Harts, previously the RAF's single engine light bomber. Their cockpits sat three metres off the ground.

At the end of the course Mardi arrived in Southampton, a 90-minute train ride south, for her temporary first posting to the ATA's No 15 Ferry Pool at nearby Hamble. Upon her arrival she received news that Richard's posting to India was imminent. Their last five days together went quickly, and she didn't see him again for two and a half years. In one respect, though Mardi was now alone, she was luckier than many of the wives left behind. She had a great job with plenty of learning to occupy her mind.

The ATA had six categories of aeroplane. Light single-engined, advanced single-engined, light twin-engined, advanced twin-engined, four-engined and lastly flying boats, deemed the most difficult. Once a pilot was trained on a specific category of aeroplane, they could ferry all types in that category. By the start of 1943 Mardi was at ATA headquarters doing the advanced single-engine course, learning how to fly Class 2 aircraft, which included fighters. After a long month of theory, she was pleased to finally transition to the first aircraft, a two-seat Harvard, with a sliding clear canopy over the cockpit.

Before flying began, she hopped in the Harvard to try it on for size. She could reach the rudder pedals, but she was aghast at how far she had to stretch to apply pressure to them. How would she manage to stretch far enough to use the brakes? Her lack of height had already caused her trouble with recruitment and she didn't want it to come back and haunt her. In the name of safety however, she bought a cushion and unashamedly flew with it.

The array of fighters the ATA pilots were expected to fly included different variants of Spitfires, all with different instructions. They began with the most basic and worked their way up. The Spitfire was like royalty – a revered performer. Its double-jointed control column meant it was flown with only subtle control inputs and its finely tuned design gave it the qualities of a thoroughbred. As wartime requirements changed, so did the design and it was the only aeroplane in production before, during and after World War II. By war's end over 20 000 Spitfires had been built at factories such as Castle Bromwich 186 kilometres west of London, and due south of there, where Mardi spent most of the war, at Southampton – the Spitfire's spiritual home where the first test flight took place at its Eastleigh airport seven years before.

After mastering the Harvard, Mardi began working with the ATA Training Pool as a ferry pilot. They eased her in gently with some Class I aeroplanes to get her comfortable again. Then she was ushered into the Hurricane – the aircraft that was credited as the most successful of the fighters in winning the Battle of Britain. It only took three flights to become familiar with the Hurricane and then she was on her own, ferrying the speedy things from their factory at nearby Langley up north to RAF bases in Wales and Scotland. The Hurricane's top speed was 295 knots (550 km/h) – more than three times the speed of the fabric biplane in which she had done her initial flight training only four years before. The Spitfire was marginally faster.

In her downtime, Mardi wrote letters home, some of which were published. One that was published in the Melbourne *Herald*, describes a workday that had the female pilots on a short overnight at a local pub. In the morning, the women raced downstairs to breakfast and were at the aerodrome half an hour later, where the fighters stood ready. When she collected her instructions, Mardi walked along the line of aeroplanes and found hers. She pressed the starter button, it kicked into life, and she then followed her colleagues out to the take-off point for the half-hour trip. She turned into wind and opened the throttle.

As the plane roared into life, she took off and trimmed for straight and level flight. Around the dash she checked her gauges and altitude, then correlated her navigation aids with her map. Over Banbury Cross she had a rare moment of song, retelling the nursery rhyme 'Ride a cock horse to Banbury Cross', as she wheeled around on a wingtip to view the town off the end of it. It was magic. But the spell was soon broken by realities on the ground. She alighted to be surrounded by a group of engineers who quickly swooped in to remove the wings.

Before she knew it, the aeroplane was swinging by a crane above her head and down into a packing crate. The wings quickly followed and by the time Mardi walked away, the last nails were hammered in and the plane was ready for shipment to the Middle East.

In mid-May 1943, Mardi ferried her first two Spitfires. She then joined 25 other women pilots on posting to the Spitfire repair aerodrome, where she stayed until she left England at the end of the following year, when her Spitfire ferry total was 233.

Around this time the women's pay was increased to equal the men's. It was the first time the British Government had agreed to equal pay for equal work, while their US contemporaries were still on 65 per cent of the men's wage.

Their work routine began each morning by collecting a chit with their name on it and the details of the aircraft they were to ferry. With helmet, goggles, maps and a small overnight bag for unforeseen stopovers, they walked to their designated aeroplane, matching the number on their chit with the number painted on the aircraft.

Fundamental knowledge such as take-off, stall and landing instructions came from the *Ferry Pilots Handbook*. This was a small folder about 15 x 12 centimetres, bound by two large metal rings at the top. It was the ferry pilots' bible, with basic information on every type of aircraft they could be called upon to fly. Once airborne, they flew in complete radio silence because radios, like armaments, hadn't yet been fitted.

Other wartime considerations were that the ATA pilots relied heavily on their personal knowledge of the countryside and supported that with their paper map. Alighting at the destination, they handed the aeroplane over and either hopped into another one to ferry it on, or waited for an airborne taxi to take them on to another airfield for another ferry flight or to take them home. Jackie Moggridge, a South African pilot based at Hamble with Mardi, wrote how unbelievable it was to most people that the ATA flew aeroplanes using a notebook as guidance, and that the first time she sat in a Mosquito, she flew it.

MARDI GETHING

If you're the type of person who flicks the wipers on instead of the indicators in a strange car, or can't find the wipers, lights or boot and fuel release button at all, consider Mardi and her colleagues with their essential notebook. Imagine hopping from a Ford into a BMW and driving around England without a map. Then getting from a truck into a Porsche. Whoa! The brakes are touchy! And where are the indicators? The thing is, the indicators vs wipers mistake will, at best, only embarrass you. But can you imagine having to stay on top of that at 500 km/h?

There were simple differences such as the Rolls Royce Griffon engine versus the Merlin engine. One turned in the opposite direction to the other, so that on take-off, the torque forced the aeroplane one way or the other. You had to push in the rudder pedal to counteract the torque and keep the aeroplane straight as it hurtled down the runway. If by accident you applied the wrong rudder you could too easily lose control and the plane would spin off into a disaster. There was so much critical information to know, which was a big ask for somebody with so few flying hours.

ATA pilots could be called on to fly a total of 40 different types of aeroplanes. Over the subsequent months and years Mardi would upgrade to the larger and more complicated Class 3 and 4 aircraft, adding significantly to the array on her daily chit sheet. Sometimes she flew aircraft across all categories, chopping and changing after as little as 20 minutes in the air. And despite the winter of 1942–43 being milder than the ones preceding and following it, there was always a great risk of getting caught in bad weather, which the ATA pilots weren't trained for. Without radios or navigational aids, these pilots were solely reliant on their rudimentary aids – map and compass – and their wits to find clear skies and useful landmarks. The tragic loss of British aviation darling (and ATA pilot) Amy Johnson only three years prior in bad weather is still talked about today. The woman who won the world's heart when she navigated, flew and serviced her open cockpit biplane from England to Australia had died because she was caught in cloud over the Thames Estuary.

As well as the vagaries of the weather and the intricacies of each aeroplane, there was the ever-present threat of being bombed. The nearby Spitfire factory at Southampton had been blown up in 1940 and production was moved to anywhere local that had a roof, including a bus depot, laundries and garages. The main factories the ATA pilots flew from were nearby Eastleigh and a secret airfield in Wiltshire called Chattis Hill, which was built after the Southampton bombing. As soon as an aeroplane was flyable, an ATA pilot would whisk its bare bones from the factory to the relative safety of the well camouflaged air force maintenance units further inland, where it would be finished off and fitted out with radio and armaments.

THE MOST CONSTANT INTERRUPTION TO DUTIES WAS WEATHER, which could have them grounded for days, then working flat out when the weather improved. After one such wet grounding, Mardi wrote about the following day's activity. This piece was published in Melbourne's *Age* newspaper on 13 January 1945, shortly after her arrival back in Melbourne:

> The next morning broke bright and clear. I went into the mess to find three aircraft delivery chits with my name on them, lying on the table, and to hear Alison's voice saying that taxi aircraft were off at 10 o'clock.
>
> For such mornings I had a routine. First, I called in at the Met. office, then down the passage and round the corner, to collect my flying chocolate coupon from the adjutant's office, then in next door, to Maps and Signals, to check on aerodrome serviceability and nomad balloons [large unmanned, tethered balloons used to block the airspace to enemy aircraft and protect

ground targets]. Back down the passage into the canteen, to cash my chocolate coupon and pick up my sandwich lunch, before going through the locker room to struggle into overalls and flying boots, tie a scarf round my hair and pull on my ancient grease-stained, but very comfortable gloves. My overnight bag, containing assorted essentials, such as maps, ferry pilots' notes, pyjamas, helmet, goggles and cosmetic case, came next. Then I was ready for the day's work.

My first job that day, was to complete the delivery of a Fleet Air Arm plane, which had been landed at our base aerodrome for refuelling. I walked across the tarmac to where it stood. The ground crew were finishing the daily Inspection, and one of them placed my parachute in the cockpit. I pulled on my helmet, was given a leg-up on to the wing and climbed in. After checking the cockpit, I gave the signal for contact; and heard the staccato splutter and cough of the engine turning over. Then it caught – and roared into life.

The sun was warm on my face through the Perspex hood, while I sat waiting for her to warm up. As the engine temperature rose, I opened her up on test. Then throttled back, waved away the chocks and taxied out to the take-off point. A green light flashed from the black and white checked control box told me all was clear. I turned into the wind and pushed open the throttle. The smooth turf blurred with speed, as I looked down to check that we were airborne before retracting the undercarriage. Wheels up, throttle and pitch back to climbing power, I slammed the hood closed and pushed up my goggles. The sun glinted dully on the river below as I circled, gaining height and then set course.

Something caught my eye. I looked back to port. A Spitfire, one of the test pilots no doubt, was coming up from behind to formate. I pretended not to see him. Soon he dived beneath me, came up ahead and stall-turned away to the right like a slender mottled leaf swept by the autumn wind.

British ATA pilot Mary Ellis, in her book *Spitfire Girl*, talks of another challenge the ATA faced, which was to negotiate the barrage balloons, used to help keep enemy aircraft away from important areas. The largest of these balloons would be 19 metres long, 7.5 metres in circumference and hoisted as high as 5000 feet. They were inflated with hydrogen and could be fixed with cable attached to a winch on a lorry and it was the hard-to-see cable that was the greatest concern for pilots. Collision would likely bring the plane down instantly and the balloons could be hidden in cloud or bad weather. They were launched over cities and strategic locations such as ports and factories. During the Blitz the balloons snagged more than 60 enemy aircraft but throughout the war downed 38 friendly aircraft also. There were procedures in place to part the curtain of balloons to allow the ATA clear access to fly through. They were dismantled in February 1945 when it was clear that the war would soon be ending.

Another difficulty was tracking the secret arrangements used for landing at camouflaged airfields. Would a trigger-happy anti-aircraft gunner mistake them as hostile and take aim? Making their way around the country, the pilots also needed to keep clear of training airfields. There was a need to remain vigilant, right up until the end of the war, which was not far away.

By spring 1944, work was increasing, and Mardi spent that time doing 25 taxi flights and 107 deliveries. She then returned to White Waltham to train on medium bombers. Light bombers could carry up to 900 kg of ordnance. Heavy bombers carried 3600 kg. The medium bombers, such as the Bristol Blenheim, carried just over half a tonne.

She clearly recalled 6 June 1944 – a day that everybody knows as D-day. The sky was filled with aircraft heading to the south-east. She continued her upgrade training and within a couple of weeks was qualified for Hudson bombers and Albermarles. The next few months were extremely busy. By the end of the summer, there was finally a reprieve as activity had moved from British shores. The Germans were being pushed back as the Allies gained the upper hand in the air.

After two years and two months with the ATA, for family reasons, Mardi cut her contract short by only a couple of months to return to Melbourne. Her ferry pool was disbanded shortly after.

She spent nine months of 1945 in Australia. During that time, she spent about six weeks on tour as the publicity/press liaison officer on the Third Victory Loan Tour as part of the *G for George* crew. It was a relaxing and happy break after all that had gone before. The huge aircraft, *G for George*, managed to cover 24 000 kilometres and 28 cities around Australia on that tour, raising funds for the country to pay for the war.

The great Lancaster bomber had been operated by No 460 Squadron in RAAF Operations in Bomber Command and safely returned all its crew from their 90 bombing operations over Europe. It now hangs as a stunning display from the ceiling in the Australian War Memorial in Canberra. At a military dinner in 2015, I sat before it, my eyes continually drawn to the warm yet strangely eerie light emanating from its cockpit some metres above.

When Mardi was reunited with Richard back in the UK at the end of the English summer, they settled in a small village outside London. Together with their two children, they undertook several RAF postings, including to Singapore. They emigrated to Australia when Richard retired from the RAF in 1960. Though finished with the military, the Gethings were not finished with flying and Mardi became a gliding instructor, soared for a total of around 300 hours and won two Australian women's gliding awards: the women's altitude record for soaring to 13 000 feet and a women's distance record. Only in her mid-sixties did she retire from gliding but continued to fly with friends as a passenger. She and Richard both passed away within a year of each other and as their daughter Mary-Jane wrote in her mother's official obituary, their 'wonderful partnership in aviation had lasted more than 64 years'.

In 2008, just three years after Mardi passed away, all surviving members of the ATA were invited to British Prime Minister Gordon Brown's residence and presented with a special veteran's badges. It was a mark of respect and acknowledgement of the ATA's wartime contributions. This was the first time the ATA had been officially acknowledged, and some of the surviving women were interviewed for a BBC4 documentary, which noted that the female pilots had taken a big step forward for women's rights. Mardi was typical of this atypical group of women whose ability to step into the role freed up important RAF resources required at the time.

By the late 1990s, when machinery from World War II was relegated to museums and a flight in a Spitfire cost thousands of dollars (if you could find one of the two-seaters that was actually serviceable), one of the Victorian women pilots remarked to an ageing Mardi that she couldn't believe that she had flown Spitfires. Still sharp as a tack, the ex-ATA pilot flashed one of her twinkling smiles and said, politely and with great understatement, 'Well … I did!'

Nancy Bird in 1933, kitted out for open cockpit flying, including her seat booster cushion.
State Library of NSW

Mardi Gething in 1943 in one of the many military aircraft she flew as a ferry pilot while in the Air Transport Auxiliary. *Mardi Gething, personal collection*

Left to right: Newcastle's Elizabeth Beeston had a commercial licence and Heather McDougall had a private licence. Pat Graham (Toole), flying from Tamworth, would collect them on her way through to Bankstown for AWPA meetings (1951). *Pat Toole, personal collection*

Early flying lessons for Pat, sitting in the cockpit of a Tiger Moth at Coffs Harbour Aero Club, circa 1950. *Pat Toole, personal collection*

June 1953: Gibbes Sepik Airways' Auster, VH-KSK after Pat Toole force-landed on the bank of the Keang River, New Guinea. Apart from bending the right undercarriage leg and shearing the propeller tip and a wingtip, the aeroplane escaped unscathed. The plane was carried out, repaired and Pat flew it again in late July. *Pat Toole, personal collection*

After completing her record-breaking solo flight around the world in 1989, Gaby Kennard undertook a fundraising trip around Australia in 1993, during which she raised more than $200 000 for the Royal Flying Doctor Service. At Charleville, Queensland, she received flowers from young Chloe Brayley. *Photo by Annabelle Brayley*

Marion McCall flew 1700 hours over 23 years with her husband David McCall as he undertook his roles as Bishop of Willochra, South Australia, and then Bishop of Bunbury, Western Australia. Marion won the Dawn to Dusk Challenge three times, the half Dawn to Dusk once and twice won the Tiger Club medal for longest distance flown. *Marion McCall, personal collection*

Marion at home in Adelaide, 2017, with the Australian Women Pilots' Association 2019 Nancy Bird Walton trophy she was awarded for the most noteworthy contribution to aviation by a woman of Australasia. The silver trophy is sponsored by the family of the late Nancy Bird Walton. *Photo by Kathy Mexted*

The dash of the brand new Seminole, VH-CZE, which Lyn Gray and Kristian Kauter were forced to ditch in the Pacific Ocean on their ferry flight from the USA to Australia in June 2006. A month later, Lyn successfully ferried the same type of aircraft, one serial number different, across the same route. *Photo by Lyn Gray*

Lyn now operates her own flying school in Cowra, New South Wales.
Lyn Gray, personal collection

First Officer Deborah Wardley (Lawrie) at the controls of an Ansett Boeing 727 in 1986. In 1979 Deborah became the first female pilot to fly for a major Australian airline after winning a legal battle against Ansett in the High Court. *Wardley v Ansett* became a milestone case after the introduction of the *Equal Opportunity Act* in Victoria. Deborah went on to enjoy an aviation career that spanned more than 50 years. *Deborah Lawrie, personal collection*

Aerial application pilot Georgia Maxwell, at home in Gunnedah and leaning on the cowl of the Cessna 188 Husky in which she did her first spray job. *Photo by Kathy Mexted*

Georgia Maxwell atop VH-LIU, an Air Tractor AT-502, at Krui airstrip in New South Wales. She had just got her turbine rating. *Georgia Maxwell, personal collection*

Sitting in VH-LIM, an Air Tractor AT-802, as high off the ground as the top front seat on a double-decker bus, Georgia (front), laughs with her best mate Bernadette Pickering. *Photo by Blaine Pickering*

Nicole Forrester refuels the Cessna 150 on her first flying job, working on an outback station as an aerial mustering pilot. *Nicole Forrester, personal collection*

Nicole flying a KC-30A Multi-Role Tanker Transport (MRTT). It is a heavily modified Airbus A330 airliner, and enables the Air Force to conduct air-to-air refuelling and provide strategic air lift. It features advanced communication and navigation systems and an electronic warfare self-protection system for shielding against threats from surface-to-air missiles. *Photo by Jeremy Sequeira*

Hard work and persistence paid off for Esther Veldstra when she became a pilot with the Royal Flying Doctor Service (Central Operations) based at Port Augusta in South Australia. Pictured behind Esther is an RFDS PC-12 aircraft.
Royal Flying Doctor Service

3

PATRICIA TOOLE
DOWN IN THE NEW GUINEA JUNGLE

I have fond memories of the first female pilot to fly commercially in New Guinea. When I interviewed you in Sydney I told you that you would fly [only] Austers carrying freight ... How wrong I was. You quickly graduated to Norsemans and became the first choice as pilot ... in Wewak.
Bobby Gibbes 5/11/97

(Handwritten inscription in Pat Toole's copy of the memoir *You Live But Once* by Bobby Gibbes DSO, DFC and Bar, OAM)

Bad weather sent the whole thing to hell in a handbasket and almost brought her undone. In June 1953 Patricia Toole was on a routine trip in a single engine four-seat Auster, loaded to the gunnels with freight. Her run along New Guinea's north coastline was from Wewak to Vanimo, back to Tadji and then up to the hilltop village of Lumi. It was going well until she got to Tadji, three-quarters of the way home. From there it should have been an easy hop to Lumi then back to Wewak.

New Guinea's weather is an unpredictable and punishing beast. Without much warning, the intense tropical heat draws moisture up from the jungle floor to form clouds and pushes them sky high. The hotter and more humid the day, the thicker the clouds. Gloomy Lumi was named so for a good reason.

Pat left the coast and flew towards Lumi in the Torricelli Mountains. Five minutes out and, Voomph! The rising cloud swamped her. 'It was sudden and complete.' Like flying in a bag of cotton balls, she was immediately blinded, with no chance of outclimbing it. Lumi was there and then it was gone.

Suddenly, all Pat could see was the inside of her aeroplane and the alarming story from her basic instruments. She was justifiably terrified by her spinning dials. Snap! Focus! Which way is up? She levelled, then climbed. The little Auster strained. It was built for aerial observation, not for hiking around the mountain tops of New Guinea. It was a great workhorse, but it was no thoroughbred. Pat pushed the under-powered little thing up into the thinning air. Too much higher and she'd need oxygen. Reality, now stark and immediate, enveloped her like the fog that besieged her.

There was no hope of making Lumi. She couldn't see it. She couldn't see anything. She followed her bouncing compass east, aiming for Maprik airport on the East Sepik river flats. Hopefully the cloud would break up and she would be able to see again. Maprik was 120 kilometres away; just under an hour.

Alone and frightened, Pat watched the fuel indicators steadily edge down. Without a radio, she had no way of calling anybody. Would she ever see her new husband again? In the slim chance that she survived, would she be found in time, or ever? Soon the engine would cough and cease. The only sounds then: gushing air and a pounding pulse. Pat would have to make a gliding descent through the cloud – definitely into the dense and steaming jungle and most likely into a hillside. The highest peaks were between 600 and 1700 metres. She just couldn't see them.

THIS SCENARIO WOULD BE EXACTLY WHAT PAT'S FATHER, Walter Graham, feared in 1952 when his only daughter shared her exciting news. Unbelievably, she had a job as a pilot. She was going to New Guinea. It was not that long since Walter had fought the Japanese in the New Guinea jungles. He knew the country and its challenges all too well.

Pat was close to her parents but after a childhood moving around NSW because of her father's work as a road contractor and then the war years commuting from Sydney to Tamworth for boarding school, she was not inclined to settle down, though she had tried. While her brother was at university and her parents recovered from a period of ill health, Pat had managed a couple of her father's hairdressing salons in Coffs Harbour to fund the family. Her future there was secure, but uncomfortably set. Until she found flying.

She'd become enamoured with aeroplanes after a friend flew in as a regular family guest. She was too young to ride in his plane then, but years later when a gleaming DC-3 descended into Coffs Harbour airport, the notion took hold. 'That's when I decided to test my mettle,' said Pat. She headed off for a joy flight at the Coffs Harbour Aero Club and immediately set her sights on getting a pilot licence. She sang all the way around the circuit on her first solo in January 1949.

Ten months later, on her twenty-first birthday, Pat earned her private pilot licence. To expedite her unrestricted and commercial pilot training she returned to Tamworth and reconnected with her school community at Church of England Girls School (now known as Calrossy).

Nothing delights a teacher more than student success and the headmistress, Miss Horton, excitedly embraced Pat's brave new venture. As Pat later recalled, 'She was a tower of strength and so very helpful', when she offered Pat free board at the school and the use of its library. In return, Pat supervised the girls in the boarding house after hours and earned extra cash doing haircuts.

Pat's daytime hairdressing wages in town went straight to the Newcastle Aero Club (Tamworth Branch) flying school as she worked her way through her courses. That required long evenings sprawled across the library floor with charts and paperwork. While Pat studied her maps, Miss Horton poured them a sherry each and joined her in coming to grips with the fascinating mathematics required for navigation.

Finally, Pat grasped the elusive equations as she could now see where they were taking her. One place they took her was flying over the New England Range from Tamworth to Coffs Harbour, cocooned in layers of warm clothes, topped with a padded flying suit and fleecy lined boots. In the Tiger Moth's open cockpit there were some cold calculations made for both the instrument and night components of her commercial licence.

One trip recorded in Pat's diary tells of her climbing high on a freezing August night with her scarf tucked tightly under her goggles. The solid ice that formed around her mouth possibly numbed the cursing because ice had also formed in the carburettor. Carburettor icing is frightening enough at any time because it makes the engine run rough or even stop. But to do a night flight over mountains knowing that it's a real possibility takes some bravery, particularly in an old Tiger, which is designed to protect itself (and inexperienced students) from carburettor ice with a heating system that is permanently switched on. One main drawback is that the more power you ask of the engine the less efficient the carburettor heat is. In extreme circumstances the fix is to reduce power to the point where maximum heating is restored and hopefully the ice is then cleared. It's counterintuitive at any time to reduce power when the engine is already struggling, but on a cold dark night over the New England Range with your face exposed to the elements, it's enough to make you seriously question your motives for flying at all.

There is a daytime flight however, that Pat remembers well. It was the day she flew to Bankstown Aerodrome in Sydney to what became the inaugural meeting of the Australian Women Pilots' Association (AWPA). Fifteen months after gaining her private licence, Pat got her commercial licence. In 1952, after flying and training for three years, she joined the worldwide queue of qualified but unemployed women pilots. Most flying jobs were taken by the returned servicemen, one of whom had set up an airline in New Guinea.

Bobby Gibbes, a nuggety World War II RAAF fighter ace founded Gibbes Sepik Airways (GSA) in 1948. GSA was a bush airline operating out of Port Moresby in the south and Wewak on the north coast. Bob knew Pat's brother Greg, who was working in agriculture in New Guinea (which was at that time a colony of Australia). As GSA had recently shed eight staff through resignation or sacking, Bob sounded off to Greg about how none of the wartime pilots would return to this confounded place. He needed pilots to fly those planes!

As they considered the conundrum, Greg recommended his sister. He'd enjoyed flying with her and could see this as a good solution. It was unheard of, but Bob was despairing and so he suggested Pat write to him. In his book, *You Live But Once*, Bob writes: 'She had been employed by me to bring my male pilots down to earth and stop them line-shooting about the difficulties of flying in New Guinea.'

The difficulties of flying in New Guinea can never be overstated, but Bob offered this unproven young woman weekly wages of £10 while training, to be increased to £20 pounds like the men once she was up and running. 'Sort your own uniform,' he added as an afterthought. Of course, she accepted, thrilled to have a job with a well-established company and to be leapfrogging the dull prospects on offer in Australia.

First jobs first, Pat headed to Sydney for some custom-made white drill culottes. They were tailor made, but the shirts were men's off-the-rack because they had the shoulder tabs for attaching epaulettes. Black shoes and white socks completed the kit and so New Guinea's first female commercial pilot was ready for work.

Back in Coffs Harbour, Walter's health improved so he wrote his own job application and gained a management position in the town of Rabaul on the island of New Britain, which lies to the east of the main island of New Guinea. When he informed Frances, his somewhat weary wife, she declared that if any of her family wanted to see her, they'd have to come home to Coffs Harbour because she had no intention of moving up there with the rest of them. For now though, the Grahams were on the move.

ON A SUNDAY MORNING IN MAY 1952, PAT STEPPED INTO HER new world; the steaming tarmac at Port Moresby's airport, Jackson's Strip. The place was memorable for its smells of betel nut, sweat and dogs, and for the groups of locals curiously eyeing the machinations of western society.

But despite her nerves and excitement at finally arriving, it was an empty welcome. Bob's intention to surprise everybody with his newest recruit was complete, because he forgot she was coming at all. Under the louvered windows of the terminal shed, instead of a hearty greeting, all she heard was the virtual sound of crickets.

Standing there on her lonesome, Pat looked about hopefully and saw in the distance her waving brother and his wife. Together they tracked down the surprised GSA manager who in turn introduced her to her new boss, the Dutch chief pilot Marinus (Rinus) Zuydam. This was the beginning of a friendship between Pat and Rinus that was marked by adventure.

On the Wednesday morning Pat climbed up into a 20-seat Lodestar to start her co-pilot endorsement. The Lodestar was intended as a passenger service and she was to be its first officer. They departed on her first flight, a 140-kilometre trip north-east over the majestic Owen Stanley Range to Popondetta.

It proved to be an exciting trip to Popondetta that day. The flight was to track through the wide Kokoda Gap and past Mount Lamington volcano, still smouldering after its recent eruption. Unfortunately, the Lodestar was also smouldering, with black smoke pouring from its portside engine. Air traffic control spotted the impending crisis before the plane even left the circuit and radioed to suggest an immediate return to Jackson's.

It was quickly obvious that this was no glitzy airline. GSA was a small company that advertised 'We Fly Anything, Any Place, Any Time'. They filled the gap where larger operators were unable or unwilling to go. In the 12 months to September 1952 they moved more than 900 tonnes of freight, 15 tonnes of mail and 11 341 passengers. GSA serviced the most remote and rudimentary airstrips that the old-time pilots called 'A Hairy Do'. Sixty years later, a new bush pilot described the place as 'f****** terrifying'. The local pilots called it flying in the chocolate box clouds because you never knew when you were going to get one with a hard centre; the cloud so often hiding a mountain within.

There was plenty to be fearful of and some of the military trained old hands questioned Bob's judgment in employing an inexperienced woman with no concept of the country. But Bob was used to confrontation, and he knew the dangers of New Guinea. In their four years of operation, at least four GSA aeroplanes had crashed. He'd had a near miss himself just before Pat's arrival and so, tough as he was, he always hammered home the need for self-preservation. He insisted on familiarisation flights above and beyond the basic requirements of the Australian Department of Civil Aviation, which was also responsible for aviation in New Guinea. With all eyes upon her, Pat worked at getting everything right. She studied the maps, the contours of the land, the cloud patterns and how terrain and weather related to each other.

After its engine blew up, the Lodestar was permanently retired and Pat moved onto the four-seat Austers and the larger Norsemans. She would ultimately, and rather quickly, be pilot-in-command flying these little aeroplanes around the mountains as a single pilot, instead of serving the long apprenticeship she was recruited into.

The company had ten Austers and they were all purchased new, carried a payload of 270 kilograms and travelled at about 130 kilometres per hour. She considered the Norseman 'a gentle, lovely workhorse powered by a reliable Pratt & Whitney engine'. An engine that, she hoped, wouldn't catch fire while she was flying it. The Norseman was designed to seat seven passengers, but these ones had bench seats with seat belts and floor fittings. They were then legally allowed to carry 16 passengers in the cabin. This was a bit of a shock for a new pilot. Rules and regulations still fresh in her mind, Pat was astonished at so many extra passengers, plus their knives, axes and cooking pots crammed into the space.

With all this unusual cargo, she and Rinus headed off to slippery airstrips hidden around mountain corners and one-way strips hacked out of the bush that would barely pass muster back in Australia. From behind their seats came the clipped sounds of the native languages as excited locals nursed their equally excitable and precious livestock.

Within three weeks of starting the job, Pat and Rinus were sent to the GSA maintenance base at Wewak, about 750 kilometres north-northwest, to swap over one Norseman for another. They were expected to be gone for a week so she carefully packed for ten days. She didn't get back for 18 months.

Departing at sea level, VH-ASN climbed to negotiate the New Guinea Highlands that form the island's spine. In her diary, Pat recorded this as being her 'first sighting of the magnificent mountains in those beautiful Highlands'. Understandably, as they came in to land at Goroka on a 40-kilometre-long valley floor at 5000 feet above sea level, she was awestruck by the mountains that towered two and three times that again, encircling them to create a stunning valley in the sky.

The next day they swooped over the palm-fringed coast of Wewak where word had filtered through about the new recruit. The GSA boys, gambling on her being an old bat, lined up at the airport to eye the new arrival. The men all lost the bet when the 23-year old blonde with fabulous hair stepped from the cabin. As they stood there agape, one of them nudged the boss, 'What are you going to do with her?' Cool as a cucumber, Colin Toole replied with a wry smile, 'Marry her of course.'

As the expat community in Wewak only comprised 29 adults and 23 children, it was a fair chance that someone would try.

But could she fly? There was plenty of work to be done and as base manager, Colin had a huge backlog to get through because for some reason the fleet of Norsemans was experiencing engine troubles and were grounded while the problems were rectified. He promptly dispatched Pat and Rinus in a different Norseman, VH-BLM, on a 25-minute charter to Angoram out on the Sepik River. The 1100-kilometre Sepik is the country's longest river and curves around a large catchment of towering mountains, swamps and tropical rainforests.

It was Black Friday, 13 June 1952. With the usual high-density seating arrangements in place, Rinus and Pat climbed southeast out of Wewak, hauling the passengers and their possessions up into the hills. In a short ten minutes, all went sickeningly silent as the propeller came sharply into view and the engine stopped dead. 'It was a great pity to see that engine fail,' said Pat years later. 'Because it was the only one we had.'

Rinus 'did a superb landing' in 1.2-metre-high Kunai grass on a ridge and, fearing a fire, he and Pat bailed – each out their own cockpit door. But as fast as the pilots were, the locals were faster and they made a clattering disappearance into the bush, trailing the possessions they were carrying home to their villages. Pat marvelled at the speed of their exit and wondered if any of them would ever fly again. She wasn't sure if they were frightened, or if they thought that was just how planes landed. Either way, they were all gone, leaving the young Australian woman and her Dutch colleague alone on a hilltop with nothing but the clothes they stood up in and the precious Norseman logbooks.

The pilots began the inevitable walk, which offered plenty of time to discuss the merit or otherwise of flying without radios. It was not mandatory at that time to carry a radio and company policy was to remove them. They weighed around 4.5 kilograms each and their reception was unreliable in the remote country. That weight allowance could be utilised for freight, which converted to plenty of payload over a 1000 flying hour cycle.

After five hours sliding over boggy mountain tracks, Pat in uncomfortable new shoes, the bedraggled pair stumbled into the village of Tring, where some locals agreed to paddle them back to Wewak. But in less time than it takes to lie back in a rudimentary canoe and dream of Wewak, it ground to a sandy halt and the occupants were rudely thrown from their seats. 'Everybody out!' the locals ordered. The sea was too rough.

It took another five painful hours following the swinging hurricane lamp of their young local guide, to emerge from the jungle about three kilometres east of Wewak. The search party was on a different track so word was sent to retrieve the retrieval party, while the pilots got themselves home around 2 am in a borrowed jeep. It had been a ten-minute flight to the grassy ridge and an excruciating ten-hour walk back. They were given leave to attend a dance the following night barefooted.

As word quickly spread about their expedition, one of Pat's contemporaries was concerned about her being 'a slip of a girl with shiny wings, with only a few hours in her logbook, getting her aerial baptism over some of the toughest flying country in the world'. Two engine failures in the first three weeks was tough stuff alright, but she was determined to make it work. Whether it was the busiest base, or perhaps for some other reason, GSA decided to keep her on in Wewak to begin her area familiarisation in the small Auster. Rising at dawn, she flew almost every day.

Her small neat logbook entries include co-pilot flights to Yang, Maprik, Telefomin, Goroka, Vanimo and other places as she completed the requirements for all new GSA pilots. It would take five times over any one route and at least three landings on any one strip before she was allowed to go in solo.

Most of her training was done with Peter Manser, a 31-year-old ex-RAAF pilot. He arrived in New Guinea after the war as a store clerk. He once asked a customer if she'd like her broom wrapped or would she rather ride it home? He was a riotous social companion and undoubtedly a better pilot than salesperson. In his few years with GSA, Peter had already endured one serious crash and was well-qualified to mentor Pat about the tricky strips that she had to master.

Due to the high volume of flying, it only took four months to finish her 200 hours familiarisation and then she was cleared and 'Good to go, happy to be an economic unit and at last pulling [her] weight.' Her turf was about 32 000 square kilometres of jungle, towering mountains populated by people of many different tribes, with many snaking rivers and slippery, difficult airstrips.

She worked alongside the men and settled into the lifestyle where, like any good colonial outpost, 'we worked hard and we played hard'. Though Bob employed her to do the same job as the men, he couldn't avoid having to house her separately. A lack of privacy in the men's long bush hut meant she dined in the GSA mess but lived alone in a simple company dwelling made of local materials.

Maybe it was while relaxing here in the shade of the verandah after work one day that Colin, the base manager, made a difficult admission to Pat. He thought he had fallen in love with her. He even dared to mention the M word. It was an astonishing moment for the young professional who was just hitting her straps and establishing her career.

While a breeze rustled through the coconut trees, Colin held his breath. But Pat was painfully slow to reply. 'No' she said gently shaking her head. 'No, that's not what I want. I'm too young and I'm not looking to settle down.' Dejected, Col walked away. Envy however, is a fickle friend and that evening she spied Col go across to the tiny hospital to visit the matron who he'd been stepping out with before Pat's arrival.

Sixty-five years later, she recalls that solitary moment with great clarity.

'Did you follow him?' I asked.

'No! But I got so bloody jealous I thought I'd better marry the bastard!' she said, roaring with laughter. 'I tracked him down the following day, hoping it wasn't too late to change my mind.'

It wasn't and soon enough the romance was all on. But first there was drama at the hospital. In a perfect case of bad luck and worse timing, before they'd even announced their engagement, Pat got really sick. And with his fiancée under the care of his ex-girlfriend, Col thought it gentlemanly to tell the matron of his intention to marry, not her, but the dengue-ridden woman in one of her hospital's four beds.

Pat lay there in extreme pain, unable to even move her eyeballs and flinched at the stream of abuse blasting up the hall as matron quite roundly told Col what she thought of him and his plans. Pat recalled that the necessary injections that were administered by the jilted matron felt as though they were launched from the doorway; the painful syringe a physical symbol of Cupid's misdirected arrow.

Despite being so ill, Doctor (Mac) MacInerny, who was no stranger to domestic disasters, stood by his patient and muttered, 'Pat, I think you might be better off recovering at home.' Pat departed the melee, not stopping to question his orders, and matron left Wewak. She wasn't hanging around for the festivities.

Walter Graham, now managing a trade store at Kavieng on an outlying island, hosted his daughter's wedding on New Year's Eve 1952. Her engagement ring had come out of a catalogue, the beautiful classic bridal dress was made by the chief pilot's wife, the matron of honour wore 'something that she had' and the wedding ring arrived the day before the wedding only to be found too small and require a set of tin snips to expand it. On a later visit to Sydney, Pat reluctantly removed the disjoined ring to have a jeweller rebuild it. It never left her finger in the 63 years afterwards.

Pat's mother Frances came from Coffs Harbour for the event, realised what she was missing out on and fell in love with the place. She stayed until she and Walter retired, about a decade later, meaning the whole family was now in different parts of the same country.

Col and Pat honeymooned at Rabaul on the nearby island of New Britain, then returned to a rudimentary house made of tent poles and iron sheets, with woven grass floors. Looking out to sea from their cliff-top location, the newlyweds 'watched the moon rise and set across the water, quite convinced [they] were in paradise.'

On the work front, Bob Gibbes returned from a trip to Europe to find the company in disarray, with all seven Norsemans grounded with engine failures. It was later revealed this was caused by an outdated and faulty maintenance directive for the 1000-hour engine overhauls. Bob arrived in Wewak to negotiate with the workers as he fought with the Australian government and his creditors to stave off bankruptcy, preserve his contracts and seek financial assistance. In a drastic reshuffling of affairs, he tried to reduce Col's wages and to sack Pat but immediately reinstated her when she said the opposition was keen to employ her.

It was a shaky start to the year and that first six months of 1953 brought more harsh life lessons, starting in March. Pat was meant to be on a joy flight with the doctor, Mac, in his Auster but was offloaded at the last minute, in favour of some more important passengers. On departure from Vanimo Mac stalled the plane into the bay. His passengers survived, but Mac did not and the close-knit expat community felt the tragedy deeply.

For all the safety systems put in place, necessity sometimes gave way to some fairly unorthodox invention. The pilots had a well-established system of mid-air refuelling for times when they were caught out by weather and required more endurance. When Pat flew important medicine to a distant and isolated patrol officer, she hesitantly adopted this questionable refuelling system.

When the belly tank fuel was exhausted, she selected the other tank and set the plane into trim so it would fly straight and level and hold its course. She then moved a blitz (fuel) can onto her lap from the passenger seat. She forced her door open against the slipstream and in a gymnastic manoeuvre, leant out and down below floor level. She was literally hanging out of the plane. She gingerly removed the cap of the belly tank's refuelling pipe and inserted the hose from the can. After the precious last drops drained into the tank, she gently screwed the tank's cap back on, retracted the can and pulled the door shut, all the while hoping the aeroplane stayed in straight and level flight and that she wouldn't fall out. I'm about the same height and I tried the same manoeuvre in a stationary Auster. Even with the advantage of being 30 years younger and more nimble, it would be a difficult and frightening thing to do.

Not surprisingly, Pat didn't love the mid-air refuelling but she had earned respect for her flying. A prominent local mining personality specifically requested her as his pilot and it was a brilliant endorsement. So, it must have been an uneasy conversation then for John Arthur, the director of civil aviation, to front the popular pilot and deliver bad news from the United Nations, which ordered her to stop flying over its uncontrolled Western Territories unless accompanied by a male pilot. They feared for her safety should she come down in such wild and unforgiving country.

Pat rightly pointed to her fully endorsed commercial licence. It had no restrictions, she was familiar with the area and intended to continue working – solo. Bob Gibbes didn't earn his stripes by being told what to do either and he didn't employ Pat as cargo, so they reached a stalemate. She agreed to carry a gun.

She continued with her work and in early June 1953 went to the rescue when Peter Manser hit a stump on approach to Vanimo airstrip. He flipped one of the only three re-engined Norsemans onto its back, leaking battery acid into his own and his passengers' eyes. Pat answered the distress call and, arriving in the small Auster, surveyed the crippled aeroplane and the precious little room left on the strip to land.

'God, here we go!' she thought as she lowered the nose, kicked on one rudder pedal and moved the control column to the opposite direction, reining the plane in at a 45-degree angle, known as a sideslip. This manoeuvre can easily be mishandled, but if done right, allows a steep approach and pinpoint control of the landing, which was vital in this situation to enable her to come in high over some trees. The difficult sideslip was exacerbated by water at both ends of the strip, tree stumps on the first third of it and the upended aeroplane across the middle. As soon as the wheels kissed the ground, Pat stamped on the brakes to slow up enough to steer around the Norseman.

She collected the walking wounded and then, with the extra weight on board, she had a group of men hold onto the tail while she revved the aeroplane for a racing start. She only just managed to become airborne on take-off, almost pitching into the bay. As she flew away, wondering if her wheels were wet, she was thankful that the passengers' eyes were bandaged so they didn't see the departure that Pat could not forget. She was still rattled when they landed back in Wewak after a two-hour flight.

Two weeks later it was Pat who was in trouble.

CLIMBING HIGH AND BLINDED BY CLOUD, PAT TURNED FOR the Sepik Flats. Almost out of fuel after circling for a while, Mother nature thrust one final chance into her lap. Unbelievably, a tiny hole appeared in the cloud to reveal a stretch of riverbed; a rare piece of flat ground upon which to put down.

With great anticipation, Pat flicked the joystick sideways, declaring to herself, 'That'll do me'. She dropped a wing and spiralled down, making for the only clear patch of land in miles of mountainous jungle. Alarmingly though, as the ground came closer, the boulders grew larger and the riverbanks got steeper. Her 'last chance' was not giving it up easily.

With a pounding heart, one shaking hand on the throttle and the other on the joystick, she aimed for the river. The steep terrain either side left little room to glide in, but she was committed to the landing.

Hoping the freight wouldn't dislodge behind her, Pat put the Auster precisely down on dry stones and shingles in a clattering, hair-raising arrival. Decreasing from about 40 knots (75 km/h), the aeroplane sped across the stones, bouncing towards huge trees that loomed in its path.

In a time-critical move, she stamped hard on one brake and flung the Auster around in a sweeping ground loop. As she slewed around, a boulder violently snapped off the right undercarriage leg and also took care of the starboard wingtip and the propeller tip.

The sturdy little aeroplane ground to a shuddering nose-down halt against the bank, with its chequered tail pointing at the clouds. Unbelievably, its pilot had survived. But she was quickly out and gone, fearing a fire. Pat ran down to the water's edge where her shaking hand instinctively reached into her pocket for a smoke. How on earth had she survived this ordeal when so many before her hadn't? She lit up a cigarette and took stock of her situation.

It was only 10.30 am on a Monday. She was alone with just two cigarettes, two bags of salt, two bolts of fabric, a tin of condensed milk, a packet of barley sugar, four litres of fuel and no communications. Oil on the windscreen confirmed that during the whiteout she'd been inverted.

She prayed that a search party would be dispatched at the standard half hour past her expected arrival time, which was about the time she connected with the rock. From among the freight, she unfurled a roll of white fabric and spelled HELP using dark stones, pointing the correct way because a search plane would only see her if it approached from the north; if it could get through at all.

In the still of the morning, she couldn't know the disposition of the villagers she'd flown over on descent but she vainly belted an empty blitz can to try and attract their attention. She hoped she hadn't landed in the wilds of the Western Territories among the hostile tribes that were the source of the UN's angst. Nobody answered.

Back at Wewak, panic set in. Dreikikir Station, 150 kilometres west-southwest had reported that an aeroplane had circled overhead in the bad weather. It was estimated that was about the extent of Pat's fuel range. GSA's first search run failed to find any sign of her and it only added to her family's distress when ABC radio reported that she was missing. The searchers assumed they'd be looking for wreckage.

Bob Gibbes was used to worried wives, as there had been a few forced landings over the years, but now he had to manage a pacing husband whose normally fine sense of humour had abandoned him. It turned into a long night for everybody.

Squashed in the back of the aeroplane, an alien figure deep within the jungle, sleep was impossible for Pat. She cursed the stifling heat as she tried to plump the bags of salt, damp with humidity, to rest her head. Bathed in sweat, she braced against the onslaught of mosquitoes needling into her clammy skin. The river water, so enticing, could only be used to rinse her dry mouth and then spat out, for fear of dysentery. She decided she'd give it three days and then she'd have to walk.

Based on the information from Dreikikir, the next morning Mandated Airlines passengers kept a lookout from the eight or so seats of their Dragon DH84. They flew across ridge after ridge of mountains and valleys covered in jungle canopy that could easily swallow a downed aeroplane. By fluke, it was Wewak's district commissioner who happened to spot the silver Auster on the dull riverbed. Pat waved frantically and the aircraft circled a few times and dropped a box, which smashed down on the other side of the waist-deep river.

She waded to the other bank, thrilled to find cans of fresh water in the splintered box. The boys had also pooled their smokes into an Ardath screw-top cigarette tin, which had unfortunately burst open among the thick riverbank reeds. She hoped the pilots had made a good note of her position on their map and would return the next day.

Now hot, dirty and wet, Pat slung her uniform over the wing and settled down in her underwear to have some water and to dry the cigarettes. Suddenly, a Qantas Drover, another eight-seat aircraft,

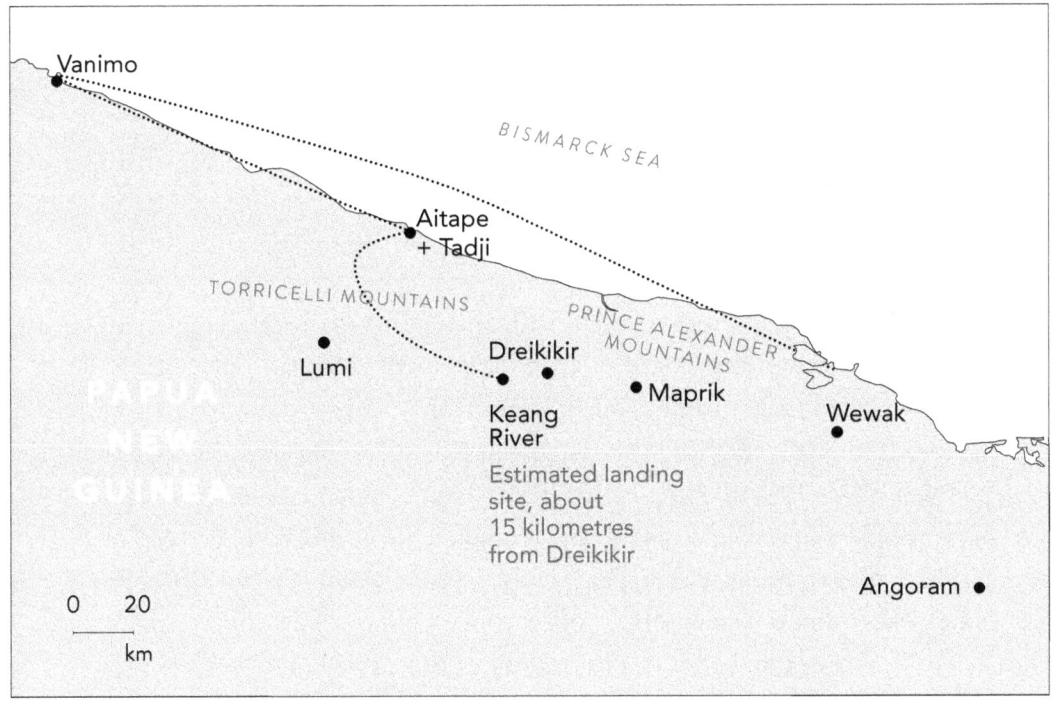

Wewak and Sepik District of PNG, showing Keang River
where Pat Toole force-landed the Auster

droned through the gloom and Pat's heart leapt when her husband of six months parachuted out of it.

But the mirage was short-lived. The husband was actually a kitbag wafting beneath a small 'chute. Col, an ex-paratrooper, was in the Drover but had been unable to find a parachute for himself. And his fear ramped up, as even though they'd finally located the grounded Auster, they did not see his wife.

Even in such dire circumstances, Pat wasn't one to gallivant about half naked and was frantically pulling on her clothes before stumbling into view. She hauled the heavy bag back through the river, left it on the bank, then waded back and folded up the 'chute.

Of all the items she would have lamented not having for that trip – a radio, survival rations, even some insect repellent – she had forgotten the most important: the Department of Civil Aviation's gun. She dived into the survival kit and pulled out a strange pistol and ammunition. Turning it in her hands, she eyed the cold hard Luger and thought she'd better learn how to load and fire it. Her shot rang out unheard by anyone else.

Next in the pack was more fresh water and then out came some old wartime K-rations. These were three meals in a tin, wrapped in heavy waxed greaseproof paper. The horrible wax paper smell had permeated the lot, rendering even the tinned camp pie inedible. The very last thing she found was a New Guinea expat staple, a bottle of Rhum Negrita, wrapped in a towel and included to numb pain in case of injury. She thought with a grin, 'Now you're talking …' It was hardly top shelf but what the hell?

No sooner had Pat started smiling at the rum than the smile was wiped right off her face. She froze as she looked up the river bend and movement slowly morphed into the shapes of men.

She quietly picked up the Luger and put it in her pocket and watched, trembling, as the group advanced. Not two, not ten, not 20. She wasn't sure how many there were, but it felt like one or two hundred naked men armed with spears, axes and bows and arrows approaching her.

As she awaited her fate, they came close enough for Pat to see the white of their teeth because, thank god, the front ones were smiling. She relaxed her grip on the Luger, fixed a smile of her own and advanced to greet the group, shaking hands with each and every one. They were from the village she had spotted on the way down and had come to investigate the aerial activity. They invited her to go back to the village with them but she thought it better to stay with the aircraft as it was clearly visible for the search party. Their offer of hospitality refused, the villagers quickly dispersed, keen to get home before nightfall.

Pat returned to the aeroplane and, with a nip of neat rum, kept a nervous eye on the river, which was rapidly rising with each inch of rain. Outside, two of the villagers, who had insisted on staying behind to guard the aircraft and its sole occupant, also kept watch. It was a great comfort, and of her time in New Guinea she recalled how wonderful the locals were to the expats.

A dedicated young government patrol officer walked into the small village later that evening, looking for the crashed aeroplane. Well, he had a tough job. Just as Pat had received the water and rations from the sky, the search party in the Dragon had flown on and dropped a rudimentary map with a circle that said, 'Proceed to the scene of the crash.' The circle covered about 300 square kilometres of forbidding jungle.

With this scant information, the patrol officer made an educated guess and set out at about lunchtime from his post at Dreikikir. The villagers informed him that the pilot was female and some miles down the ever-expanding river.

The officer, a stocky Australian who had been partly raised in New Guinea, was used to walking for days on patrol in this country and without hesitation continued overland into the night with his three local police assistants. They hacked their way down the last few kilometres of steep and slippery jungle at around 10 pm. When he fired a couple of shots into the deep night to signal his approach, Pat replied with a couple of rounds from the Luger but her shots echoed from the steep canyon walls, unheard.

Through teeming rain, she stared into the blackness and waited. Eventually, a hurricane lantern lit the very welcome face of the 21-year-old patrol officer, Jock MacGregor. They introduced themselves and then Pat, rising to the occasion, turned to her new friend and enquired, 'Jock … Would you like a rum?' 'Christ!' exclaimed her sandy-haired saviour. 'I walk for eight hours in the jungle. I find a white woman – alive! – and she offers me rum. You bloody beaut!'

The police assistants erected a grass shelter as Pat and Jock crouched under the Auster wing. Precious rum splashed into a couple of pannikins, five glugs each, and as Jock rested his feet, Pat handled the drinks and began her debrief. Oblivious to the mosquitoes and the river rocks, they finished the bottle and fell into a relieved sleep around 3 am. Pat had been out there for more than 40 hours.

ON WEDNESDAY THE CREW CLEARED THE BANK AND LASHED the Auster to trees on higher ground so it wouldn't get swept away in the flooded river. Engineers would be in soon to salvage it.

Another airdrop came and it contained a letter from Col. That letter has been lost to time, but whatever it said quickly reduced his young wife to tears and brought poor Jock awkwardly rushing to console her. He thought it was bad news, but he was in fact witnessing Pat having an emotional response to events as much as to the letter. Pat partly walked and partly rode out of the river on a sedan chair for much of the journey back to Dreikikir. She flew home the following day with the Bishop of Wewak and was soon returned to the loving arms of her husband. When things settled down, Col joked, 'Any other pilot takes five hours to do that trip. Not my wife, she takes five days.'

It was straight back to business as usual and Pat flew a dozen more hours, then took a holiday to Australia with Col. Her last assignment was a five-hour return trip to Goroka on 31 July 1953. She was back in the repaired Auster, which an engineer, Mr Brearley and his assistant Mr K Haslett, had dismantled at the crash site and carried out to Dreikikir. They replaced the leg and propeller and spliced timber into the main spar. Peter Manser flew it home to Wewak.

Pat hadn't lost her nerve. And she hadn't wrecked the aeroplane, for which her boss was most grateful. In fact, Bob Gibbes later recalled that had she not hit the rock, Pat could very well have flown the Auster out again.

Pat and Col returned from leave to find a staff reshuffle and reduction had left Col in limbo and Pat grounded without explanation. There was talk of the company starting a base in Madang, 300 kilometres east along the coast, but as Bob and John Arthur from the Department of Civil Aviation worked together to bring GSA's affairs under control, ten employees were let go, reducing wage costs by 25 per cent.

Pat and Col repaired to the Highlands to wait it out but Bob then stopped communicating with them and they resigned in frustration. That marked the end of Pat's commercial flying career, grounded through no fault of her own. It had been three years in the making and 15 life-changing months in the doing. She never did get that pay rise.

This turn of events pushed them into starting Kalanga, a Highlands coffee plantation, a few years earlier than planned. In an underfunded operation that was literally carved out of the bush, they slept on a grass palliasse (mattress), drank boiled water from the river and settled in for the five-year wait for their coffee plants to produce fruit.

The famous aviator Nancy Bird Walton visited in 1956. The Australian Women Pilots' Association, which Nancy had founded, and was by then six years old, had one charter member's signature missing. Nancy didn't trust the important document to the mail, and it was a perfect excuse to visit her brother in Lae and then spend a week at Kalanga so Pat could sign the document.

It might have been a rare opportunity for Pat to debrief with another aviator, particularly as the Dreikikir incident was only a few years behind her. Nancy was especially proud of Pat and the week was filled with flying talk. It was a great example of why AWPA was formed – to facilitate camaraderie among women pilots.

With her flying days finished, Pat settled into married life and built the coffee business alongside her husband. They socialised, entertained and embarked on a great adventure, producing award winning coffee at the farm.

'Everybody loved Pat,' said Ann Munro, a neighbouring coffee grower. 'She was so capable. She plumbed their house. She could do anything. When I handed Pat my nursing book on how to deliver a baby in case mine came early, she took one look and said, "It's a big book!" as she accepted the task.' Thankfully for all, Pat didn't need to deliver the baby.

Alongside the hard work and equally energetic socialising, Pat and Col had four children. Right into old age, Pat carried the trauma of losing their last baby at birth, though she recorded it in her usual matter-of-fact style, shifting the focus of her grief to the challenges of everyday life in New Guinea:

> In 1962 our fourth child, Bill, was born. The birth was breech and quite difficult and was too much for the baby who did not survive the ordeal. Some time later, I was looking for [middle child] Margaret and found her in the wood shed with the Meri [native woman] who looked after the children. Margaret had the big axe poised over her hand. I quietly grabbed the axe then asked what it was all about. Margaret told me the Meri had told her she had not shown how sorry she was because the baby had not lived. To show she was sorry she should cut off a finger – the number of joints removed indicating how close the death was and that a complete finger should be alright for a brother. I was so pleased I had arrived in the nick of time. Margaret was only five and the axe was large. She would have mutilated her whole hand had I been a little later. I tried to explain to the Meri and Margaret that that was the native fashion and not our way at all.

In January 1969 as Independence approached for New Guinea and the two eldest children were at high school in Australia, Pat and Col decided to *go-pinis*: 'go and finish', the pidgin term for final farewells. Kalanga was sold to Miles and Norma Barne.

When they came home to Queensland in January 1969, in their luggage was the Auster's damaged propeller. It took a good 12 months or more to settle in after 17 years in a foreign land because nothing was familiar.

In Brisbane their various businesses included a Buderim ginger farm, a Palmwoods sawmill, a small property subdivision and finally a Brisbane timber laminating plant. Through good fortunes and bad, Col and Pat had lived and worked together since Wewak in 1952 until their sons took on the timber business in the late 1980s.

Pat felt the passing of Colin in 1993 very deeply and filled her time with travel and family, including an around-Australia drive with a fellow woman pilot, stopping off with AWPA members most of the way.

In 1998 a fellow AWPA founding member, Dorothy Herbert, invited Pat to a Women in Aviation conference in New Zealand. Pat decided to get relicensed. She joined AWPA again and enjoyed flying for another five years up and around the Brisbane coast. For a 72-year-old though, the relentless radio chatter became difficult to decipher and she knew it was time to give it away. She claimed there was a time when you were too old for it, whether you wanted to admit that or not.

She wasn't too old for a motorised glider joy flight though, which in a fateful moment had an engine failure after take-off. The pilot put the plane down safely in a paddock and said to Pat, 'You were very calm.' She smiled as she replied, 'It's my third forced landing.'

When the 2016 AWPA annual conference organising committee was searching for a guest speaker, they invited Pat as one of only five AWPA founding members still alive, three of whom were still Association members. Her talk had 150 people spellbound as she related her stories of a time without navigation aids, employment contracts or weather reports. A time that was as remote to most of the audience as the location itself. She finished without flourish but stood frozen with surprise when the crowd rose for a teary standing ovation.

The day after the speech, the 88-year-old was spotted deep in thought beside an Auster at Aldinga airfield, but had to refuse a ride. The legs that delivered her so gracefully down from the aeroplane at Wewak in 1952 could no longer lift her back up.

HAD PAT NOT BEEN ENTANGLED IN GSA'S CRISIS OF 1952, SHE may have continued her commercial career. By 1954 Bob Gibbes had saved GSA and four years later sold it to Mandated Airlines, which then sold out to Ansett in 1962.

If she'd continued to fly after she had children, would the new companies have kept her on as they did Peter Manser? It was another 15 years before Deborah Lawrie took Reg Ansett to court for the right to fly as Ansett's first female airline pilot. Pat's love of the job and flying ability would easily have found a place had she been born 60 years later.

Pat died just two weeks after appearing at the AWPA conference, where she had spoken of her enduring respect for the little Auster VH-KSK, which she said treated her very gently in the Keang River. Pat's will requested that, upon completion of its latest restoration, VH-KSK carry her again to release her ashes into the open skies north of Brisbane.

Pat Toole was remarkable for seizing the opportunity Bob Gibbes provided, even though he did it, he said later, to hold her up as an example to pull the men into line. She quickly proved her worth and set a precedent for future women pilots in one of the toughest flying environments on earth. She, and those who knew her, were proud of her achievement.

Of GSA's ten Auster aeroplanes, eight were written off by the company's pilots. Papua New Guinea remains an unforgiving environment and as the first Australian female commercial pilot to try her hand up there, Pat proved that gender is no barrier to skill, although few have dared to follow her.

Jan Goodhew worked for Talair out of their Wewak base in the 1980s. She recalls other women who flew in PNG as pilots: Eileen Steenson, Juliette Chubb, Cathy Burrows and Honor Egger. Air Niugini's first female jet pilot is Captain Beverley Pakii who began flying the Fokker 100 in 2018.

Jan met Pat much later back in Brisbane and they shared many stories. 'Even 30 years after Pat's ground-breaking time, working as a commercial pilot in PNG remained a combination of privilege and challenge,' says Jan. 'Although the aircraft were then predominately single- and twin-engine Cessnas, the ten-seater twin-engine Islander and turbo props, the unrelenting mix of difficult weather and airstrips located in mountainous terrain remained. Pilot accommodation had vastly improved. However, the regular loss of power and or water, combined with the lack of food in the trade stores toward the end of each month before a new batch arrived by ship, remained stark differences to living in Australia. The incredible bond and respect between pilots who have successfully taken on the challenge of flying in PNG remains unbreakable.'

4

GABY KENNARD
AROUND THE WORLD SOLO

*I found a dream and that brought hope
and a new way of looking at things.*

(Gaby Kennard, 1989)

In the equatorial air approaching Majuro in the Marshall Islands, just west of the International Date Line, Gaby Kennard was thinking about Amelia Earhart, the famous American aviatrix of the 1930s, who was thought to have disappeared around Majuro more than 50 years earlier on a round-the-world attempt.

Within a few years, Gaby would become the first Australian woman to fly around the world in a single engine aeroplane. According to earthrounders.com, a list of all the people who have circumnavigated the globe, Gaby is still the only Australian woman to have done so; alongside 11 Australian men and 127 people worldwide.

As Majuro revealed itself, the pilot in command casually mentioned, 'This is the area where Amelia Earhart was lost.' Gaby was flying with Jim Hazelton, co-founder of Hazelton Airlines, from California to Sydney on one of his more than 200 light aircraft crossings as a ferry pilot.

It didn't take long for Gaby's long-time interest in the famous American aviatrix to be piqued again. Back in Sydney Gaby dived into anything she could find on Earhart's and other pioneering aviators' stories. As a pilot herself, she felt a natural alliance to Amelia.

BORN IN MELBOURNE IN 1944, GABY EMBARKED ON A NURSING career that then took her into a role as a pharmaceutical rep. For a decade in that job she routinely drove past the South Coast Airport at Albion Park, also known as Illawarra Regional, Wollongong, and now Shellharbour Airport. She had always yearned to fly and later learnt it was in her DNA as her father James was an American pilot who had been killed as a passenger in an aircraft accident departing Amberley Air Force Base near Brisbane during World War II.

She loved the sensation of flight, the surge of the take-off and the challenge of landing. And so, in 1977 the 33-year-old pulled into the South Coast Airport to enquire about lessons.

It took courage to make that big step through the door and announce, 'I'd like to learn to fly.' She was not the first to experience trepidation but perhaps one of the few who experienced the terse response she received from the instructor: 'I don't believe in women flying so I'm not going to teach you to fly.'

That instructor totally misread the motivation of the woman standing before him. But before the quietly spoken potential student could flee, the receptionist intervened and summoned the chief flying instructor, Ron Berry. He was impressed with Gaby's determination.

As a single mother of daughter Mimi, who was only a toddler at the time, she sacrificed many extras to reach her goal (and pay for it). She soaked up everything Ron had to teach her. Because she always needed to cut costs, the aero club also became her rare social outlet. There Gaby could relax with like-minded people. And her little daughter Mimi enjoyed her weekend visits, flying with her mum. Once she had gained her private pilot licence, Gaby had ambitions to fly higher but this time the RAAF Reserve confounded her with the blunt statement, 'We don't have women.' When she asked why, the officer replied, 'You'd have to change an act of parliament for that.'

In 1983, a few years after gaining her licence, Gaby spent a final year with her mother, Patricia, who was gravely ill. Patricia encouraged Gaby not to let her hard-won flying fall by the wayside and so, after her marriage to Neville Kennard that year, Gaby continued her training to include a commercial licence, multi-engine command instrument rating, and a seaplane endorsement.

In 1987 Gaby and Neville went to the USA to collect a new floatplane that Neville had bought. Unfortunately he flipped it in Florida's alligator-infested waters and had to swim to shore. The aircraft was a write-off and Neville lost heart for flying it. Although this was a blow to Gaby, she flew the replacement aircraft to Torrance, California. There, she was strongly advised not to attempt the flight across the Pacific because the seaplane, with its top-mounted engine and the enormous fuel load required, was deemed too unstable and dangerous for such a flight. Instead, she came home with Jim Hazelton in a light twin-engined aircraft as an introduction to long-distance flying.

Having had the experience of flying across the Pacific with Jim, Gaby researched and sought permission to ferry her family's seaplane home via the north Pacific rim – USA, Aleutian Islands, Russia, Kuril Islands, Japan, Philippines, Indonesia and home – but the Russian government refused her permission to transit their territories, thereby thwarting nine months intense work.

It was a big blow. But Gaby rebounded with a more daring and fulfilling challenge – she planned to fly around the whole world, not just halfway as previously planned. It was a huge and quite overwhelming undertaking, but she took to it with great conviction. The more she was discouraged, the more determined she became. She just needed an aeroplane, money, contacts, visas, a babysitter and a solid plan. She began by seeking the people who could provide the all-important moral support, useful information and necessary introductions. The next year was one of intense and focused planning.

Being the first Australian woman to fly solo around the world was not the original intent when she planned her trip. In fact, Gaby didn't even realise that was a title to be won and was shocked when asked if she was doing it for the publicity. Nothing was further from the truth. The publicity was simply a by-product. Her motivation was nested in self-fulfilment; to know that she could do it.

She settled on two agendas. To raise funds for the Royal Flying Doctor Service (RFDS) and to retrace, as closely as possible, the final flight of Amelia Earhart. She set to gaining the airspace and visa approvals for the 21 countries she'd transit and collated charts and advice for the trip. While juggling a job, two children and a mortgage, she approached sponsors, mortgaged her house and imported a single-engine 1981 model Piper Saratoga from the USA and registered it in Australia. VH-GKF was designed to carry six people and it had a Lycoming engine, which Gaby would rely on to get her across vast expanses of ocean and unfamiliar and inhospitable terrain.

Qantas was quick to help with logistics such as diplomatic clearances and kindly offered a briefing and some practical help for the trip, which began on 3 August 1989. And just before her departure at Bankstown airport, as an eleventh-hour gesture, Gaby's brother-in-law Andy pressed US$4000 into her hand, which she hid in the instrument panel. Nancy Bird Walton later joked that the money bought about a million dollars worth of publicity. And boy, there was a lot of publicity. Once she departed on her trip, the publicity took on a life of its own. The compromise in her escape would be the whole country breathlessly following her around the world, vicariously living an adventure few were able or willing to pursue. Australian current affairs program *60 Minutes* installed cameras in the aeroplane, which she sometimes found intrusive and occasionally turned off.

The morning of her departure dawned clear and Gaby flew off at 8.55 am. She was an hour late leaving because of media commitments. She flew north carrying a debt of $150 000. She was escorted out of Bankstown by her husband and the two children and some other aviation supporters. She was elated to be finally getting away and as the other aeroplanes peeled off to return to Bankstown, Gaby continued on the first leg of her planned 33-day, 54 000-kilometre trip.

The journey had all the hallmarks of a gripping tale, though some of her friends, including Ron Berry, who was by then very fond of Gaby, were extremely anxious about her plans for this tough undertaking. Qantas Captain Les Haywood, responding to a reporter's questions about the flight, said, 'I sincerely hope she makes it, but I'm not going to put a number on it. I'm not a betting man …'

Though it made a good snippet for the nightly news, Captain Haywood's concern was not about Gaby's ability, but rather at the disappointment she would endure if something were to go awry in an unlikely part of the world and maintenance were not available, causing the trip to be called off.

ON THE FIRST LEG OF THE FLIGHT – SYDNEY TO CAIRNS – THE Omega satellite navigation system started playing up. An RFDS pilot in Cairns had warned her not to rely on it and he was right. The Omega, an early form of GPS, worked intermittently throughout the whole trip and so she relied on dead reckoning for navigation, together with the VOR and DME ground stations, which are useful only when within a few hundred kilometres. Most airports had transmitters that could be picked up by an aircraft with the correct VOR and DME receivers, but they were no use out across the ocean or in remote areas where none existed.

The next leg, across the short Torres Strait to Papua New Guinea, was the first over water and preceded having to tackle the notorious Kokoda Gap. Thankfully Ron had worded up his old mates at the Port Moresby Aero Club to lay out the hard facts of flying in this treacherous country. So, with a life-saving hand-drawn map in hand, Gaby departed Port Moresby and was forced to duck and weave at an altitude of 12 000 feet above the Owen Stanley Ranges. The mountains are a couple of thousand feet higher than pilots should fly without oxygen so it was an eyes-wide-open flight, knowing which mountains to weave around in turbulent, ever-changing weather without a second pair of eyes to keep watch, map read, or offer prior knowledge.

In the 30 years since Pat Toole had to negotiate the same terrain, some things that had changed were the quality of the navigation, the speed of the aeroplane and the fact that Gaby had communications. What hadn't changed was the size and threat of the mountains and that cloud hides them. The biggest difference was that Gaby only had to do this once, but she had to do it alone and get it right the first time.

AUSTRALIAN WOMEN PILOTS

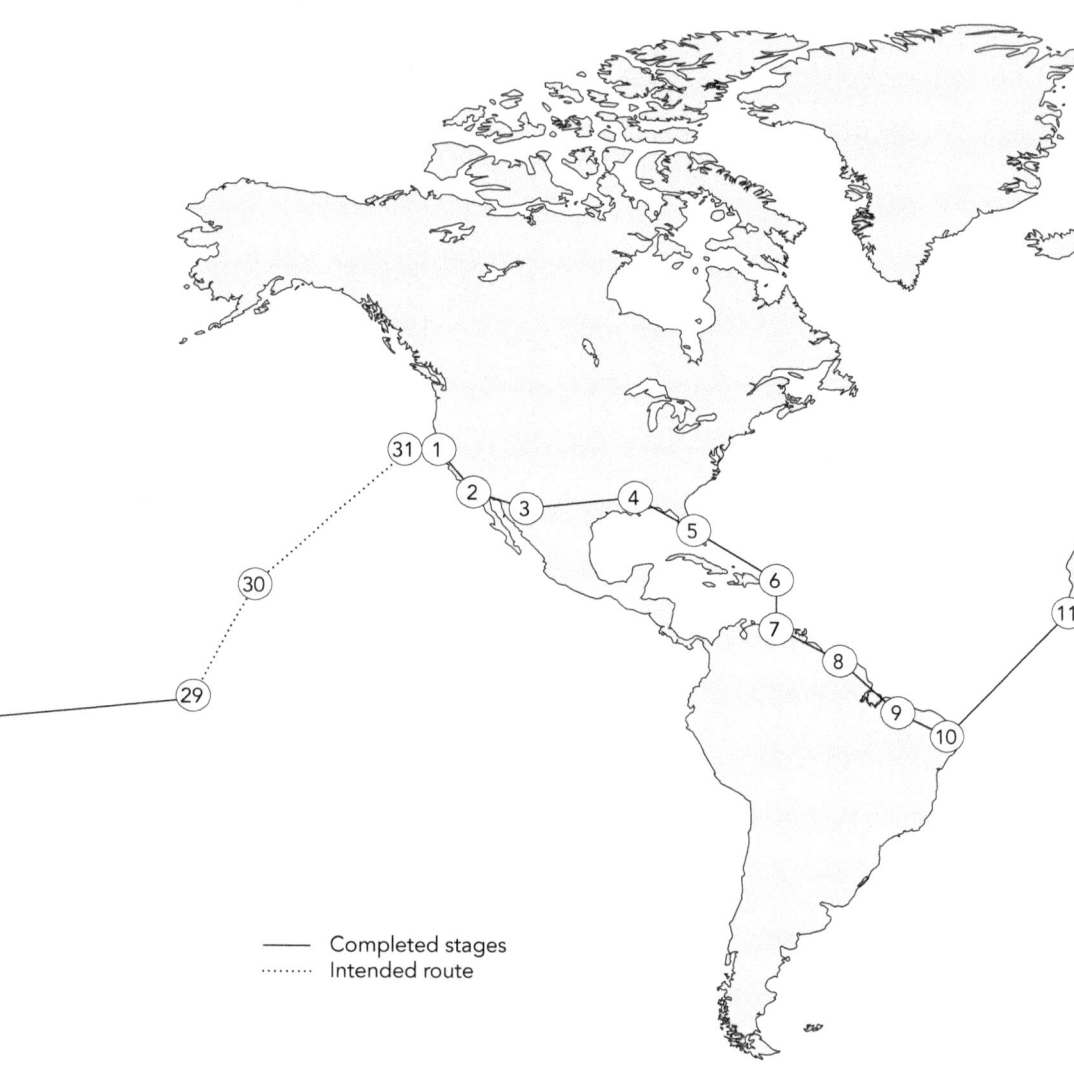

— Completed stages
······· Intended route

1 Oakland	12 Dakar	23 Singapore
2 Burbank	13 Geo	24 Bandoeng
3 Tuscon	14 Fort Lamy	25 Saurabaya
4 New Orleans	15 El Fasher	26 Koepang
5 Miami	16 Khartoum	27 Darwin
6 San Juan	17 Massawa	28 Lae
7 Caripito	18 Assab	29 Howland Is.?
8 Paramaribo	19 Karachi	30 Hawaii
9 Fortaleza	20 Calcutta	31 Oakland
10 Natal	21 Akyab	
11 St Louis	22 Rangoon	

Route of Amelia Earhart's 1937 attempt to fly solo around the world

She left early to avoid as much building cloud as possible and flew around carpeted mountains that met like entwined knuckles. Far below, rivers slithered around their deep ravines like trapped serpents and she breathed a sigh of relief as PNG's north-eastern coastline came into view and she knew she'd made it through, where far too many had failed before her.

PNG is no place for complacency though and more cloud forced her down to around a hundred feet, which is well below the minimum allowable. As quickly as it came, the cloud dissipated and she landed near Lae in clear skies.

Strangers are just friends we haven't met yet and two of them appeared at the airport to greet this woman pilot they'd heard about. Amanda and Doug Wright's welcome was the first of many unexpected kindnesses from strangers. It was also her first encounter with Amelia Earhart's actual flight path, and the Melanesian Hotel, where Gaby stayed, had a bar dedicated to the American pilot. Though it opened 28 years after Earhart's visit, photos and information recounted Earhart's time in Lae. A small overgrown concrete memorial opposite the old airfield was cleaned up for Gaby to lay a wreath at its base, and her companion was an old lady who had been present at Earhart's departure (along with her navigator Fred Noonan) so many years before.

Gaby waggled her wings the next morning at 50 feet above the runway from which Earhart had departed, then climbed into the sky thinking about two things: Earhart's ill-fated flight path, which she was now following, and closer to home, the DNA inherited from her father, James.

Gaby felt an affinity with Earhart as she flew out to sea. For the first 150 kilometres, under a cerulean sky, she was escorted by a PNG Defence Force DC3 for her three-hour trip to Rabaul on the northern tip of the island of New Britain, which lies to the east of the main island of New Guinea. Rabaul was to be just a quick stopover to slightly shorten the Pacific leg to Hawaii. Quick enough for a sleep and a tough early lesson in being adaptable: during the night somebody robbed her plane of her precious survival gear.

Gone was the borrowed state-of-the-art life jacket, which included flares, lights, mirrors, waterproof matches, fishing lines and a survival beacon. Also gone were field glasses, spark plugs, a plug wrench and vacuum pump. It was not enough to pressure her to admit defeat by any means but when the Marshall Islands airline office told her they'd been robbed 25 times, the futility of her frustration became clear. By 5.30 the following morning she was wearing an inferior replacement life jacket and clipping a lead attached to the remaining life raft to her wrist – ferry pilot Ray Clamback had warned her that the life raft is the first thing to float away or sink after ditching. The risks of the looming Pacific crossing could not be overstated.

At 6.09 am Gaby left Rabaul and focused on her first long water crossing. Finding Majuro in the Marshall Islands would really test her navigation skills. After almost 2600 uninterrupted kilometres over water without a navigational fix, the twinkling lights of steamy Majuro welcomed her and offered a second Earhart encounter.

The next morning, Neville Hill, the New Zealand–born manager of the local airline, turned to see the Australian, faint and hot in the tropical humidity, leaning against his office wall. She'd walked a long way for a weather briefing. Conversation inevitably led to the Earhart mystery and to 80-year-old local Oscar de Brun. Oscar recounted to Gaby how, when he was 28 years old, he had seen Amelia Earhart taken away by the Japanese.

Gaby completed her flight plan by torchlight the next morning and departed into an electrical storm that soon turned to blue skies for the 3500-kilometre leg to Honolulu. But blue skies don't always mean smooth sailing and after careful in-flight calculations, she estimated that there would be 14 hours and 37 minutes flight time.

AUSTRALIAN WOMEN PILOTS

1 Sydney	14 San Juan	27 Luxor
2 Cairns	15 Barbados	28 Bahrain
3 Port Moresby	16 Paramaribo	29 Karachi
4 Lae	17 Cayenne	30 Bombay
5 Rabaul	18 Belem	31 Madras
6 Majuro	19 Fortaleza	32 Phuket
7 Johnston Atoll	20 Natal	33 Singapore
8 Honolulu	21 Dakar	34 Bali
9 Oakland	22 Agadir	35 Darwin
10 Winslow	23 Alger	36 Alice Springs
11 Bartlesville	24 Tunis	37 Parkes
12 Memphis	25 Iraklion	38 Camden
13 Miami	26 Cairo	39 Sydney

GABY KENNARD

Route that Gaby Kennard took in 1989 to become the first Australian woman to fly solo around the world

The only navigational fix on this long ocean crossing was a tiny dot called Johnston Island, a high-security US military base that doesn't welcome uninvited visitors. And they didn't welcome Gaby when she realised that the winds had slowed her up by over an hour and if she didn't refuel, she had every chance of running out. It was gut-wrenching. But in perfect time, a break in the clouds revealed the tiny island and she landed, declaring it an emergency.

The US military were serious about their security and greeted the drop-in with eight military rifles pointing dead at her. On shut-down, she was met by a gruff military man who barked orders at the startled pilot to 'disembark and stand by your aircraft', then demanded to search it.

When the camp commander casually arrived to grill the interloper, the mood changed. He was lovely. A fleeting smile and a slight show of solidarity from a female underling also brought enormous relief for the pilot and once airborne en route to Honolulu the funny side of the charade revealed itself.

This confronting theatre is recognisable to me. Arriving at Burlington Airport in Vermont, USA, to refuel, a uniformed officer bawled at us to get out and stand by the aircraft – he was shouting like a furious headmaster. The charade lasted about 15 minutes until he'd satisfied himself that we were in order. Was he armed? I don't remember, but it was a bloody awful welcome. For Gaby to experience that alone and with guns pointed at her must have been terrifying.

In Sydney the next day, Gaby's children James and Mimi watched Channel 9 newsreader, Brian Henderson, report that '16 days after leaving Australia, Sydney pilot and mother of two, Gaby Kennard, has arrived safely in Hawaii after the most dangerous leg of her world solo flight. She almost didn't make it across the Pacific. With fuel running low she was forced to land at a top secret US air base.'

This report was followed by footage of their smiling mother's pre-dawn arrival in Hawaii, after a 16.5-hour flying day. The

Channel 9 crew who met her in Honolulu took her to the Sheraton Hotel, where she rang her children to warn them of the story and then fell into bed at 5 am.

Gaby had placated the children prior to her departure with, 'Well, I know how to fly and so I'll be fine.' Even though she was scared and knew it was dangerous, she spared the kids that worry. Mimi believed what her mum said but secretly thought the flight would not go ahead. They only ever doubted her safety when journalists put the idea to them.

Honolulu was a good place to relax and to manage flight planning for the next leg of Gaby's trip, to Oakland, California. Ten days was excessive though, as she waited (and waited) for the head-wind to still or ideally turn into a tail wind. This leg was even longer than the previous one, without the bonus of any landmark, such as she'd had with Johnston Island, and it was a necessary exercise in patience.

She did a short hop to the town of Hilo, on the easternmost island of Hawai'i, to give herself half an hour's head start.

BY THE TIME THE TAXI FOR THE AIRPORT FINALLY APPEARED, Gaby was late leaving for the almost 3700-kilometre over-water leg from Hawaii to Oakland. With a couple of extra long-range fuel tanks just fitted to her aeroplane, she was confident of making Oakland with fuel to spare. This leg would be her longest of the entire trip and she needed to get cracking.

Hilo was reduced to a pinpoint and blinked its goodbye as VH-GKF, heavy with the extra fuel, gingerly climbed northeast above the Pacific Ocean. The mood in the cabin was as calm as the 16-hour night ahead and it was a relief to find that the Omega navigation unit was working for this leg.

An hour into the flight, Gaby did a routine switch from the main fuel tanks to her no. 2 auxiliary tank. She checked her flight plan then cast her eyes back to the horizon, when a bright green glow ascended from the ocean. So far from anywhere and in the realms of her surreal situation, her first reaction was, 'Good God. It's a UFO!' She searched her mind for a rational answer but logic failed her. The light slowly grew larger and as it rose from the oceanic depths, the apparition revealed itself: it was the moon. It lit the stage and then departed, leaving the Saratoga to continue into the ink-black night.

Most of the cabin space was taken up with auxiliary fuel tanks, leaving the pilot's seat nestled in front of and beside them. Strangely, the no. 2 auxiliary tank seemed to be consuming little fuel. It indicated an extra 90 minutes useable beyond its limit. She stayed on that tank until it was almost exhausted and then switched to tank 1. As she puzzled over the calculations, there was a heart-stopping engine cough then nothing: the reaction was like an electric shock and a real 'oh shit!' moment.

She very reluctantly pushed the nose down to avert stalling the aeroplane and spinning into the water. From 8000 feet, Gaby lost 1000 feet of altitude and had only a few minutes to come up with a solution. Still nothing happened when she switched back to tank 2.

'I thought this was probably the end,' she said in late 2016, 27 years later. 'Even if I had to ditch I couldn't see the water to land on it. I had a flash of understanding about how panic kills people.'

In a technicolour moment, her children Mimi (then 16) and James (six) passed before her eyes. This drove her back on task. She knew she had to work it out. In those frantic seconds, Gaby closed the throttle to prevent an air blockage in the fuel lines, then switched to the main tanks. Opening the throttle, the aeroplane responded. She held her breath and climbed back up to 8000 feet as emotion took over and her body shook uncontrollably.

Should she continue to Oakland? She was a third of the way there, but either direction was beyond the endurance of just the main tanks. She'd need to revert to the troublesome auxiliary tanks whichever option she took. The only thing that had changed on this leg was the new gravity-fed tanks fitted in Hawaii.

She decided to continue on.

She drained the new tanks into her no. 2 tank, disconnected the hoses and taped their ends to prevent the escape of any more of the deadly fuel vapours that she could smell in the enclosed cabin. She put her nose out of the tiny 'storm' window, which is about the size of a hand on the pilot's side of the cabin. It was a great big empty nothing out there. She drew in some crisp breaths and returned her attention to the cabin.

Having set the autopilot, Gaby left her seat to do some physical checks down the back of the plane, where four passenger seats would normally have been. In the claustrophobic cabin, she bent and squeezed between the two large metal tanks, hoping not to unbalance the plane and send it spinning. The cause of the fuel problem wasn't obvious and so in a process of elimination she reluctantly switched back to the no. 2 tank, which now held the fuel drained out of the new gravity-fed tanks fitted in Hawaii. If it ran, she should be fine.

With a trembling hand on the switch, Gaby defaulted to her chequered Catholic upbringing, her interest in Buddhism and to any deity who would listen – probably even the lucky rabbit's foot gifted by her children. She said a quick prayer in what she thought could be her final living moments.

After this short one-sided conversation, she turned on the electric fuel boost pump and shifted from the mains to the no. 2 auxiliary tank. White with fear, she begged the fuel to feed to the engine. She began counting … 12, 13, 14, nothing. The engine stopped again. She wanted to throw up.

Holding her breath, she flicked the selector back to the main tanks with a clammy hand. She had no option but to continue systematic trials and on the next move tried auxiliary no. 3. Counting to ten, she thanked her lucky stars when the engine kept running, but realised that no. 3 and no. 2 were draining simultaneously.

Like a game of Russian roulette, the engine would cut out or not each time the tanks were changed. By the time she switched to no. 4 tank, the fuel was draining normally, while also not drawing from tank 2 or 3. The flight plan indicated there was five hours flying left and seven hours worth of useable fuel. Hopefully the whole show would hold together. The engine had cut out four times.

Just as she was starting to settle down, a subconscious but very present voice prompted, you can turn the boost pump off now. This one-time auditory hallucination, commonly associated with trauma, was akin to a bunch of pioneer aviators looking over her shoulder, sharing their collective guidance. Gaby realised later that this psychological phenomenon is common to people alone at sea. Whatever it was, it helped enormously.

Now back on straight and level flight, the night edged out and a perfect rising sun stretched its rays over a golden fog bank. The sight brought on an overwhelming adrenaline-induced euphoria and less than five hours later there were floods of joyful tears when the enormous Golden Gate Bridge came into view. Gaby had survived the longest night of her life.

By the time she touched down at Oakland 16 hours after leaving Hilo and having lived through what one newspaper reported as 'Solo Mum's Terror Plunge', Gaby rushed to do two things: touch the ground and receive a comforting hug, in this case from her friend Iris, a member of the 99s (the International Women Pilots Association). There was nobody to take over the stress, but there was a friend to offer respite from it.

Another crisis came when Gaby embarked to leave a week later. Paralysed by fear, she cancelled her flight plan for the next leg. The same thing happened the next day. But then in a waiting room at the briefing office, she happened to see a television program on motivation and overcoming fear. Fear was the one thing she was trying to conquer. As she weighed her options, Gaby heeded the program's message and submitted an amended flight plan. It was tough getting back into the plane but once she got airborne, she was in control again.

That experience taught her not to be so hard on herself. She had to manage delays, diversions and a myriad of other things she couldn't control. She had to let go of the things she couldn't control and manage her concerns about the things that she could, and this became a motto for life.

Throughout the USA trip, from California across to Florida, Gaby let go of her reservations and unwillingness to impose on others, and enjoyed the experiences and graciously accepted the warm-hearted hospitality when it was offered to her. Even now, she says that self-doubt is a burden she has to constantly shift. Australian aviator Dick Smith was a backer who truly believed in her. His magazine *Australian Geographic* was a sponsor of the journey, and it was Dick who entrusted a piece of fabric from Kingsford Smith's aeroplane, the *Southern Cross*, to her care. He told her that anybody who carried this fabric always returned home safely.

And so, with a determination to make the most of the trip, one of the most joyous highlights was being graciously welcomed into Earhart's home-town of Atchison, Kansas, where the mayor presented her with two keys to the city. One key was to keep and one was to be returned in person a year later. Alone in Earhart's childhood bedroom, now a museum, Gaby found a sense of connection with the place and the young girl who once inhabited it.

The women pilots in the USA epitomised the camaraderie that is the intent of the 99s, founded by Earhart in 1929 and which today boasts some 5000 members across 35 countries. It was a highlight of her trip, in which there were many ups and downs over the next couple of months as she flew through South America, Africa and Asia. Very few 99s though, were in countries other than America.

Leaving the comfort of the English-speaking USA, Gaby's nerves resurfaced as she departed Fort Lauderdale, Florida, for San Juan, the capital of Puerto Rico. This time though, she managed the fear, even when her radio went silent while passing the notorious Bermuda Triangle (also known as the Devil's Triangle). The devil wasn't home, you see. He was waiting over the Atlantic.

As she was heading down the South American east coast for her Atlantic launch point of Natal in Brazil, she knew she was crossing into territory that was much less technologically sophisticated, and she had one great windfall in discovering the services of 'Boston Bob' from 'Weather Service Corporation'.

Bob advised that Hurricane Hugo was brewing in her path and for Gaby to get cracking. She island-hopped across the Caribbean to Barbados, off the coast of Venezuela, then over endless kilometres of Amazon jungle until she was forced down by a big storm into Zanderij Airport at coastal Paramaribo in Suriname – a country run by a military dictatorship and a place she had been warned to avoid.

Being a single woman (and blonde to boot) in a possibly hostile environment was an unsettling thought, but there was no choice. She put her faith in one friendly taxi driver. This was contrasted 24 hours later when she made her destination of French Cayenne, a city 750 kilometres further down the coast and as cosmopolitan as Paramaribo was unsophisticated.

As Boston Bob carefully monitored the hurricane, she departed the next day over the immense steaming Amazon jungle, an exercise in navigation and keeping her imagination in check. She followed a pencil line through a portion of map that read 'elevation unknown', while the grave concerns of the Qantas team perched precariously on her shoulder. She finally arrived in Belem, a Brazilian city of two and a half million people. Unable to communicate with air traffic control due to language difficulties, she nevertheless made a perfect landing before being hit with the full force of Brazilian red tape over the next three hours, not the least of which complications was an expired visa.

The next day a chance encounter with some local pilots pointed her towards a maintenance organisation that discovered a problem with the hydraulic oil reservoir, which they were able to patch up. It was a relieved woman who flew away from Belem and its mountains of paperwork, fees, fines and poverty.

In Natal, three and a half hours south of Belem and the last stop at the point closest to Africa, the frustrations she had encountered in Belem were forgotten in the face of the kindness of the Brazilian Air Force and its commanding officer. The hydraulic leak was fully repaired while Gaby gathered her thoughts at a beautiful beachfront hotel. Her children were always at the forefront of her mind and she called them every chance she could. On the almost deserted beach, tracing her toes through the Atlantic waters she was about to brave, gentle thoughts of home surfaced.

With another heavy fuel load for her third long water crossing, Gaby carefully flew the Saratoga off the Natal airstrip and, as five Brazilian fighter jets formed a salute to say goodbye, she also said goodbye to the Americas. Next stop – Senegal in West Africa, 3070 kilometres to the north-east.

The moonless night beckoned like a siren of the sea. She was not looking forward to the south Atlantic crossing and, in the empty dark sky, yearned for company. She made a broadcast on her HF radio in the vain hope that someone might hear. To her utter surprise, the radio crackled in reply and an English radio enthusiast monitoring a maritime frequency asked who she was. Astonished at her endeavours, he provided some useful advice on frequencies for her arrival in Dakar and wished her well.

Just as she said goodbye and thought she'd avoided some thunderstorms she'd been warned about, a faint flash in the darkness ahead made her shiver. That familiar feeling of vulnerability returned, and it was justified. A tiny dot high in the sky and a thousand miles out to sea, the Saratoga flew into unavoidable and intense thunderstorms. The storms over the Atlantic are known to range from 1000 feet up to as high as 50 000 feet. The aeroplane, so secure and stable in calm skies, was tossed about like a toy and cracking lightning relentlessly lit the cabin from all sides. Ducking and weaving between the storm cells, without the aid of a storm scope to warn of turbulence, lightning or wind shear, Gaby flew a violent marathon for survival. One of many electrical malfunctions had the undercarriage extend and retract uncontrollably, which varied the airspeed dramatically and with all the electrics then switched off, the battle continued for three interminable hours. During this time, the Omega system got confused and then finally failed.

Through it all, thankfully, the engine kept turning. Gaby knew she was only as good as that engine. Then, like waking from a nightmare, calm was restored, except to the severely rattled pilot, who managed an 'adequate' landing at Senegal, due to the night's ordeal. But, rocky landing or not, she had made it past the half-way point.

Again, the kindness of a local taxi driver named Souheil brightened her arrival. Entering her simple accommodation, she was pleased with the serenity of the place, until opening the bathroom door and finding very rudimentary plumbing. After an ill-advised meal, wave upon wave of nausea and diarrhoea rendered her immobile as the mysteries of African microbiology revealed themselves in her gut.

A scheduled *60 Minutes* link-up from the fortified radio station, where the family's images blinked onto the screen, was an important boost for Gaby, who was by then at a low ebb. Only the fear of dying alone so far from home was enough to get her off the hard, lumpy bed and out of there a week later.

From Senegal, Earhart flew due east across sub-Saharan Africa to Mali, Chad, Sudan and Ethiopia, but that route was now unfeasible due to political instability. Gaby would fly north around the African coast to Morocco, Algeria, Tunisia, Crete, Egypt, then across to Bahrain, and on to Pakistan.

Souheil saw her safely to her hot aeroplane and, weak and sick, she left Senegal behind, though Senegal didn't leave her. The stomach bug played havoc for another week.

Against warnings about three civilian planes recently shot down on her intended route, she followed the coast north through thick desert haze for stopovers in Agadir and Algiers. Friendly and efficient Tunis was different and the preferred place to wait out the weather again and regain some strength. It provided all the exotic experiences that the previous weeks had not, but most importantly, it had clean food to counterbalance her physical and mental weakness.

She didn't realise how vulnerable she'd become until the six-hour water crossing over the Mediterranean when the UK radio enthusiast again made contact. Filling him in on her Atlantic dance with the devil, the full horror of it resurfaced and once she signed off, the radio banter gave way to a deep indulgent cleansing howl.

There were so many fears to face: death and failure being a couple of them. A yearn to travel is often attributed to a dissatisfaction with home, but there is nothing like bone weary travel fatigue to make the light of home burn brighter. And there was still so far to go.

CROSSING THE HALFWAY MARK GAVE GABY A MENTAL BOOST but it came with a greater degree of difficulty as thunderstorms had knocked out the Omega system and so navigation was reduced to a rudimentary dead reckoning like the pioneers before her had used. There were at least three water crossings ahead and precious little English-speaking territory across the Middle East and Asia.

The challenges kept coming and began with two air traffic controllers in Cairo who were giving different instructions. One gave clearance to land, while the other broke in urgently, telling her she was at the wrong airport and to go around. As she retracted the wheels and flaps to go around, the first controller told her to land. She quickly reversed what she'd done and put the aeroplane down at the end of the enormous runway. A perplexed American 747 captain waiting to depart came onto the radio and said, 'Lady, I don't know how you did it, but that was a beautiful landing.'

There was no time to waste in Cairo. She'd seen its greatest beauty from the air as she flew over the pyramids. On the ground the fuel agents almost used the wrong fuel, which would have presented a huge problem and time delay to drain and clean out. And the Middle East brought unique stresses around the vulnerability of being a single female. Qantas had advised her not to miss her time slot to traverse Saudi Arabia as that permit would probably not be re-granted, so trying to get out of Egypt on time became imperative. It cost her $1000 in 'fees' with a handling agent, with whom she didn't have time to argue.

In her room that night, Gaby pored over her map for the next day. Scrawled across it in thick pencil was, 'Under no circumstances make a landing in Saudi Arabia!!!!' Against this warning from her navigation teacher in Sydney, it was an odd comfort to have the Saudi controller call her 'Sir' each time they talked on the radio. Perhaps he couldn't contemplate a woman flying as at that time, in Saudi Arabia, they were not even allowed to drive. It would be another 26 years before the *Arab News* reported the Saudis had trained their first female pilot.

She passed their borders without a problem but then it was a nervous flight out of Bahrain through Iranian airspace. The Iran–Iraq war had ended the year prior and a year later allied ships gathered for the Gulf War of 1990.

Flying along the coast of Iran was as incident-free as the stunning coastal arrival into Karachi, Pakistan was difficult, with complicated instructions that diverted her unnecessarily 100 kilometres out to sea and back again. Gaby refused to honour the extortion attempts of the handling agents and spent three hours in customs for her trouble. It was almost worth it for the sake of the victory. She was wising up to their corruption and hostility to women.

In Bombay, on the Indian west coast, a couple of local 99s knocked on the hotel door, one of whom was an Indian Airlines captain. That connection was so refreshing because she had hardly spoken to a woman since Florida. They organised a press conference and somebody noticed Gaby's locket of Indian guru Sathya Sai Baba. It was a good luck gift given to her by friends in Sydney. The press were intrigued.

On departure from Bombay as Gaby was rotating off the runway, the air traffic controllers completely changed the approved flight plan. They directed her to climb to 2000 feet on the same track. Imagine the horror when she noticed through the thick smog that a tree branch and a chimneystack almost brushed her wingtips. In describing this event, Gaby said, 'The bloody idiots had directed me into a hill!'

Crossing India, she was forced to fly at 12 500 feet in unpleasant weather and by the time she landed in Madras, on the east coast, Gaby was happy to be staying at a very modern hotel. Owing to some paperwork issues, she had to stay in Madras for the weekend and she was invited by a friend of one of the pilots in Bombay to fly to Bangalore, about 350 kilometres to the west, to visit Sai Baba's ashram, 'Whitefields' about an hour's drive north of Bangalore. They flew across on Indian Airlines and Gaby had the chance to visit the cockpit and chat to the pilots. They ran a busy schedule with few luxuries.

On this expedition, Gaby had time to be silent and reflective. She enjoyed the weekend immensely and returned to Madras with a profound sense of calm. It was possibly the inner fuel she needed to continue her journey, because every port and leg presented some fresh new trial or incident.

Singapore was almost the last of her stops. Even the locals were surprised when the aircraft maintenance company reported the escape of a metre-long green and yellow snake from her aircraft's cabin. It shot out from under the auxiliary fuel tanks, slid down the startled engineer's leg onto the hangar floor and slithered into a drain. He didn't care to investigate or discuss it any further. The only place she'd parked on the grass was Rabaul, PNG, and Gaby thought that was a hell of a long way for a snake to travel.

She departed Singapore in the pouring rain, heading for a fuel stop in Bali. She knew she'd have to face the media back in Australia; a stark contrast to the solitude of her experience, but before that she had a good rest and spent an enjoyable evening with a friend. Departing the beautiful island the next day, she undertook her last water crossing, longing to see the land.

WHEN THE AUSTRALIAN ACCENT OF AN AIR TRAFFIC CONTROLler uttered the words 'Welcome home', Gaby Kennard became the first Australian woman and the fifth internationally to fly around the world solo. Only three more (non-Australian) women have done it in the 30 years since.

Thirty kilometres out from Darwin, the Australian Womens Pilots' Association Darwin branch radioed a message: 'Gaby, welcome home. We are truly proud of your magnificent efforts and applaud you as you join other aviation legends like Amy Johnson, Jean Batten, Amelia Earhart, Ross and Keith Smith, Bert Hinkler and Charles Kingsford Smith.' To the strains of 'Waltzing Matilda', the pilot emerged, beaming, to a crowd of 200 people.

Darwin had been Earhart's only Australian stop and there Gaby farewelled her ethereal travel companion, then settled in for a comfortable night at the Hilton with her sister.

Later, flying in over Sydney Harbour, Gaby informed Dick

Smith that she had safely returned the fabric from the *Southern Cross*. Ryan Campbell (the youngest person and first teenager to fly solo around the world) and Jessica Watson (youngest person to sail solo and unassisted around the world) both carried the same piece of cloth on their journeys in the decades after.

Pride and relief swept over Ron Berry, Gaby's flight instructor friend from Illawarra Airport, as he stood with a group watching Gaby land in the rain at Bankstown. Emerging from the cockpit in her flight suit, she hugged him with great affection. It was an incredible honour for the instructor to see his former student succeed, remembering his lessons and using them to avoid trouble.

Approaching the Sydney Town Hall in a motorcade with her children beside her, she was deafened by a brass band and crowds that clogged the city streets, many of them women who were thrilled to show their support. The whole country was excited to see her home. Alderman Jeremy Bingham, the Lord Mayor of Sydney, presented Gaby with the key to the City of Sydney. She was only the thirteenth person to receive it.

She finally slept soundly that night, in her own bed, in the same house as her children, and awoke to headlines that hailed her achievement. The planned 33-day trip had taken 99 days, and she had travelled over 54 000 kilometres.

FOR THE NEXT FIVE YEARS GABY WAS RUN OFF HER FEET with media commitments and the promised RFDS fundraising tour, where she flew herself around Australia and raised over $200 000. It was a big shock to be skyrocketed into having a national profile. Eventually the attention became somewhat overwhelming.

At the urging of a publisher, she pulled together her notes scribbled on various hotel letterheads and restaurant notepads and, together with Kerry McAloon, wrote *Solo Woman*. The book was released in 1990 and endorsed by Hazel Hawke, Nancy Bird Walton and Dick Smith. Ron's copy is inscribed, '… Lots of love to you and thanks for your wonderful teaching.'

In 1994, five years after her return, the family moved to Colorado, USA. They stayed for a decade and it was there that Gaby finally pursued her long-held interest in art and completed a two-year degree in Liberal Arts at Colorado Mountain College.

HER REMARKABLE FLIGHT WAS AN ACHIEVEMENT THAT PUT Gaby into the record books. It improved her confidence and sense of self, but she will readily admit that she still strives to be more assertive and self-confident.

Solo pilot Ryan Campbell paid the following tribute to the woman almost 50 years his senior, for her dignity and example:

> When I completed my round-the-world flight, thousands welcomed me home but I knew that Gaby was one of only two who truly understood what was now behind me. I loved her calm and humble approach to her achievements. It's one thing to do something great but a bigger challenge to manage success and stay true to who you really are.

Flying gave Gaby some of the greatest memories of her life. The pilot's logbook detailing her pioneering trip has been packed away in her home, along with a mountain of newspaper cuttings. They are relegated to history as the young 70-something-year-old has become immersed in her art.

Now living in northern NSW, she wakes to the pungent smell of the rainforest to find her breakfast companion is a koala watching from high in a tree, and the resident python's recently shed skin hangs limp from the verandah's eaves. Fresh artworks adorn her walls; warm, colourful and sharp, they are the inner expression of a woman who knows that, whatever the pursuit – painting, flying, living – it all takes courage.

5

MARION McCALL

DAWN TO DUSK WITH THE BISHOP

My mother's words came back to me, 'Remember who you are.' Right then I was the winner of the Dawn to Dusk Challenge, with 100 people waiting for me to make a speech.

(Marion McCall on the first of her three acceptance speeches at the Royal Air Force Club in Piccadilly, London)

A perfectly polished English accent echoed down the line from London to Marion McCall at her home in Bunbury, Western Australia. The voice belonged to one of the judges for the international Dawn to Dusk Flying Competition.

This competition was established in London by the Duke of Edinburgh to demonstrate a pilot's abilities in undertaking a day's flying, between dawn and dusk, to achieve some kind of commendable objective. Pilots need to set a challenging goal, with a theme, keep a detailed log of preparations and then execute the challenge.

'I had lunch with Prince Philip yesterday in Buckingham Palace,' announced the caller. 'And he said to me, "Get that Australian girl to defend her title!" so I'm ringing to ask you to do that.'

Marion thought she couldn't possibly go into the competition again. She had done it two years prior, in 2004, and it was so much work. The annual awards dinner though, held at the Royal Air Force (RAF) Club in London's Piccadilly, was so much fun. Prince Philip is the competition's patron.

Having already brought the first prize trophy back to Australia once, Marion had counted it as a wonderful life experience and left it at that. But when a request comes directly from the Duke of Edinburgh … She suppressed a grin and took up the challenge.

This enthusiastic invitation was at odds with the first time Marion and the Duke crossed paths. At a Buckingham Palace garden party a few years before she'd even heard of the Dawn to Dusk, Marion and her husband David were part of the 1998 Lambeth Bishops' Conference. In a designated area of the palace lawns, the Archbishop of York introduced the Australian couple to Prince Philip: 'This is David McCall. He is the Bishop of Willochra, South Australia, which covers an area six times the size of England. And this is his wife. She flies him around his diocese.' In that setting, under those circumstances, that was Marion – a Bishop's wife and a flying taxi driver.

Prince Phillip, a pilot himself, asked Marion if she was connected with the Royal Flying Doctor Service because he knew about that. She told him she wasn't but she flew over the same area, to which he nodded acknowledgement and moved on. With so many guests to manage, Marion thought perhaps her flying wasn't important enough to further investigate at a crowded garden party. But back in South Australia her flying was very important because the Anglican Diocese of Willochra covers over 80 per cent of the state. The ability to fly it changed David's workload, changed Marion and brought some timely equilibrium back into the relationship.

At 50, Marion transitioned from mother of five, choir leader and chief bottle washer at the Bishop's House, to the bishop's pilot, accompanying him on every trip. They now worked together, instead of her standing at home, waving him off for days at a time. And though nobody at the palace garden party back in 1998 seemed to know about her new skills, within half a dozen years they did. Marion returned to London by invitation three times. The first two times were to collect the first prize Dawn to Dusk perpetual flying trophy, donated by the Duke of Edinburgh and worth £12 000.

MARION CONSIDERS HER LIFE TO HAVE BEEN FORTUNATE, with parents who adored each other and their meshed-together family. Her mother, Thelma, had married a radio operator/rear gunner who flew in England with the No 10 Flying Boat Squadron. Sadly, he was killed during the war in a flying tragedy. She subsequently married Heywood Le Breton. Heywood was a mild-mannered bachelor of 33 and it was his warm-hearted way of nurturing Thelma's three sons that clinched the deal. Within a year of their marriage, Marion was born. Inevitably, Heywood formed a special bond with his daughter and they shared a wicked sense of humour and a love of music.

The Le Breton kids had a cultured upbringing, entrenched in Anglican ethos and backlit with music. For as long as she could hold a thought, Marion had wanted to be a performer. The love of music that her father washed across his precious Bechstein baby grand piano flooded down to the nine-month-old child who took her first steps underneath it. The Bechstein, among the best of baby grand pianos, is a prized heirloom and was one of the last exported from Germany before World War II. Marion danced and sang her way through childhood and later, as a teen, took inspiration from Julie Andrews. Maybe she was a little show-off but showing off is really just playing to an audience. Her desire to sing and act was lifelong.

Though a younger sister and brother came along, Marion says her three older brothers shaped her character and taught her cricket and football skills. She did her utmost to keep pace as the family moved around Victoria every three years because of her father's role as postmaster. From Mornington where Marion was born, they moved to Kaniva, Rosebud, Bright and then St Arnaud where she became the under 13s 100-yard sprint champion. On the last move, to Seymour, she was elected school captain after only one term at Seymour High School.

Every January, as a return favour for kindness shown by her parents, the O'Day family would host Marion at their large house in the gentrified Melbourne suburb of Kew. Mrs O'Day was actually Dr Una Shergold – a specialist at the Royal Children's Hospital.

During these breaks, Marion was 'polished up and taken on day trips to places like art galleries'. She dined at the exclusive Lyceum Club where she was pushed to speak French throughout lunch, and exposed to as much culture and art as could be squeezed into a week. The large house and another family's routines were rather terrifying for a nervous country girl and by week's end the lure of home was strong. Mrs O'Day's education, however, would stand her in good stead.

After school Marion studied teaching and in her third year was recruited to the Victorian Education Department Music Board and studied singing at the Conservatorium. It was an important appointment, and she was perfect for the role. The beauty of teaching for Marion was in standing at the front of a class and teaching singing. Even the classroom was a platform and the music, transporting and transformative, soothes your nerves, lifts your spirits and makes the soundtrack to your memories. Best of all, it keeps you company.

After two years of teaching, Marion bought a passage to London. She joined friends on the SS *Orcades* and sailed off on a 12-month adventure. One of their inevitable cash shortages was solved by selling their blood. The Greeks knew that Marion's O-negative blood was worth bottling and paid her a premium for it. Full of experiences but without the stamina to continue the trip for the year as planned, Marion had that overwhelming urge to get home that eventually affects most backpackers.

She left her friends in Europe and returned to a perfect directional change; she applied for and was accepted by ABC Radio for an announcer's job in Melbourne. With nine months to fill in before starting the position, her parents, now in Wangaratta, took the chance to pull her close, and the music students and Wangaratta Cathedral Choir benefitted.

She got to know the cathedral's bishop, who invited the family to dinner because, fortuitously, his son David was in town. And that was the end of the ABC before it even began! Six months later the choir were singing at the marriage of Marion Le Breton and David McCall.

'I was quite chuffed to think I was married to a priest. It's an incredible vocation and he is a man of substance, integrity and vision. We are opposites. I've got a short fuse but he has only raised his voice once in 48 years of marriage. I might lose my temper three times a day on average!' says Marion with wicked good humour. 'We have the same values and similar upbringings and so there's no conflict on parenting or personal standards.'

Marriage brought exciting change and the McCalls had four children over the next six years. They thought the Riverina in southern New South Wales would always be home until David was asked to relocate to suburban Goodwood in Adelaide. Marion enjoyed Goodwood's wonderful music tradition at their beautiful old church and she undertook extra training to become conductor of the parish choir and work with a youth orchestra. She also taught music from their parish home and had her fifth baby.

Singing and church were non-negotiable for the children and when one of the children's friends asked why all the McCall kids had such beautiful voices, the child joked, 'Mum drowns babies who can't sing.'

For ten delightful years the family immersed themselves in the community and family life, until a Thursday night in early 1987 when a phone call changed everything. The priest at Willochra, an enormous diocese a couple of hours drive north of Adelaide, asked if David would put his name on the ballot to become bishop. With one night to decide, the caller's reassuring sign-off was, 'You're probably not suitable anyway but it'd be nice to have another name on the list.' You'd have to think it was a set-up because the next day he was elected. The decision weighed heavily on both partners because it would be the end of family life as they knew it and a huge change in circumstance. The diocese covers 90 per cent of the geographic area of South Australia and includes more than 50 churches.

Marion's father saw the move as an opportunity though, and surprised Marion when he said, 'Your whole life has been a preparation for what you have to do now.' He knew that her great capacity for compassion together with her experience in public speaking, leadership and teaching equipped her well to handle the role of bishop's wife. Her father's confidence was some comfort as Marion packed over the next five months, then billeted the three eldest children with trusted friends to finish the high school year and arranged for boarding school the year after. The rest of the family moved 200 kilometres north to Gladstone, population 689. It was a wrench.

Seven-year-old Rachel and 11-year-old Elizabeth couldn't believe their luck when they arrived at the beautiful 17-room stone Bishop's House at Main Road North, on the hill above Gladstone and across town from the church. The huge house and associated land were a kids' paradise, not to mention the privilege of having their mum to themselves. In their youth, they didn't notice her deep sense of loss about the splintering of the family or of her musical life left behind.

The new role meant David was gone most weeks, leaving his wife in charge of the two girls, Tosca the kelpie, and a lot of housework, hospitality and gardening. The 70-year-old house was to be home for the next 13 years, but Elizabeth was gone after two.

As a backstop, in a place where she was often on her own while David was away and her daughters at school, the church assigned a 'spiritual director'. This young single priest's first task was to repair a malfunctioning computer, and he quipped that the computer would be easier to sort than the woman who owned it. The conservative bishop's wife feared the counsel this progressive upstart might offer her, but it was actually a perfect match. She blew off steam and he offered alternative viewpoints.

The young priest's brief was never specifically stated but it's safe to say that he never told her to fire up an aeroplane. She did that by herself.

WHEN ELIZABETH LEFT FOR BOARDING SCHOOL IN 1990, IT was time to take stock. 'What are you going to do with yourself, Marion?' asked a concerned friend visiting from Victoria. 'You're almost 50 and not challenging your brain. You can't just rot away in Gladstone being the bishop's wife!'

These blunt words were confronting when some challenging family concerns were being managed remotely. But the friend was right. What would she do? Perhaps she could study acting. The thought of that training was appealing, but really, it had no practical application out there.

Elizabeth wonders if the flying ambition started after she and Rachel and their mum flew with Hugh Usher in his four-seat Piper. David had been away for weeks and Hugh, who was part of the Diocesan Council (an adviser to the bishop), collected the family to meet with David when he arrived in Whyalla. The trip reduced a long drive to a mere interlude and brought into sharp focus the amount of driving that David was doing. He was tired.

The novelty of the bishop's job wore terribly thin on Marion's forty-eighth birthday in 1991, when he drove off to whoop-whoop, working. She went alone to dine with friends down in Clare, an hour south. The longer the dinner went on, the better the flying idea seemed. It would be a practical way for Marion to work with her husband and streamline his schedule. She had been for a fly with her brother the year before and enjoyed it immensely.

By dessert it was decided that if every parishioner in the diocese bought a $10 share in Marion, she'd have enough to pay for the whole licence. Times were good in agriculture and as each of them peeled off $10 notes to place before her, the 'Wings over Willochra' campaign to get Marion flying was born. The necessary $10 000 would be fundraised by a committee or donated in $10 lots – they hoped. As bizarre as it sounds, it turned out to be a brilliant plan.

Des O'Driscoll, a respected bush pilot and instructor from Pinaroo (400 kilometres south-east of Gladstone) came highly recommended. He'd never taught a bishop's wife to fly before but he reckoned it should be interesting enough. Des would stay at Bishop's

House for five days at a time and together they would work through the aviation syllabus. For radio calls they talked into spoons across the table from each other. Marion called from the 'aeroplane' and Des replied from the 'tower'.

Using the steady flutter of money that came in from around the diocese, Marion and Des then hired the Port Pirie Aero Club's four-seat Cessna 172 and got to work on the practical skills. On one circuit Marion landed too far down the runway and the aircraft overshot the runway completely and landed in a ploughed paddock.

As the wheels slowed and sank in the dirt, they took Marion's good spirits with them. What the hell was she doing trying to fly an aeroplane anyway? It was far removed from all that was familiar: music, drama, community groups, meetings, praying, cooking, chasing kids, an inordinate amount of entertaining, and tending to everybody's needs. She was so far outside of her comfort zone that she didn't think she could cope. Fear, she came to know then and in a dark sky many years later, starts in the pit of your stomach and creeps up, then lodges in your brain. Marion reckoned she'd give away the flying and send each of the contributors back $7.50 and thank them for their support. But each of the three times she tried to quit, something got her up again and back into the aeroplane.

Things became even more intense on the cross-country flights. Des dispatched her on her first solo in a one-hour triangle from Port Pirie, east to Burra then north over the top of old Koomooloo Station and back to Pirie. Around Burra the few roads that a pilot can use for navigation disappear underneath thick saltbush. Suddenly she was lost. About half an hour on, Marion turned right (south) and found the Murray River at Waikerie – the only South Australian river town with a silo. She turned right again and followed the large river on its north-west course until she reached Morgan, where it does a sharp turn. Marion continued on her heading as the river disappeared to the south and she picked up the road back to Pirie, where she landed in a state of despair. It was no big deal to Des. She'd used her brain and got home. But she was deeply distressed by her inadequacy and its effect on her undertaking. In perfect timing, the next day she opened a letter from an old lady in Yorktown who was thrilled by the prospect of the bishop flying in. Within the paper folds was a crisp $10 note.

Marion feared she didn't have the abilities to pilot a plane and then a friend from Adelaide arrived and pointed out some harsh realities to the student pilot. The friend quickly lost patience and told her, 'Oh marvellous, Marion! You're so used to being capable, and now you've come up against something that's not easy and you want to throw in the towel. There are some things in your life that you have never faced.'

Her friend's words of advice forced Marion to cast a beam into the deepest crevasses of her soul. The inevitable awakening was hard to face but it made her realise that in the end, we are not judged or identified by our list of achievements, but by the person that we are, and in that mindset she returned to the aeroplane for another go. She would rather fail than quit.

The flying fraternity around her didn't see the insecurities. Brian Condon, who also flew from Port Pirie, thought she was a real go-getter and admired her enthusiasm and determination.

Back in the air, she found that roads that were lost under canopies of trees could now be identified by the fact that there was a straight line of trees. Lakes dried up and disappeared but rivers rarely did. Towns looked the same from above but some had a grain silo, easily seen from the air. Sometimes she would find an airport and land to figure out where she was. Des went back to basics and sent her on a flight that went from silo to silo, coastline to coastline and back to a silo. To ease her nerves, she resorted to her music and sang aloud for most of the trip. Her anxious hands must have accidentally squeezed the switch on the press-to-talk microphone and so finally she got her wish to sing on the radio, albeit not the ABC. Des pipped her about her singing when she proudly returned.

And so she finally got the hang of flying. After seven months, at the end of 1992, Des issued her licence. David said a prayer of thanks and hopped in the passenger seat for his first flight, up to Woomera. For almost every one of her 1700 flying hours over the next 23 years, David was with her. Flying the bishop, after all, was Marion's job.

Rachel, the only child left at home, was often plonked in the back and carted all over the state and everybody thought it was exciting, except Rachel, and Marion's mother, who thought that Marion would either orphan her children or widow her husband with all this flying.

Rachel left for Walford boarding school in 1992 and Marion and David became a tight team. Reverend Trevor Briggs was an occasional passenger and was always impressed with the way Marion carried herself in public. He thought she was respectful of David's position and she portrayed the regard his family held for him.

She also had the happy knack of turning most things into a joke, while being mindful of not taking jokes too far. Elizabeth backs that up with, 'Mum always knows where the boundaries are and with her humour she is able to tread that fine line. Sometimes it is a fairly fine line.'

David's eight-hour drives were now reduced to an hour or two of flying. Marion came to know and love the people they were working with and to see where her husband had been disappearing to each week during their first three years in Gladstone. His role involved overseeing the churches and parishes in his diocese, checking the welfare of priests and their families and other people in need who approached him. There were also many ceremonial functions to attend or preside over.

Sometimes on formal occasions Marion would arrive at a remote airfield in her casual flying clothes, then dash behind a bush to change for official duties and change again for the flight home. Once, on a four-day trip they were heading down the Eyre Peninsula when halfway across the Spencer Gulf, Marion asked David where her bag was. Among other things, it held her outfit for a priest's induction and a civic reception. The man who never raises his voice meekly replied that from a scan of the back seat it would appear her bag was still at home on the bed. For the next half an hour his wife, wearing shorts and a t-shirt, imparted her thoughts on that matter and a few more for measure. By the time they landed, David was well aware of his sins. A parishioner kindly lent Marion a Massimo Osti dress – the stretch fabric that was fashionable for old ladies in the 1970s. She urged Marion to keep the dress, saying that it was from her mother, who no longer needed it because she was dead.

The unlikely story of the bishop's wife gained attention and in 1993 ABC television program *Australian Story* did a 15-minute profile of Marion. In the film, David praised his wife and her place in his work, while Marion reflected on her unrealised dreams of becoming an opera singer or actor. Her performances, she told the viewers, were now on a much grander stage and the life she lost in Adelaide, she had now found in Willochra. She began to be invited to speak all over the country.

Then one day, in 1997 while crossing between Adelaide's Parafield Airport and Port Lincoln, Marion started seeing double. Ten days of testing returned a devastating diagnosis: Myasthenia gravis, a chronic autoimmune neuromuscular disease that causes weakness in the skeletal muscles.

The diagnosis explained why she'd always been so tired. Her specialist ascertained that she had contracted the condition after a bout of measles when she was six years old. It explained her slightly drooping eye, and why she could win the sprint but would puff out doing cross-country. She clenched her fists when the doctor said she would be in a wheelchair within two years and end her days in a nursing home. She was 51. If it came to the nursing home stage, Marion told David to put her there and continue his work. But he surprised her when he replied that he would resign and care for his wife.

With great determination Marion defied the grim forecast and embarked upon a course of medication. For the next 24 years it has worked beautifully, though she still needs a bit of a lie-down occasionally and getting out of bed in the morning is a drawn-out affair. From one of her books a four-line poem titled 'Afternoon' says it simply:

> They ask me how I am
> I sweetly smile and say
> Then by the afternoon
> My strength just slips away.

That moment of diagnosis was a grave time, lightened by the arrival of many friends, among whom was another student pilot and his wife who came from Jamestown, 200 kilometres north of Adelaide, and who insisted that she go and do her flight review with Des. She passed and received her medical pass as well. It was the kindness and love of that man encouraging her to get back into the aeroplane that got Marion back into the air again.

FLYING AROUND THE OUTBACK, SOME OF THE INSTRUCtions from property owners to pilots didn't differ much from those issued to Nancy Bird in the 1930s. Instructions such as 'just land in the home paddock along the fence where the crop duster lands' were common but on arrival Marion might find a mob of sheep following a ute doing circles in a paddock, with no indication of where she should be landing or which way the wind was blowing.

She raised the topic of difficult flights a few times at the aero club. How to tackle navigational challenges, managing changing weather, finding and landing on remote outback strips with obstacles, and reviewing decisions and mistakes. But the men were closed about it. 'Why is that?' she asks. 'I know they've had frightening experiences as well, but they don't talk about it, whereas women do. I think it's important to think about it or else you think you're a bit unusual.'

The self-confidence that Marion gained by learning to fly gave her the confidence to share her poetry and stories. She published a small book of her works and four more have followed.

In 1999 the McCalls bought an immaculate four-seat Cessna 172. Its call-sign Juliet Charlie Sierra (JCS) was affectionately renamed Jesus Christ Superstar. In Parafield one day they bumped into Des who asked if it was their aeroplane because he recognised Marion's voice on the radio, but not the call-sign. He ran off to check it out and gave VH-JCS the big tick of approval.

Less than a year later, Marion joined many other pilots when she flew JCS down to Lameroo, near Adelaide, for Des's funeral. She cried with the rest when the missing man formation flew over the cemetery. His name lives on, as the Lameroo airfield is now named after him. He would have loved what came next and to know that his good teaching went with Marion as she flew David over to the west.

After 13 years at Willochra, David felt he needed a change and, out of the blue, Bunbury elected him. It was a surprise. As the Bishop of Bunbury, his diocese was 170 kilometres south of Perth and hugged the south-west corner of the state. It felt like the other side of the world, not just the other side of the country, but in March 2000 they left the entire family behind, including the dog. The aeroplane's back seat held a cat in a cage on top and a gifted bottle of Grange underneath it. The welcome was warm, they settled in quickly and the flying was now over waving wheat fields and pearly white beaches.

In 2004 the Bunbury Diocese turned 100 and Marion decided to celebrate and fundraise by entering the Dawn to Dusk Challenge.

This event was instigated in 1964 by Prince Philip – an athletic man who enjoyed a bit of healthy competition. After completing an air race, he announced he'd like to create one with a more sporting approach.

The challenge is '... to encourage the most interesting employment of a flying machine within the limits of competent airmanship and to demonstrate the capabilities of pilot and machine in a day's flying, during the hours between Dawn and Dusk, in terms of furthering some original and praiseworthy objective.' So very English.

Using the Wings over Willochra fundraising model, Marion and David decided to 'Beat the Bounds' of the diocese. Beating the Bounds is an English tradition where church members take an annual walk around the parish boundary and stop at significant places along the way to pray for various reasons that are possibly now relegated to folklore. Part of Marion's challenge was to carefully manage fuel stops along the way and to enlist various volunteers to officially verify her movements and achievements. Weather of course was a major consideration. It required a lot of coordinating, and faith in volunteers to turn up and do their allotted job.

After weeks of bad weather, the sky shone blue on 6 March 2004. With David in his religious attire, the engine's roar cut the morning sky in Bunbury. Around the diocese, the parishioners were in prayer. The national women's church group that Marion belonged to did the same. And in Woking, just outside London, a small order of nuns who had served in the Diocese of Bunbury put their hands together.

The first stop out from Bunbury was 40 minutes up the coast at Mandurah where they spent 20 minutes with the parishioners and David ceremoniously stamped his bishop's staff on the ground to claim it for the diocese. Departing to the west they flew just over an hour out across the wheatfields to Narrogin, where 80 parishioners were having breakfast. Ten minutes later they departed for Corrigin, 45 minutes to the north-west, where 50 people were having morning tea. With just enough time to say hello and depart again, they flew

40 minutes to the famous tourist attraction Wave Rock at Hyden, hoping that Keith Urley, the local ag pilot, would remember to appear with a drum of avgas to refuel them. Fortunately, he did.

They waved goodbye to Hyden and headed 66 minutes south-east to Ravensthorpe, where the wind indicated Marion should land on the smaller strip running crossways to the main one. But on closer inspection this strip appeared long neglected and so she had to execute a more difficult crosswind landing on the main strip. This would have been fine except lined up along the length of the strip was a welcoming committee: every Anglican in Ravensthorpe poised in their cars with picnic tables. Managing to keep the aeroplane straight so as not to wipe out the entire congregation in one go, Marion and David landed safely, enjoyed lunch and took off on a short hop for Bremer Bay.

The dozen or so parishioners at this tiny outpost invited another 50 townsfolk for an afternoon of jocularity, which by the time Marion landed was becoming quite jocular indeed. In fact many of the revellers appeared to have forgotten why they were gathered and wondered what she was doing there.

From Bremer Bay to Albany they tracked along the coast, with the 95 minutes from Albany to Augusta the longest stretch. The day was drawing out and as the coastline came and went and the Southern Ocean rocked below them, David closed his eyes. Even the radio fell silent as Marion monitored her instruments, listened for any deviations in the hum of the steady engine and kept an eye on the time. With all that water below and the remote and rugged coastline offering little chance of an easy rescue, Marion poked David in the ribs to wake him up.

From Augusta, they rounded the headlands and turned north to Busselton. The waiting gang at Busselton had decided against hosting a barbecue and instead put on Sunday evening champagne and nibbles. As the shadows lengthened, the champagne took effect and

PERTH
Corrigin
Hyden
Mandurah
Narrogin
WESTERN
AUSTRALIA
Bunbury
Cape Naturaliste
Ravensthorpe
Busselton
March 2004 Dawn to Dusk: Beating the bounds
April 2008 Half Trophy: Sea to air
Augusta
Bremer
Bay
Black
Point
Windy
Harbour
Cliffy
Head
Torbay
Albany
0 20
km

WESTERN
AUSTRALIA
SOUTH
AUSTRALIA
Kalgoorlie
Rawlinna
Forrest
Cook
Ooldea
Immarna
Malbooma
Tarcoola
Coondambo
Pimba
Hesso
Port Augusta
Great
Australian
Bight
0 100
km
2006 Dawn to Dusk: Crossing the desert

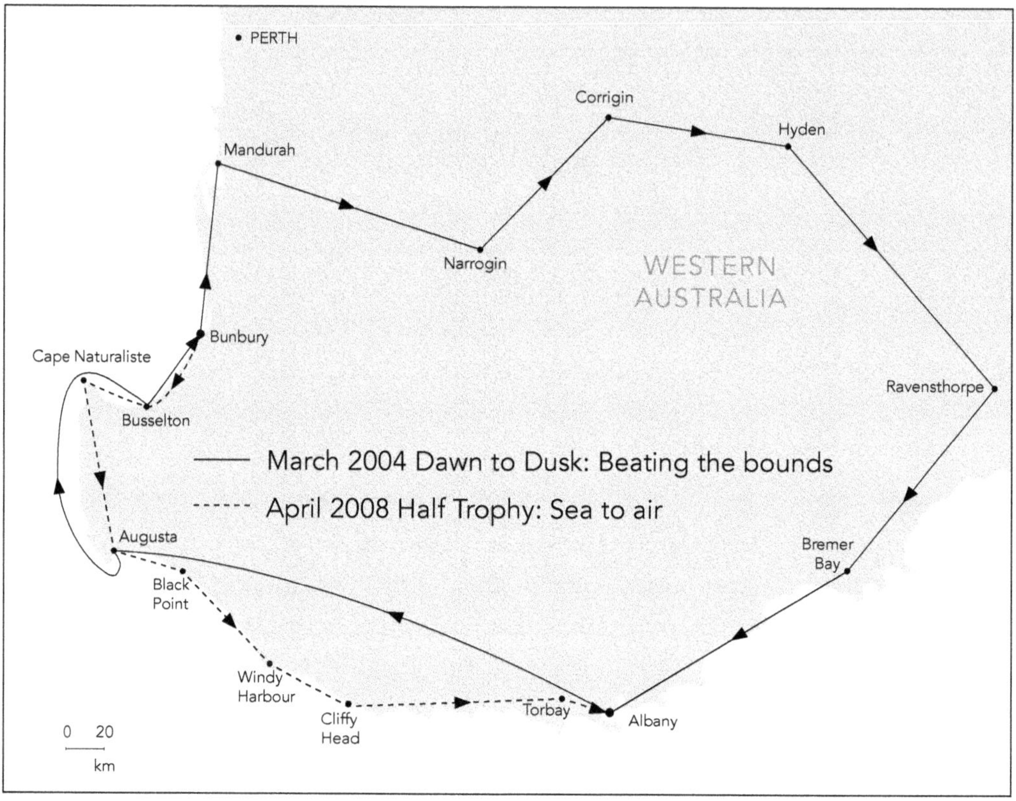

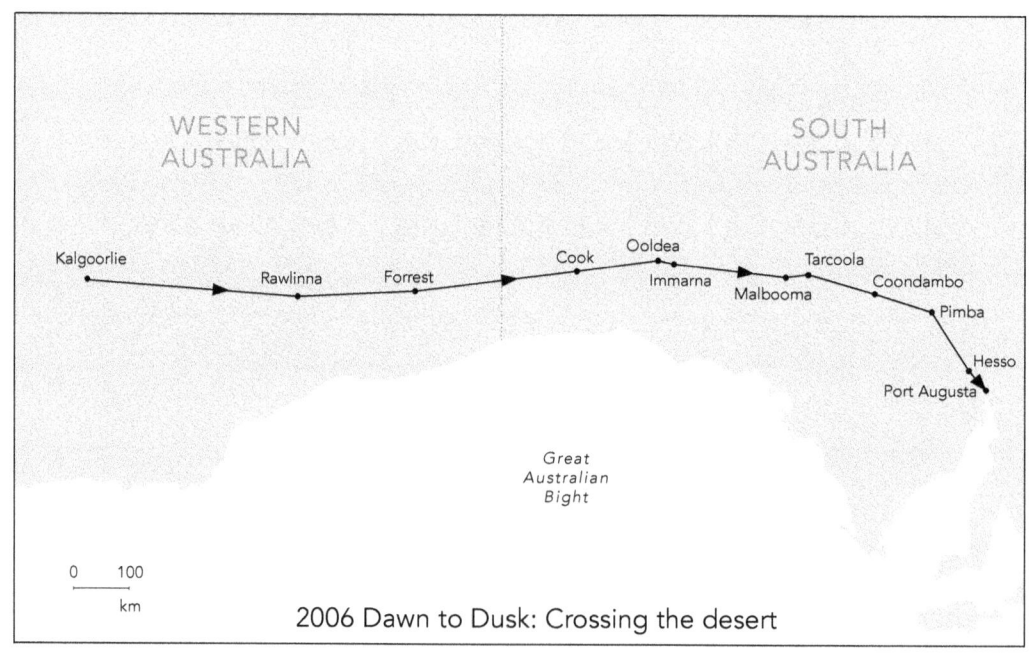

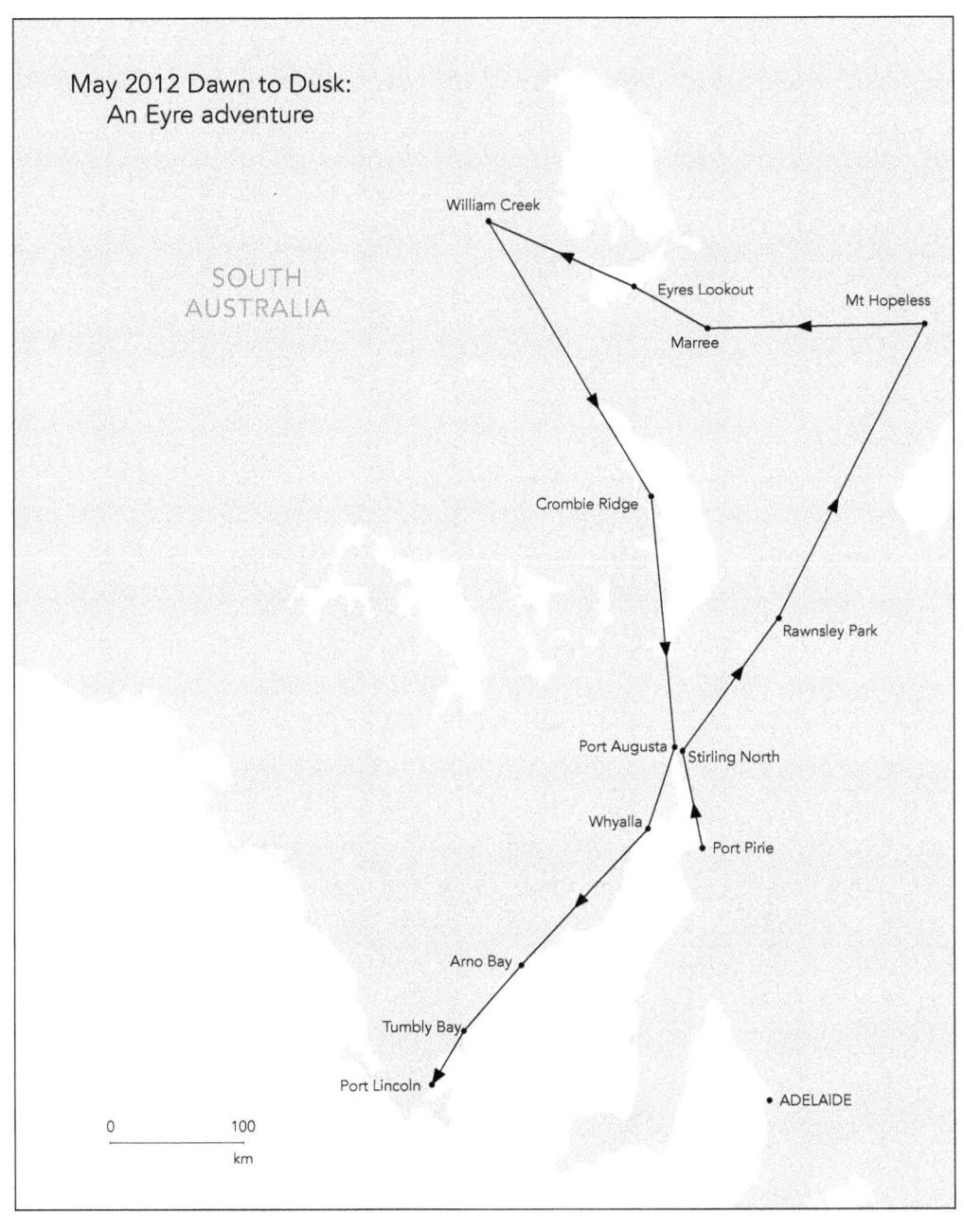

Marion McCall's Dawn to Dusk routes

the group enthusiastically but mistakenly welcomed three aeroplanes before finally, at 6.42 pm, Marion emerged out of the southern sky.

They arrived back home three minutes after their estimated arrival time. They had been gone 12 hours and 48 minutes and flown 1345 kilometres around an area that they flew regularly in parts. It was effectively their workplace, but they had never seen it as a whole before. It had been a huge day with ten landings and 670 people to greet.

The flight log was dispatched to London and a long silence followed. Then a letter arrived, informing them that the presentation dinner at the Royal Air Force (RAF) Club in Piccadilly had to be postponed until January and was there any chance of attending? The McCalls replied that it would be nice to see their daughters Elizabeth and Alexandra, now studying music in London, but considered the distance, time and cost in going so far just for a dinner as a bit indulgent. 'I can put it no more strongly than you should move heaven and earth to be here,' came the swift reply from one of the organisers. With that kind of motivation and travel plans now afoot, Marion excitedly called a couple of previous entrants from Victoria who informed her that even if she'd won, there would be no allowances to make a speech because the evening was so formal. Aghast, she replied, 'I can't go all the way to London and not open my mouth!' and so devised a ruse. She got approval from the RAF Club to present a photo of the landing back in Bunbury with a few well-chosen words to accompany the presentation. Marion set to work on her speech — it would be hilarious — and she would enjoy her moment in the sun.

In mid-winter London, wearing a velvet skirt and top in deep red, her favourite colour, Marion approached the RAF Club with David at her side and two of her daughters and their partners closely following. Though she felt comfortable in her clothes, the opulence and colour of Piccadilly in Central London and the history and pomp of the Club was overwhelming.

Up the half dozen front steps and through the large polished timber and glass doors, a starkly different world awaited. In varying shades of gold and gilt, the light reflected off wide, deep-framed photographs and oil paintings, portraits, battle scenes, the framed crest of every imperial Air Force squadron, and photos of Bristol box-kites from the 1800s to Chinook helicopters in Iraq in the early 2000s. It was all there, lining the richly painted walls and holding up traditions and values and a sense of national pride that spanned the Club's 80-year-old history.

It landed like a slap. Marion turned to David and timidly uttered, 'I … don't … think … I … can … make … that … speech.'

'Ohhh, no-no-no. Mm-mm,' mumbled David, quietly pursing his lips and inspecting his feet.

In the dining room the couple perused the remarkable logs of their 14 rivals and it didn't seem even remotely likely that they could win any of the prizes. They settled down for the silver service dinner while Marion, sick with nerves, tried to figure out how to wriggle out of her humorous speech.

Across the table was a judge's young Italian wife. Confident in her surroundings, she presented with typical European flair in a plunging neckline, leaving Marion to feel decidedly colonial. But when they went to powder their noses, Marion confessed her fear of the silly speech, to which the young Italian replied, 'Oh sock it to them. They're such a stuffy mob!' So she did.

Feeling sick to her core, she rose to speak. Fear, the Siamese twin of bravery, reduced her to the plain postmaster's daughter from St Arnaud. She felt out of place and out of her league. But combating her nerves was the knowledge that her husband of 35 years, the father of her five children, her co-pilot and the man who promised to nurse her in ill health, was sitting six metres in front of her and beaming. She kept her focus, not daring to look at him.

Elizabeth proudly watched her mum's speech bring light and

humour to a very conservative place with a strict sense of order. But contrary to that, the people were warm and friendly and, not only did her speech win them over, so did her flying – Marion won first prize! She was the first Australian and the fourth woman to have done so in the race's 40-year history, and she was in shock. Everybody was – particularly the couple of polished young British airmen who came second. She followed it up by also winning the Tiger Club medal for the longest distance flown. The whole thing was thrilling and unbelievable.

The substantial trophy was a World War II Tiger Moth compass. The Duke of Edinburgh had had it set in oak with a sterling silver casing and Waterford crystal dome. The McCalls took it with them that night to drink champagne and toast this incredible success. David lugged the thing onto the flight home disguised as hand luggage, doing his best to pretend it weighed less than its 10 kilograms. At the Bishop's House in Bunbury, Bishop's Court, the uninsurable item lived under the bed and Marion lived in fear of getting robbed. She playfully nicknamed it Phil and when an email from the Duke of Edinburgh, via David Hamilton (a Dawn to Dusk judge) joked about the value of the trophy he quipped that he didn't want to hear that Ned Kelly had got hold of it. He also asked, 'Now that you're the best after-dinner speaker in the world, are you charging double?' Marion replied that she now gets two spoons of sugar instead of one – a sly hint that usually her payment for appearances is a cup of tea.

Enjoying the win, Marion hauled 'Phil the trophy' to a conference in Wangaratta, Victoria. In a 'touché' move, she had David take a photo of her handing it over to a life-sized replica of Ned Kelly. There was no reply from London until a couple of years later when the request came for Marion to defend her title.

Surely, she couldn't win it twice? But the idea gelled when she considered the fundraising possibilities.

The Bunbury Diocese had a relationship with Highveld in South Africa. The McCalls had met the Bishop of Highveld at a Bishops Conference and in 2003 went over at his invitation to visit. While she was there, Marion nursed a dying baby girl. It had a profound effect and so she formed a charity to feed AIDS babies. A respectable amount was handed over to the locals to get things going. There was no response and no follow-up and Marion thought the project had foundered. Fourteen years later, the Highveld church newsletter reported on the continuing success of the charity that started with the money raised through the 2004 Dawn to Dusk campaign. For the 2006 challenge, $12 000 was donated to an Australian women's charity.

This time the trip would involve Marion carrying a letter from the Western Australian governor to the governor of South Australia, by crossing the Nullarbor from Kalgoorlie to Port Augusta, following the railway line. Marion's biggest problem was again securing fuel in the outback. It was the middle of summer and the resulting turbulence over nine hours of flying left her declaring to anybody who would listen not to ever let her do it again.

At the presentation dinner in London, the master of the Guild of Air Pilots asked Marion if she was nervous. She said she was satisfied to have won the Challenge once. He replied, 'Nonsense! You're the most competitive person I've ever met!'

To her great surprise and delight, Marion won first prize again, as well as another Tiger Club medal. She beat her nearest rival by 45 kilometres. She had also been invited to make another speech but didn't have anything new to say. Heckling, an art perfected by the British, came from the front table when somebody muttered loudly enough for her to hear, 'We've got a right one 'ere …' The Australian object of the quip thought, 'Blow you Jack!' and gave it her all. Her speech was so endearing that a copy was requested for the RAF Club archives.

Marion entered the competition a third time, in 2008, this time accompanied by Anne Hamilton, the wife of a British pilot she'd met at the previous dinner. They flew a half marathon and followed Matthew Flinders' route from Bunbury to Albany. They then returned inland back to Bunbury.

Thelma Pye, an Australian Women Pilots' Association (AWPA) friend from Adelaide, said it was marvellous to see the delight of audiences who'd not heard any of Marion's funny speeches before. Ever self-deprecating, Marion endeared herself to her audiences. She is an actress, after all, and even now, in her seventies, still agrees to about one talk per month.

Nancy Bird Walton, herself well-versed in speech-making, heard one of Marion's talks and they became good friends, phoning each other regularly. As Nancy's health deteriorated, they spoke more often and when Marion rang to say she'd be away for six weeks to attend her third Royal Aero Club function in London, Nancy simply finished the call, 'Goodbye Darling.'

Sadly, Marion knew what that meant and when the time came shortly after, in January 2009, regretted that she could not join the other women pilots at Nancy's funeral. But Nancy would be the last person to suggest that Marion stay home instead of receiving another trophy in London.

The following year, David retired and the couple moved back to Adelaide to be near their children. Marion began 2011 by being awarded an Order of Australia Medal and a few months later won the AWPA Nancy Bird Trophy for an Outstanding Contribution to Aviation.

She and David competed in their final Dawn to Dusk and were informed by phone in early 2012 that they'd won again. In all, Marion has won the Dawn to Dusk three times, the Half Dawn to Dusk once, and twice won the Tiger Club medal for the longest distance flown while doing the Challenge. Her successes eventually defined her public life and launched her onto many stages.

With retirement came the sale of VH-JCS. After 15 years together, the Cessna was sold to Jonathon Rasheed and is still based in outback South Australia.

David continues to consult and support his colleagues where requested. As he said to the *Australian Story* team all those years ago, he married a teacher who became a mother, choir conductor, bishop's wife and pilot and he wasn't sure what would come next. But he only had to look to the $500 that had been sitting in an unused account for about five years to get a hint.

Geoff Broad, a Western Australian businessman sitting next to Marion at a formal dinner, talked about dreams: what were Marion's? An idea had gestated after a conversation 15 years prior with an old South Australian woman who talked about the tough prejudices of her childhood. With that understanding, Marion determined that she would like to do something to assist Indigenous women.

Broad wrote a $500 cheque to the Marion McCall OAM Scholarship Fund, which was just a vague idea at that time. Marion was able to later add to it. Once the scholarship was established in 2017, her South Australian AWPA colleagues committed to perpetuate it by adding funds themselves.

The AWPA Marion McCall OAM Scholarship Fund is to financially assist an Aboriginal or Torres Strait Islander woman resident in South Australia, Northern Territory or Western Australia to train up to solo flying standard. The annual amount of $3750 will cover that cost. If she has already gone solo, then the money can be used for further solo flights.

'The day that I flew solo', said Marion, 'I gained an enormous amount of confidence that combatted the roaring insecurities I'd carried all my life. I hope this scholarship, by enabling a young Indigenous girl to go solo in an aeroplane, will give her the same encouragement – not necessarily to become a pilot – but perhaps to pursue whatever is important to her. I just want it to give her the confidence to see that things are possible.'

Fundraising every step of the way, pushing herself to get back into the aeroplane when all seemed hopeless and taking a big bite at her opportunities; Marion herself learnt that many things are possible. You just have to figure out who you are and remember that, then give it a go.

6

LYN GRAY

FERRY PILOT WITH A WET FOOTPRINT

There's a lot of aeroplanes and aviators down in that water. Thank God I'm not one of them.

(Pilot Lyn Gray's thoughts as she sailed away from her aeroplane, adrift in the Pacific)

In June 2006, 1600 kilometres out across the Pacific Ocean, 28-year-old Kristian Kauter swung to his right and looked quizzically at Lyn Gray, the pilot-in-command of the four-seat twin-engine Piper Seminole. 'You're calling out the Coast Guard?' he asked in disbelief. 'It's that bad?'

Lyn didn't want to alarm her co-pilot. It was his second ferry flight delivering light aircraft from the USA into Australia. It was her tenth. In a guilty moment, she wondered if she'd understated the risk of flying a light plane from Santa Barbara, California, to Sydney over great stretches of water.

She was a seasoned ferry pilot and he was a young commercial pilot working towards an airline career. He'd done most of his flight training with Lyn so they knew each other quite well. Kristian was focused on his future and was enjoying the process of building hours, but when he forked out the cash for a seat on this flight, he hadn't asked for this. Then again, as Kristian says, neither had Lyn.

Lyn had to steel herself; I can't control this and I can't make it seem better, she thought.

Kristian's next enquiry, about what had happened to all the fuel, drew an unusually short response. 'I don't know where it went. I couldn't care less. It's not there,' she snapped awkwardly.

In the back of the Seminole, Lyn rolled up one of the long-range fuel bladders to assess its volume. The GPS said they had eight hours and 35 minutes to Hawaii. There was only enough fuel for six hours. That's when the 47-year-old knew she was going to get wet.

Suddenly there were many things to manage: ditching, rescue and her justifiably anxious co-pilot. This was a true emergency, but Lyn was no stranger to keeping a cool head. She'd practised it from a young age.

LYN AND HER BROTHER GARRY, WHO WERE CLOSE IN AGE AND spirit, were kids of the great outdoors. They were guided by their energetic father, Brian Miller, a toolmaker and TAFE teacher, who used his practical skills to tutor his young'uns in camping and outdoor pursuits near home in suburban Castle Hill on Sydney's outskirts, and in the Blue Mountains an hour's drive further out.

Despite its inevitable growth, only 40 minutes by bus from the CBD, the suburb still has shades of the rural vibe that drew Lyn's parents to what was in the 1960s still a small orchard and dairy town. Brian and Heather provided their kids with a secure, happy-go-lucky childhood. It all came with the companionship of various family dogs and her affinity for dogs and her love of the outdoors remains.

As Lyn approached high school age, Bankstown Airport, 26 kilometres to the south-east, was increasingly busy as general aviation in Australia reached a peak of activity. Importing aeroplanes became big business, and would be a major part of her future. But before flying, Lyn took up shooting at age 14. By the late 1980s she had been three-times pistol national champion and by the time she retired from the sport in 1995, she had been NSW state champion seven times. As a champion Australian pistol shooter, she was also one of the best ten in the world and competed in various international competitions in Venezuela, England and Australia as part of the Australian team. It was a sport that taught her patience and focus.

Lyn qualified as a primary school teacher in 1981 and at Easter that year the 21-year-old teamed up with a fellow club member, Ray Gray, at the National Pistol Titles at Blacktown. 'We kind of knew each other from hanging out with the same group of friends. I used to collect badges and he had one on his jacket that I hadn't seen before so I walked up to him and said, "stand still" and got my pocketknife out and cut the badge off. He asked me out for lunch,' Lyn said.

'Was it a bit brash?' I ask.

Lyn laughs. She laughs a lot anyway, but she laughs at the memory of this meeting. 'Ah, well. You've got a knife and he's gonna stand still. It was only a little pocketknife and I was just cutting the threads off. It's not like he was a stranger and I started hacking at his clothing.' By Christmas they were married.

The teaching and shooting both gave way to flying after Lyn's thirty-seventh birthday in 1997, when her brother gifted her a flying lesson at Schofields Flying Club at Bankstown Airport. When the instructor asked if he'd see her again, Lyn hastily replied, 'Yeah ... Tomorrow.'

After handling the controls, she fell in love with flying. At 153 centimetres tall, she needed a booster cushion in order to see comfortably through the windscreen, but her height was no barrier and she spent weekends and holidays training and in 18 months had her licence and later her instructor rating. Teaching aviation students from 6 am until 8 am, Lyn would then whip over to school and teach her primary school pupils, then return to the airport in the evenings.

She had no intention to make flying a full-time career, but the flying school bought a new four-seat Piper Archer, which had to be imported from Vero Beach, Florida, USA. To defray the cost of ferrying it into Australia, Schofields ran a raffle. First prize was to accompany the ferry pilot in the Archer across mainland USA and the other prize was to accompany him on the Pacific crossing back to Australia.

The Club secretary won the Florida to California component of the raffle and sold it to Lyn for $1000. She then made her way across Bankstown Airport to the Clamback and Hennessy hangar and introduced herself to the ferry pilot, Ray Clamback, who she would be joining for the ferry trip. The next time they met was at Orlando, Florida. They drove together to Vero Beach to the Piper Aircraft Manufacturing facility. She'd only had her licence for a few months, and felt herself to still be a raw beginner, but to Lyn's surprise Ray told her to go and check out the aircraft, which was on the ramp, while he obtained the documentation. 'Jump in', he said. 'Into the left-hand seat?' she asked. 'Yes', he replied. And so Lyn flew as a pilot under instruction across the USA.

As the changing landscapes of Florida, Mississippi, Texas, New Mexico, Arizona and California unfolded beneath them on that trans-continental journey, the wonders of aviation beguiled her. Over the next few years Lyn began ferrying as a paying passenger for the experience.

As she worked towards her instrument rating, Ray Clamback offered Lyn a job with Clamback and Hennessy at Bankstown Airport managing fuel, baggage and passengers on weekends to pay for her instrument, commercial and instructor ratings. Paying passengers were often trainee pilots. They were welcomed as company for the ferry pilots and it worked well for the passengers, who were able to build hours or to gain the experience of a long-distance over-water flight. Lyn was a co-pilot/passenger on four or five ferry trips just for the experience, including Australia to USA, Perth to Thailand and South Africa to Perth. Once she started ferrying as a pilot, she often flew alone from California to NSW.

IN OCTOBER 2004 LYN WAS AGAIN CROSSING THE PACIFIC, this time along with Ray Clamback, his wife Aminta Hennessy and her co-pilot Simon Matthews. Ray and Lyn were each flying a single-engine Cessna 182. Aminta was piloting an empty Cessna Caravan, capable of carrying up to a dozen passengers, with Simon as her co-pilot. Pleased to have the long California to Hawaii leg out of the way, Lyn and Ray set out at daybreak to fly their planes the nine hours from Honolulu to Kiritimati Island (also called Christmas Island) in the Kiribati chain. Aminta and Simon departed an hour later in their larger and faster aeroplane, but flying the same route. Shortly before Aminta passed Ray and Lyn, drama unfolded.

'I could see Ray the whole time we were flying,' said Lyn. 'I was behind and below him so I could always look up and see him in my windscreen. I noticed that he was slowing down so I radioed to ask why.'

'I've got a problem with the plane,' he said. 'I think it is fuel injectors.'

Lyn figured that problem could easily be fixed at Kiritimati Island. She recalculated his flight time and reckoned he'd still make it OK. A few minutes later Ray stated calmly, 'The oil pressure light has just illuminated.' That meant engine trouble.

'Ray. There's just been a big puff of white smoke,' said Lyn.

Sixty kilometres behind, Aminta heard her husband's last words on the matter. He said, 'The motor just seized. I'm going in.'

Devoid of power, Ray was heading for the water. Lyn asked if he had his life jacket on. He did. She relayed wind speed and wave direction and followed him down. In a notebook on the passenger seat she wrote the life-saving GPS coordinates.

Aminta radioed San Francisco, the controlling body for most of the Pacific Ocean, around 4500 kilometres away, to call out the US Coast Guard. She says, in her story, published on their company website:

> My HF [high frequency radio] was working well, but talking to San Francisco in amongst the rest of the world trying to communicate on the same frequency was hard. I asked San Francisco to call out the Coast Guard please as we had an aircraft in trouble (at this stage he was still airborne). They seemed to me to ask a great number of questions in an emergency. Finally, I said, 'Call out the Coast Guard, the aircraft is now in the water.'

Down on the water the four-seat aeroplane was immediately flipped by a wave, exposing its oil-stained belly. From a few hundred feet above, a horrified Lyn thought she saw the life raft and a person, but quickly lost sight of them both. She circled at 500 feet and to her horror, within two or three minutes, the aeroplane gurgled into the briny deep, leaving her nothing to focus on but her GPS coordinates and the endless blue Pacific. When the US Coast Guard came within range of Lyn's VHF radio, she gave them the coordinates of the ditching. She had extended a stage of flap so she could fly slower but all she could see was a wheel spat and some navigation charts afloat.

Lyn was fairly sure she'd spotted Ray exit the plane in his life jacket. Well into the afternoon she continued the lonely business of searching but did not spot him again because above the heaving ocean's two-metre swell and whitecaps, all that she could hope to see was his dark head. She had come down as low as 100 feet and seen the empty life raft. Unrecognisable flotsam suggested a hard landing. The Pacific Ocean is the largest ocean in the world, covering about 165 million square kilometres. It is, without a doubt, the loneliest place on earth. Lyn was alone and distressed, and Ray appeared to be gone. She called an overflying Air New Zealand jet and said she didn't need any help but just wanted to talk to somebody while she was circling down low by herself.

The abrupt captain showed little interest but then she got onto a guy named Sonny who was flying a Gulfstream to Kiritimati Island. Flying back past the crash site on his return, he advised that the runway lights were not working there and suggested she arrive before dark. Aminta had also advised Lyn to land before dark. She had gone ahead and had organised the runway lights and cars to shine their headlights if required.

When the US Coast Guard lumbered in at 500 feet with their white C-130 Hercules with the distinctive red stripes wrapped around the belly, Lyn cleared the airspace for them by climbing to 1000 feet. She continued searching above them until they urged her to leave in plenty of time to make Kiritimati. 'We don't want to be looking for two planes,' they told her.

It was cold comfort. She continued to question whether she had in fact seen Ray exit the aircraft as she'd thought, or whether it was wishful thinking. Eventually, the auxiliary fuel warning lights came on. It was time to leave. She knew that down in the water, if he'd survived, Ray would be trying not to think about drowning, dehydration or the unbearable possibility that he would never be found. By now Lyn had been circling for over four hours.

She switched to her main fuel tanks, farewelled the US Coast Guard crew and set course for Kiritimati Island. It was a three-hour flight, and she was distraught. Wondering if her best had been enough, Lyn sobbed for the first hour and was numb for the next two. But she had to pull herself together for a night-time arrival. As she flew the last of her circuit pattern, about one minute before landing, Poof! the lights came on and she landed safely, though traumatised, one minute before last light.

She sat in the aeroplane, exhausted, in the deep darkness. The feeble light from the airport revealed a crowd of people she knew she'd have to face, but first to the aeroplane door was Aminta, a stoic determined pilot with 50 years experience whose mild English accent has never left her. Lyn sat helpless in the pilot seat and by the look on her face it was obvious to Aminta what was coming. All she could say to Aminta was, 'I'm sorry.'

At the besser block hotel, Aminta, Simon and Lyn picked at their meals, and Lyn stayed fixed in her seat when a phone call came for Aminta from the Coast Guard. Lyn didn't want to get bad news but as the call went on, curiosity got the better of her.

In the upturned aeroplane, Ray had escaped his seatbelt and struggled out with the lifejacket tight around his neck. The raft, which he'd been unable to inflate, then inflated itself and floated off. For the whole time, he'd been treading water and holding the lifejacket away from his neck. With his back to the wind to avoid spray in his face, the western sun burned his head and hands. Trying not to gulp seawater, and with his legs cycling beneath him, Ray watched in hope that his employee or the US Coast Guard would find him. He knew that Lyn had stayed in the area. She'd flown right over him a couple of times but hadn't seen him. If she had, she'd have waggled the wings – an aviator's wave.

At the hotel, when she learnt that the Coast Guard had footage of Ray climbing into their life raft, her mood was too deep to shift. 'It's not quite the release you think because you're in the midst of grieving,' said Lyn. 'So, when we got the news it didn't make the big difference that I thought it would. I found this episode much harder to digest and process than when it was me who went in the water two years later, because I had no control over what was happening to Ray. If I hear a mayday call when I'm flying now, I get upset until I know what's happened, whereas if it's my own mayday call, I know what I'm doing. It's a different situation.'

The following day, with Ray onboard a P&O Nedlloyd container ship heading for Melbourne, Lyn continued on and flew the 2300-kilometre leg to Pago Pago in American Samoa, with Aminta in radio contact the whole way. Waiting another day wasn't going to make things any better and she wanted to complete her job.

In her few onboard possessions, Lyn always carries something to read, but over the Pacific when she picked up the golden cover of her current book, *Smithy*, by New Zealand–born author Ian Mackersey, she stopped reading at Chapter 27, 'Final flight'. She closed the book solemnly. It's well known that Kingsford Smith went into the sea off Burma. She didn't need to relive it.

From Pago Pago to Australia, Lyn flew off into some wild weather en route to Coolangatta, Queensland, and eventually arrived at Bankstown. The following week, their ordeal made headlines Australia-wide, and from New York to London.

Ray said in an interview that he knew Lyn and Aminta would be talking to the Coast Guard and that they would come looking for him. At 3.45 am Hawaiian time, a huge ship pulled up alongside Ray, a tiny speck in the ocean, and that was the most frightening moment of the whole ordeal.

It was his second rescue at sea. In 1999 Ray and his co-pilot spent ten hours in the Pacific when their engine failed. The weather had not been as kind that time.

Speaking to the press after the rescue, he said, 'I realised that all I had to do was to survive, I thought I had a reasonable chance of doing that, so I was just determined to hang on as long as I could, which I did for about six and a half hours.' He realised this time, at 67 years old, he'd been a lot weaker than the first time he ditched. He concluded by saying he might quit flying single-engine aeroplanes and stick to flying twins.

Lyn escaped the media storm in Sydney and flew to Melbourne in a new Cessna 182 to train some students. As the passenger, with a friend at the controls, she flew out across Port Phillip Bay to circle the Nedlloyd ship as it passed through the heads. This time, looking down from the aeroplane, she saw the head that had eluded her in the Pacific Ocean a week before; Ray Clamback was waving from the ship's bridge.

After this dramatic episode, the team was quickly back to work and Lyn pressed on with her career. Two years later, she and Ray had an unwelcome role reversal.

THE FLIGHT FROM CALIFORNIA TO HAWAII STARTED WELL enough, with clear skies and a good speed. Everybody (Lyn and her co-pilot Kristian Kauter, Ray Clamback and his co-pilot Tom Caska) was keen to get home after a few delays in the US. Kristian had phoned his wife to say they were finally leaving and he'd be in Sydney within the week. She was keen for him to get home. Delays are the norm in general aviation, which can be trying for everybody.

It was worth Kristian's time to persevere though, as he was keen to log flying hours, and so it was his hands on the controls a couple of hours later when the aircraft gave a large shudder. What a heart starter. Would the engine seize? The instruments indicated no problems and without any further clues, the pilots had to assume it was some sort of turbulence. It wasn't enough to put Lyn off her banana pudding or Kristian off his peanuts.

Within the hour, however, brown marks and what looked like a small hole in the portside engine cowling appeared. They didn't think much of it but Kristian photographed it to monitor its size. They would investigate further when they arrived in Hawaii 14 hours later.

In view of the cowling issue, Lyn reached behind her to pat the rubber bladder containing the extra ferrying fuel, just to check that it was taut and full. It wasn't. Kristian went back to check the contents and Lyn asked hopefully, 'Would there be 50 gallons [190 litres]?'

'No,' he replied.

'40?'

'No.'

'30?'

'Maybe 20,' came the sombre reply. About an hour's worth.

Alarmed, Lyn ducked back into the cabin and found only a few gallons left in the ferry tank. She quickly shoved their personal bags underneath the bladder to raise one end. It was imperative to push the remaining fuel forward towards its pick-up hose.

The airline pilots monitoring the 123.45 frequency on the California–Hawaii 'Delta route' suddenly put down their coffees when they heard a woman on the radio discussing fuel load and her lack of it with Ray, who was flying within five or ten miles of them in the same model aircraft with 23-year-old Tom. Trying not to raise any alarms yet, and acutely aware of all the ears listening in, Lyn calmly mentioned to her boss the marks on the left engine cowling. Though it was never ascertained if that and the lack of fuel were connected, Lyn deduced that if there was leaking fuel in the left tank and it caught fire, it would probably melt the wing off the aeroplane. There was nothing calming about that idea.

Ray said he would contact the US Coast Guard and he recommended that the portside engine be shut down. From its 8500 feet cruising altitude, the Piper Seminole descended to 4500 feet under less power, and settled there, just above a layer of cloud. Ferry fuel is pumped from the ferry tank into the right wing tank from where it is cross-fed after that. Engineers at Bankstown later discovered that the cross-feed system had failed and fuel was inadvertently leaking into the left tank and out the overflow.

Up around 40 000 feet, the airwaves were all achatter as the airline pilots tripped over each other offering assistance. With such a height disparity, radio contact could only be maintained for about 15 minutes with the high and fast-flying jets, so each captain soon settled into a pattern of handing communications over to the next jet behind them. Ray asked the airliners to alert the US Coast Guard to the probable ditching of VH-CZE, and the information they acquired from Lyn about latitude, longitude and airspeeds was also relayed.

Kristian quickly came up to speed with the situation and together they worked towards the awful moment – expected to be six hours away – when they would make the unavoidable descent into water. The eight-hour flight to the town of Hilo on the eastern side of Hawaii was two hours beyond their endurance.

Too soon, they were pumping air out of the empty ferry bag and swapped onto their main tank. As Lyn said, 'We just had to put one foot in front of the other.' If the feet were methodically plodding through the problems, the thumbs were getting a workout in the back of the plane as Lyn studied the aircraft's manual, seeking long-range cruise endurance settings while juggling the fuel bag and talking to Ray on the radio.

Despite knowing what was to come, it was surreal for Kristian to hear it out loud over the radio. It was hard to digest the reality, given they were flying in fine weather with full main fuel tanks and he had his instructor beside him. Everything should have been OK, but it was not.

'If there'd been bad weather or flames and fire then it would have felt like an emergency,' he said later. 'But it was a beautiful day and everything was fine, except we were in deep trouble.'

They were already flying west, so decided to keep flying with the sun, rather than turn back towards California and risk ditching in cold water and late afternoon light. Over the next 1100 kilometres Lyn identified herself as Charlie Zulu Echo to each new airliner flying past above: Qantas, United, Aloha, Southwest and a business jet. At one point, a US Airways jet took over for the 15-minute contact and identified themselves using their nickname: 'Charlie Zulu Echo, this is Cactus (followed by the flight number). We are with you now.'

'Cactus?' was Lyn's deadpan reply. 'Shit mate. We're the ones that are cactus!' Surprised at the airline's self-appointed nickname, Lyn's reply was somewhat laconic, given the gravity of their cactusness. There was silence from the Americans, who didn't understand the meaning of the Australian slang.

In the variety of people that they spoke to during those next few hours, it was the comforting accent of a Qantas crew who understood perfectly. They urged the pair to wear long sleeves to prevent hypothermia in the water and shared other survival tips. The captain then said, 'We've got a sat phone on board so if you'd like us to call anyone at home, we'd be happy to do it for you.' They politely declined – it just brought the situation into an even sharper focus.

'We might not have had a chance to say anything to anyone back home later,' said Kristian. 'But what were they going to tell our families? Yeah, we've just spoken to Kristian and Lyn and they're fine but they're about to crash the plane? The intention was good but there was nothing really to be said. But it was certainly very reassuring to hear the Australian voice.'

Lyn couldn't see the point of giving her last will and testament while she was still drawing breath. Anyway, there was so much else to focus on. Two yellow 'grab bags' were stuffed with all the important documents and any torches, strobes or flashing lights that would be useful in the two single-person life rafts. Lyn put a torch and portable beacon around her neck and they rehearsed their ditching plan. As an ashen Ray managed the radio work from his aircraft and continued to press for updates from the Coast Guard, Lyn broadcast position, track and speed every quarter hour.

Ray was calm under the pressure, drawing on his previous two ditching experiences. He slowed his aircraft to remain in sight of and in contact with Lyn and Kristian. The pilots discussed tactics and revised emergency procedures and Ray reassured his troubled colleagues that, thankfully on this occasion, the weather was on their side.

The Coast Guard were unable to find any ships within ditching range and as the severity of the situation began to register, Lyn feared the possibility of – at best – three days at sea in a life raft. In his mind Kristian was being circled by sharks.

Like an angel above, a US navy P-3 Orion aircraft en route from Hawaii to California provided more much appreciated emotional support by circling the stricken Seminole for over two hours so they wouldn't be alone way out there over the ocean. The Orion crew checked on the pilots, asking how they were feeling and reassuring them. The irony was that later, one of the US Coastguard

Hercules pilots asked, 'Is that Ray Clamback? I'm the bloke who spotted you with the night vision goggles when you were last in the water!' He had saved Ray's life and hopefully now he could save Lyn's and Kristian's.

The Coast Guard assessed shipping movements and requested a diversion for the Seminole towards a Thai fishing vessel so there would be a ship nearby for rescue. The Seminole changed course accordingly but half an hour later was diverted again towards the Maltese bulk carrier, *Virginius*. It was bigger and better equipped to handle an emergency.

The pilots moved the HF radio from the dashboard down to the floor. Everything that was not screwed down was moved to the back of the cabin and secured so it would not fly about when they hit the water. Lyn wanted nothing to be in the way of them and their exit from the plane. From deep in her nav bag, she pulled out her pocket-knife and Kristian hacked through the soft foam of her back-pillow. Taking one half each, they wedged the foam between themselves and the dash. It might just save their lives upon impact.

There was so much uncertainty in the impending water landing because it is not possible to practice it other than in theory. For a normal runway landing, the pilot raises the Seminole's nose to slow it down and touches the main wheels on the ground, holding the nose off until it runs out of airspeed. The smaller nose-wheel then settles on the runway and the aeroplane rolls to a gentle halt.

A water landing is approached the same way but consideration must be given to wind and wave direction and, with wheels up, when the fuselage finally connects with the water there is no roll. The aeroplane will only skim or skip for a few seconds before it 'grabs' and this can flip the plane over. Both pilots were well aware that their greatest risk was being knocked unconscious on impact, or being caught upside down in the aeroplane, with only minutes to escape. Lyn had already seen it happen.

Throughout the preparation of stowing goods, padding themselves and practising their drill, the pilots drank water to maintain their hydration. Who knows how long they could be out there being swirled around in the ocean? They'd been in and out of their seatbelts so many times that Kristian suggested they put their seatbelts over the outside of their life jackets and do a trial run of un-belting to ensure they didn't get tangled in the rush to escape.

Four-and-a-half hours into the emergency, the US Coast Guard was finally close enough to talk directly to the pilots via the VHF radio. They issued a new heading and a rendezvous point for the ship. Everybody stopped in their tracks when a United Airlines captain came on the radio. 'God Bless you,' she said to the surprised Lyn. 'We are praying for you.' Prayers! Lyn acknowledged the woman and then, with damp eyes, put it out of her mind.

When the GPS coordinates closed in on their target, Lyn and Kristian aimed for it. Ray and Tom, with a close eye on their fuel, had to keep on track for Hilo. Kristian's final words to Tom were wrenching: 'Please say goodbye to my wife if we don't make it.' Dumbstruck, Tom replied, 'I'll be waiting for you in Hawaii with a case of beer.'

Lyn paused. Beyond the radio chatter, navigation and flight management, she drew a deep breath as she started the descent and, deafened by the pulse pounding in her ears, wondered, Is this it? Would her life end here, 850 kilometres off the coast of Hawaii? And what about the young man beside her? She felt an overwhelming responsibility towards him.

She had run through a full range of emotions from 'we'll be fine' to 'we're going to die'. But she had to shove those thoughts aside. It was daylight, they were in control of the plane and they had rescuers standing by. They were in the best possible position given the dire circumstances and if they could keep the aeroplane up the right way the chance of survival was good. There was no feasible alternative and now she just wanted to do it. There were ten minutes to go.

MORE REFINED COORDINATES ARE AGAIN ENTERED IN THE GPS during the eight-minute descent. Lyn opens her door and wedges in a manual, a metal-bound book of Pacific Approach Plates, to keep it from jamming shut and trapping them in the aeroplane if the airframe bends on impact. The roar of air from outside threatens to overwhelm the radio so she dials the volume up to full. She thinks the open door might also make them sink and drown fast.

Her anxiety increases.

Kristian takes the one-person life raft from Lyn's lap to act as another buffer between himself and the dash. He puts the yellow grab bags on her lap. Severing contact with everybody, the pilots remove their headsets and stow them. They can't risk getting entangled. They are on their own.

Scattered cloud whips against the windscreen as they descend through it. There's the ship. They gingerly start up the ailing left engine and for that short time they are back in a normal flight configuration.

The Coast Guard's Hercules swoops past the *Virginius* to lay down a path of parallel flares. There are ten aside at 15-metre intervals to simulate a runway. The path is parallel to the starboard side, off the bow. The ship will protect them from the wind and resultant waves. The flares give perspective. An orange rescue dinghy is waiting by the bow.

From the right-hand seat, Lyn flies a left-hand circuit around the ship. Kristian holds the dual control column as a backup. At Lyn's request, he reaches down and pulls up the flap lever. The aeroplane baulks and the airspeed winds back. They will land as slowly as possible.

The stern slides by, 300 feet below them, and Lyn can see that she is too low for the flare path, but there is no 'runway' to aim for. Water surrounds them. They line up between the smoking flares and activate their emergency locator transmitter. At ten knots slower than normal approach speed, it still feels way too fast to be putting down. Not wanting to stall the plane, Lyn levels her wings. Kristian pulls on the last two stages of flap and opens his emergency window. Five seconds to go. 'Feather the engines,' she calls to Kristian – asking him to turn the propeller blades 90 degrees so they would slice through the water instead of dragging against it and possibly causing the aircraft to flip; a routine procedure, now being performed in a very non-routine landing. Everything is happening so fast.

The Coast Guard pilots and crew brace as the Seminole connects with the water in a terrifying collision of spray and metal. The crewman in the circling Hercules holding the video camera jumps as the Seminole's left wing digs into the water and jerks the aeroplane 90 degrees, forcing the engine and cowlings off the airframe. The shot is obscured.

All aboard watch, aghast. It is almost a textbook exercise, but surely nobody has survived the crash.

They soon erupt into cheers of joy.

With fear and adrenaline running so high, Lyn doesn't remember the landing, nor the water rushing in through her door to fill the cabin up to seat level, nor Kristian calling from the roof, 'Do you want to climb up here?'

'There's no point,' says Lyn from the wing. 'It's going to tip over soon.' And it does, 40 seconds later. Lyn yanks the toggles on her life vest and as the weighty aircraft lurches on the vibrant blue Pacific Ocean, the Coast Guard is relieved to see the pilots waving. And then swimming.

The next thing Lyn remembers is having her arms hooked over the edge of Kristian's life raft and – of all the things to be thinking about – being surprised at the warmth and intense blueness of the ocean.

THE *VIRGINIUS*'s LIFE RAFT WAS CLEARLY VISIBLE ACROSS the water's half-metre swell and within 15 minutes Kristian was in it, but not Lyn. On the second pass, they made a determined grab for the back of her jacket and dragged her into the boat.

Minutes later, all were safely on board the ship. On the deck, Lyn looked down to see her life raft still attached to her arm, through glasses still attached to her face. The AUD$460 000 Seminole rocked with the swell, its tail pointing skywards and its nose submerged. That's the way it remained as the *Virginius* steamed away and Lyn watched the aeroplane until it was out of sight.

There's a lot of aeroplanes and aviators down in that water, she thought. Thank God I'm not one of them. She was right. As well as Charles Ulm and maybe Amelia Earhart, there are several hundred wartime aviators somewhere in the Pacific.

MEANWHILE, RAY AND TOM FLEW ON SILENTLY IN A SURREAL shimmering misty light. Each man lost in his own thoughts, they cast their eyes sombrely upon stratus cloud spread below them like wads of finely strung cotton wool. As the afternoon wore on, they wondered how this day would end. Would their friends survive? And would their own fuel system, installed by the same engineering team, continue to function normally until they reached Hilo in three hours time?

The radio came to life and the Coast Guard advised that they had footage of the pilots climbing into the *Virginius*'s life raft and later reported that the pair were '... just a little emotionally shook up when we talked to them on the radio once they got on board the vessel'. Six thousand feet above the Pacific Ocean, Ray Clamback drew a long and relieved breath.

As the two men literally flew into the sunset, things were still unfolding down on the ship, as Kristian recalled: 'A couple of scary looking tattooed Cuban guys with sailors' beards and missing teeth showed us to our rooms and gave me some old jeans and thongs to wear. I called my wife and suggested she might like to have a seat as I explained we had a bit of a problem but were all OK. She thought she was having a bad day until I explained mine.'

Lyn reckoned a nice whisky would hit the spot about then, but the captain ran a tight ship. And a dry one.

The one-week trip would stretch to three weeks and when he hung up, Kristian settled into the ship's tiny hospital bed and slept for 24 hours. The ship's nurse found only a pulled muscle in Lyn's knee and the next day a bruise came out on Kristian's neck. That was it as far as physical injuries went.

From the ship, Lyn rang the Sydney office and informed them that the plane had sunk and the pilots had swum.

At home in Sydney, her husband Ray Gray took the daily call from Clamback's office to catch up on his wife's progress. He thought the caller was joking when he said, 'They had to ditch but everyone's OK.'

'Yeah right!' he said and hung up laughing.

The phone rang again and this time the caller persisted, advising that the plane had ditched but that Lyn and Kristian were okay and safely on board a ship.

Feeling grateful for her rescue, Lyn then faced a new set of logistics. They were heading for China, which was 19 sailing days away. She had no passport! But she was enormously relieved when in the middle of the night there was a knock on her door and a white piece of paper was thrust in front of her. They were diverting to Honolulu and would arrive two days later.

For most of her flying life, Lyn had kept journals and she lost two of them to the ditching. She still wishes she had them. At the small desk in her ship's cabin, she opened the blank pages of a tiny new notebook and began writing: '8 June 2006 KSBA – PHTO' (Santa Barbara to Hilo).

Just prior to disembarking, the pilots went in search of their few possessions. It was the only sour encounter, as one intimidating crew member withheld their lifejackets and goods, suggesting the pilots were lucky to be alive. Feeling protective of his female companion, Kristian backed away.

'We were treated well, but this guy was menacing. The captain was very good and he wouldn't have stood for this behaviour if we'd reported it. It's one thing [for us] to be in charge of an aeroplane, but another thing to be so vulnerable on a ship in the middle of the ocean, unable to speak Spanish,' he said.

Twenty kilometres off Honolulu, the *Virginius* disembarked the pilots down an old wooden ladder into a rubber dinghy that delivered them to the Coast Guard cutter *Washington*. But there was no proper relief for Lyn until she stepped off the *Washington* at Sand Island and saw Ray Clamback waiting. He had been a father figure and mentor to her in her short aviation career. She was so glad to see a familiar face.

When a reporter asked Lyn why she thought she could make it across the Pacific in such a small plane, she pointed to Ray and said, 'Well that guy has just done it in the same aeroplane'. Kristian stepped in and praised Lyn's skill.

Beyond the reporters, he could see Tom waiting to greet them. 'Kristian was initially really shaken up,' said Tom. 'He didn't want to talk much about it. He brushed it off. We had a few drinks and went to the beach.'

While the young men kept a low profile and debriefed in private, Lyn and Ray attended to business, including obtaining new passports and tickets to fly out. A Coast Guard employee thought Lyn looked like she just wanted to get home. And who could blame her? It was her forty-eighth birthday.

Back in Sydney, for a month afterwards Lyn's emotions were immovably flat until a small trigger reduced the no-nonsense woman to floods of tears: tears of tension, anxiety and eventually relief that the ditching experience was behind her and she could resume her work with a clear head.

Ray Gray could see the rawness of emotion in his wife and listened as she lamented that everybody wanted her to relive the story. Trying to placate her, he said that it was natural for people to be curious. But Lyn didn't want the ditching to define her flying or end her career, so exactly a month later, she ferried exactly the same type of aeroplane over exactly the same route. The aircraft was just one serial number different.

'Preparing for that was hard,' she says, with typical understatement. An hour into the flight though, out in a world so removed from earthly routine, her old self returned. About ten of the aircraft and aircrew were those who had been en route when Lyn was ditching. What a coincidence! The crews of many of the airliners she spoke to must have been stunned to hear she was flying again so soon, but back in their shared space she recounted to them the end of the story. Particularly delighted were the US Airways pilots who were now enlightened as to the meaning of the Australian expression 'cactus'.

AMINTA REFUSED TO FLY ANY MORE FERRIES. WHEN ASKED if she'd go again, she replied that they'd have to pay her a million dollars. Lyn was inclined to wait also, until the problem with the fuel line was discovered by their engineer, Ian Thornton, in Sydney. Ray ferried aircraft from 1969 onwards from every continent in the world and made roughly 300 Pacific crossings in his career between 1969 and 2019.

Several ferry pilots over the years have ditched in the Pacific, one of whom was another Australian, Mike Roberts. Ron Altrans, an American pilot, was ferrying an aircraft to Tahiti via Hawaii. He ditched and was never found. His last communication was with an overflying Qantas crew.

After 35 years in business, Clamback and Hennessy Pty Ltd was sold to a Chinese group that closed the Bankstown operation and moved to Mildura on 30 June 2019. The Chinese group are now training airline pilots.

Kristian did more ferry trips from Sydney to New Zealand and from Kuala Lumpur to Hamilton Island. He now flies for a regional airline based out of Sydney, with no real desire to fly light aircraft anymore. He did buy his mum a new camera though, after the one he had borrowed from her went down in the ocean.

Tom retired from flying after a hang-gliding accident and now operates a high-end unpiloted flight imaging business.

Lyn's last ferry flight for Clamback and Hennessy was to take place in March 2010. After a decade as a senior instructor and ferry pilot, and a lifetime of city living, Lyn now lives with her husband and their four dogs on their small farm at Gooloogong, 30 kilometres east of Cowra, NSW. On 1 July 2013 she opened Fly Oz at Cowra airport where they train around 130 students per year, with five full-time employees. When an airline pilot further out west needed to entrust his son to a flying instructor, he was repeatedly directed to Fly Oz. He walked through the doors and enquired loudly, 'Is the famous Lyn Gray here?'

Since the ditching in the Pacific in 2006, Lyn has had two emergencies when instructing students; the last just before Christmas 2016 in somebody else's aeroplane. When the nose wheel refused to extend, and all procedures had been exhausted, Lyn performed a textbook landing in front of all the emergency services, camera crew and onlookers.

Those with the expertise to comment were impressed with the short ground-roll due to her skilful preparation, the touchdown resulting in minimal damage to the expensive airframe. An engineer's inspection reported that the jammed wheel required brute force to release it – something that couldn't have been done in the air.

The flying school is a deeply satisfying and fulfilling business for Lyn and she is well supported by the local community. Lyn is a popular speaker and is occasionally asked to talk about her flying experiences. She is typically upbeat about her 23-year story, but that happy default setting belies the depth of skill and bravery required to live it.

Perhaps only those who have been forced to leave a wet footprint can truly understand it.

7

DEBORAH LAWRIE (WARDLEY)

IN COURT WITH ANSETT

We have a good record of employing females …
but have adopted a policy of only employing men as pilots.

(Ansett Airlines, 1979)

Twenty-five-year old pilot Deborah Wardley was sitting in a light aircraft instructing a student off the Melbourne coast late one afternoon in 1979. Over the airwaves came the voice of a helicopter pilot she'd never met but whose familiar inflection brought on a steaming anger in the normally calm young instructor.

She bristled as the helicopter pilot, Cal Pain, radioed confidently, 'AaaaaAlpha November Delta.' She knew his track. From the city helipad, he'd fly direct across Port Phillip Bay to Reg Ansett's home at Mount Eliza.

Her fury was not directed at the pilot; it wasn't his fault he was born a male, though she envied his luck to be one of the chosen species. Her emotion was aimed squarely at his passenger, Sir Reginald Ansett, because he alone had the power to introduce change and employ women pilots in his airline.

She knew that as he choppered away from Melbourne's peak hour traffic with enviable ease, Sir Reg would be shuffling through his work papers and that a fat pile bearing her name would be among them: Wardley v Ansett Transport Industries Ltd.

In his 40 years of operation, Reg Ansett, founder and owner of Ansett Airlines, had never employed a female pilot and had no intention of ever doing so. This woman was a thorn in his side though, because she had the support of the Equal Opportunity Board who were keen to see if their new *Sex Discrimination Act* had any legs.

It looked like times might be changing just in time for Wardley, because new pilots were not employed after they turned 27, a policy that ensured the airlines got their money's worth out of a pilot after the expensive training process. She was already 25. But the winds of change did little to sway Reg Ansett's opinion. He held fast to his beliefs. And there were some things he thought he knew for sure.

When Cal skimmed the cliffs to land the helicopter, VH-AND, at the 46-hectare waterfront property at Mount Eliza each night, a

DEBORAH LAWRIE (WARDLEY)

bejewelled Joan Ansett would greet her husband at the door and, with a swish of her evening gown, hand him his martini.

A woman's place in Ansett's world was at home, in the office, or – until they were married – serving onboard meals as air hostesses. For Deborah Wardley, this thinking was outmoded and unfair, and it needed to change. What might have been acceptable in the 1950s was beginning to grate by the late 1970s. In the Moorabbin training area during the 14 months starting 31 January 1979, Deb kept working as an instructor and charter pilot to pay her lawyers, while the might of an airline was pitted against her to try to prove that women were unsuitable to fly large jets.

Occasionally, when Reg Ansett's private helicopter whizzed through her workspace, she fantasised that she could turn quickly and vaporise the one man who was standing in her way. Voom-phaaa. Right out of the sky. Then the whole nightmare would be over and she could refocus on her flying, hopefully as an airline pilot.

The longer it dragged on, the more worried her mother became about Deb's health and her obsession with the court case. And rightly so. Her thinning face was endlessly plastered across newsstands and the nightly news.

The principle of the matter became bigger than the woman at its centre and a divided Australian public carefully followed the big story of the determined young pilot and the retiring transport tycoon as it careened from the Equal Opportunity Board in Collins Street to the Supreme Court of Victoria and back again, until eventually stampeding its way to the High Court of Australia in Sydney.

This showdown was inevitable and if it hadn't been Deb, it would have been somebody else. In time, that person may have got an easier run with a less determined opponent and a more enlightened society. But society could get stuffed. Deb only had two years.

THE LOT OF WOMEN HAD CHANGED DRAMATICALLY SINCE Deborah Lawrie's birth in 1953. Women were now allowed to drink in bars, and had access to equal pay, subsidised childcare and 'no fault' divorce. All of these rights would be directly relevant to Deborah as she progressed through her personal and professional life.

In 1978 the Victorian *Equal Opportunity Act* became fully operational and the Board set up to oversee the Act expected its role would simply be managing and adjudicating as the public became educated about the new direction: that it was illegal to discriminate against anybody on the grounds of their sex.

If the Act were to be tested by anyone, it would probably be (they thought) a well-educated mainstream professional. Deborah Lawrie was well educated but her profession was quite out of the box. Her opponent – a man who learnt to fly in the 1930s and started his transport business with a second-hand Studebaker car, driving it as a taxi from Hamilton to Ballarat and Melbourne – was of no mind to be managed or adjudicated. His taxi business had morphed into one of Australia's two major domestic airlines. You knew you were in Melbourne as soon as you glimpsed the distinctive 'A' logo crowning the company's multistorey headquarters at the top of its main thoroughfare, Swanston Street.

Ansett's impressive career was coloured with cutthroat corporate tactics enacted with high-level political contacts. He had been in business from the Depression, through a World War and into the Age of Aquarius. Now it was the Age of Equality and it didn't sit well with him. He thought this glitch with the woman pilot would be a storm in his fine china teacup. She thought the hearing would be a one-day affair. How wrong they both were.

With the help of her barrister John Dwyer, a pro bono lawyer Trish Roberts, and her family, Deb gathered her fortitude and stepped into the lion's den. It was her resolute belief in her right to fly and her ability to do so that sustained her through a protracted, excruciating examination of her character, her abilities and the perceived weaknesses of her gender.

Reg Ansett threw down the gauntlet and, like a true warrior, Deborah Wardley picked it up.

IN SUBURBAN MELBOURNE, NOT FAR FROM ESSENDON Airport, Deborah didn't grow up thinking her gender was weak. She was a feisty kid who stuck to her guns when she felt strongly about something.

From her home in Melbourne's eastern suburbs, Deb's mother Dorothy Barnes now reflects on her strong-willed, competitive eldest child. Unusually defiant for a girl, Dorothy thinks Deb would have been good as a boy. Perhaps her competitive streak would have been easier to anticipate. It was an unusual mix when combined with her grace and easy charm.

'She walked at nine months, and when she was three, she took her two-year-old friend off to the day-care centre up the road to join the other kids. She was independent and she was competitive like her father,' says Dorothy.

Her father, James, was a staunch supporter of education and pushed his daughter to be the best she could. This attitude drove her to try even harder. She was the eldest of four siblings, tall and commanding, and was guided by James, who firmly believed his bright daughter should eventually gain a university education.

Dorothy clearly recalls that Deb was always a thinker and when one of the nuns at her high school told the priest about Deb's relentless questioning, the priest replied, 'You have a very intelligent girl on your hands.' With that realisation, the school sent the 'intelligent girl' over the road to study science at the boys' school.

In return for helping James learn his flying checks for his pilot licence, he gave her the money for two flying lessons when she turned 16. Then there was no turning back, but she had to pay for the rest. That meant working weekends for teenage wages and flying once a month at Moorabbin, a one-hour drive with her mother to the other side of town. It took 11 hours flying and 11 months of saving before she could go solo.

After school, Deb studied maths and science at the prestigious Melbourne University, and graduated at the end of 1975 with a bachelor of science in maths, physics and chemistry, with a final-year specialisation in nuclear and upper-atmosphere physics and pure maths. Meanwhile, at Moorabbin Airport she had also gained all her flying qualifications, including senior commercial subjects (required to fly airliners) and a flying instructor rating. With those university subjects under her belt, some might consider airline flying a low career goal.

In order to fulfil her teaching commitments and repay her debt to the government for funding her education, Deb took a job at Chandler High School, beginning in 1976. Teaching would be a good backstop later, but for now it was just a hindrance to her part-time flying instructor role at Moorabbin Airport. She spent every spare moment adding to her flying hours and taking any opportunity to fly.

When a larger than life opal dealer – a friend of her father's – arrived on the scene, Deb found the perfect avenue for increasing her hours, finding adventure in the outback and maturity as a pilot. John Mules had an opal shop in Melbourne's CBD but he was most at home cutting deals and cutting opals in the grit and hustle of Coober Pedy or outback Queensland, or wherever there was a deal to be made. He was a practical man who used his words sparingly and on trips with John, Deb learnt about men in a man's world, and living life beyond the university or flying school culture and the prim patchwork of green fields around Melbourne.

These outback trips sparked Deb's love of the Australian landscape: the colours, the cliffs, the unnavigable expanses and the rivers, roads and ranges that joined it all together. She learnt that fencing wire can hold a magneto together long enough to get you home, and from her single camp stretcher in a remote opal field she learnt that sometimes life can be a bed of boulders. She was physically walking on rocky ground, but not as rocky as the ground she would encounter in the courts. Being on a trip with these men as they dug, cut and traded opals, she was exposed to a vastly different world to the one she normally inhabited. She marvelled at the opportunities that her pilot licence afforded her.

'Ah well, Deb. Must piss off,' John would say at the end of each trip as he hoisted boulder opals from the aeroplane to the boot of his car. As he disappeared into the sunset, she would clean the plane and return it to the security of its Moorabbin hangar. She would then re-enter her familiar world with the new perspective that travel affords.

She sought the company of other women pilots at the Royal Victorian Aero Club, including aviation pioneer Freda Thompson OBE, the first female flying instructor in the British Empire and a woman who had completed a solo UK–Australia flight in 1934. Deb was in good company and, together with a group of 15 or 20 other women pilots, flew in the annual women-only Freda Thompson Aerial Race Around Port Phillip Bay. Deb's competitiveness on the basketball court and in the classroom was now evident in the aeroplane as the lone pilots pitted against each other to be first to circumnavigate the Bay.

As her reputation grew, so did her flying student list. And as those young men made their way into airlines jobs, she started to grow restless and a bit resentful that her own applications seemed to be getting her nowhere. Well-meaning men around the airport, who enjoyed knowing her but didn't take her ambition seriously, told her to be content with instructing. Though a good instructor is worth their weight in gold, it was not her ultimate aim. For most pilots it is a stepping stone to bigger things and the more she flew, the more she knew how much she wanted a big aviation career. A brain like that can't do circuits forever. For some people though, it was a huge leap of faith to send a woman up in charge of a jet when women had barely won the right to equal pay. With her youthful naivety and energy, she failed to understand why this prejudice prevailed.

Ansett had already rejected a handful of women, one of whom was Lorraine Cooper. When Deb and Lorraine crossed paths at the Royal Victorian Aero Club, Lorraine's advice was to go into the Ansett office and make herself known. So, she did.

THE 1970S HAD BEEN A TRYING TIME FOR ANSETT, WITH financial strains and the threat of a corporate takeover. Now, along with those problems, women wanted to be employed as pilots and Reg Ansett wasn't having it. Lorraine Cooper had been put on the waiting list to be an Ansett pilot at age 24, left there until she was 27 and then taken off the list due to her age.

In 1975 Deb handed over her paperwork to Captain Henry Theunissen, Ansett's pilot in charge of intake training. She asked him directly to be honest with her. 'What are my chances?' He wasn't sure.

As other women were culled out with technical excuses such as age, lack of training opportunities and in some cases just no reply at all, it seemed that the time had come for Reg Ansett to face the recruitment music one way or another. His flight management team knew it because they'd been seeing the appearance of women in airlines overseas, particularly in North America, where women pilots had been hired since 1973.

After a two-year hiring hiatus, recruiting began again, and Theunissen suggested to the airline management that they needed to address Deborah's application because men who were less experienced were being taken on. In mid-1977 Deb wrote to Ansett again to update her CV. She now had 1000 hours of single-engine experience and 120 hours of twin-engine experience. It was more than enough to be considered by an airline. Theunissen replied to her that she could expect to be interviewed by the end of the year.

Around this time Deb moved into a flat with her boyfriend, Peter Wardley, an air traffic controller from Moorabbin. She was 24, and was school teaching full time and flight instructing part time.

Captain Theunissen admitted it had taken him two years to convince the company to grant Deb an initial interview, but that he'd finally done it. The interview went well.

In the 12 months that it took to get a second interview, Deb had become engaged to Peter. Meanwhile, Theunissen kept the pressure up on Ansett management and Deb was granted her final interview, despite the assumption that she wouldn't be employed. Theunissen was told to go slow with the interviewing process. Presumably they expected her to reach the age of 27, like Lorraine Cooper, and be filtered out.

In light of today's standards, it's unbelievable that the six men on the interviewing panel invited her to lay out her family planning intentions. She didn't think she would want any more than two children. Around the long oval table, they took turns leafing through her logbook and asking about any gaps or breaks in her flying career. She was asked about the danger of earrings in an emergency escape and she explained patiently that they could be removed. There was nothing in her answers to discredit her application and she was sent for psychological assessment: the last phase of the application process.

By chance, a tennis friend of her mother's worked for the psychological testing company. She'd heard that Deb had done exceptionally well. Somewhere in the top 20 per cent of candidates, and presumed this meant she'd get a job. The woman was most surprised when she found Deb had heard nothing yet. Her high marks had in fact put her in the top group of recommended candidates. There were murmurings among the staff that did the psych testing. They'd never known a female pilot to get through and waited eagerly to see how it went. Well, it went badly. The refusal was outright.

As Peter Wardley retrieved and straightened out the screwed-up rejection letter, Deborah sat glumly with her chin on her fists. While she was considered unworthy to join the jet jockeys, the men she was training were not and they filed out like ants to join the airlines, leaving her to scratch her head at the inequity of it all. Peter ventured that the new Equal Opportunity law might be worth exploring because he knew her skills and he knew her competition. Had she been a man, he was sure she would have been in the airline long ago.

Theunissen told Deb that, on average, the total hours of the intake pilots was 1500. She already had 1688. And a copy of the psychological assessment concluded that, overall, her mental reasoning abilities were more than adequate for a commercial airline pilot; and intellectually, she could function in any top professional or senior management position. 'In essence, your interests are very appropriate for a career as a pilot,' it said.

Motivated by the psychological assessment, Peter took Deb to a meeting with Fay Marles, the Commissioner for Equal Opportunity. Victoria's *Equal Opportunity Act* had only been in effect for three months when Deborah lodged her appeal on 2 August 1978. She was Complainant No 72.

Within a fortnight, Marles had also seen Reg Ansett and lodged the complaint with the Equal Opportunity Board. During his interview with Marles, Ansett appeared unconcerned about Deb's application. At that early stage he pointed out that she would be rejected because she wouldn't have the strength to handle the aeroplane if the hydraulics failed, that the Pilots Union would strike if a woman were to be employed, and that menstrual tension would hinder her performance. Ansett then brazenly informed Marles that the psychological testing was false. That was when she began to see that this would be a hard fight.

IN PREPARATION FOR THE CASE, DEB WAS GUIDED BY TRISH Roberts, who was a lawyer with an aviation background and a pilot licence. Trish introduced Deb and Peter to John Dwyer. Dwyer was in tune with Deb's plight. He was a barrister who had witnessed discrimination against his lawyer wife and her doctor mother. While he was committed to the cause, he was also sceptical about the process and about a law that had not yet been tested.

As the bills mounted, Trish offered her services gratis and John agreed to wait for settlement to finalise his fees. The hearing was set down for January 1979, but two months beforehand, Ansett Airlines applied for exemption on safety grounds, maintaining that an all-male crew would be safer. This was the first of many stalling tactics, and their 'concerns' were dismissed out of hand.

But Deb had her supporters and one was Trans Australia Airlines (TAA) Captain Ray Vuillerman. Ray knew about difficult decisions and, in a twin-engine Aero Commander, he tested Deborah in the skies above Essendon and disproved the strength theory outright. As the January hearing date approached, Deb prepared for her day in court and for her wedding a few weeks later.

More than 50 male pilots had been taken on since her letter of refusal. Ansett Airlines wanted her to reapply and go through the whole interview process again. Recognising this as a stalling tactic, or a way to fail her, Deb refused and the hearings began.

It was obvious that things were going to get dirty when, in fear of losing her job, the woman who had rung about the psychological testing signed an affidavit stating that she had no knowledge of the phone call or the test results. It was a stunning withdrawal and proved false when the documents were subpoenaed. Against the

28 pilots tested at the time, and who were to start with Ansett, Deb was better qualified than several of them.

That afternoon, the Chair announced what the Wardley team already knew. Deborah had been discriminated against. The Board ruled that she was to be included in the next pilot intake. For ten minutes she believed she'd won. And then Ansett applied for an exemption on safety grounds. That one day in court would be just the beginning of a protracted battle that would last for a year.

The hearing resumed on Thursday 1 February 1979 and Vuillerman testified as to Deborah's outstanding abilities. Ansett retaliated with two issues: compatibility of women and men flying together, and of physical appearance. The argument implied that it would be 'incompatible' for a male captain to have to fly with a female first officer. The second argument was that they didn't want to employ somebody who was not good looking! Late in the afternoon there was an injunction from the Victorian Supreme Court, which would take over the hearing the following Tuesday.

Two days later, Deb competed in the Freda Thompson Air Race around Port Philip Bay, as she had for many years. It was an event that she loved and she didn't want to miss out. It only took an hour to complete the solo race but Deb couldn't hang around for the lunch and race results. There was somewhere else she needed to be.

In the searing heat of that February afternoon, under the spotlight of the national media, Deborah Lawrie married Peter Wardley. It was to be the only night for the next 15 months that she was able to forget about the court case. The wedding celebrations lasted until dawn.

On Tuesday morning it was back to the courtroom. The case was gathering momentum. Sometimes it was overwhelming. When the Supreme Court ruled that a new Board of the Equal Opportunity Commission be established to hear the case, the matter was delayed for four weeks. Deb was then invited to a new job interview with Ansett Airlines and then had it 'deferred' via a telegram from the company. These delay tactics were frustrating and expensive, but the Wardleys vowed to fight on, despite Deborah's mother's concerns. Dorothy felt the full weight of the stress that her daughter was feeling. 'It was frightening to be so directly in the firing line and it made me really upset,' she said. 'I felt it was ruining my daughter's life, but Deb wouldn't walk away from it.'

It was early April 1979 when they returned to court to start again with a new Equal Opportunity Commission Board. Reg Ansett came in with a more senior high-profile barrister and a revised attack. Rather than pursue the line of female lack of strength if faced with a hydraulic failure, they came in with a pregnancy and childbirth argument. Time off for childbirth, they said, would be disruptive to Deborah and expensive for her employer. Expensive for Deb too, as it turned out. She had been told in her interview that she'd be placed on leave without pay from the moment she announced her pregnancy until six weeks after the birth. But, she'd still be expected to contribute to the superannuation fund. She had agreed to that, and the two children she suggested as a possibility were fed back to her in the witness stand as evidence of her wish to have a large family. How things got twisted!

As the court adjourned for another couple of weeks, Ansett Airlines delayed their next pilot intake. At the same time, the Women's Electoral Lobby in Perth had forwarded a pivotal letter to Deborah, dated only a couple of months prior. The Lobby had written to Ansett Airlines stating their intention to boycott the airline until Deborah's case was resolved. The official reply included a line that Ansett '... for safety reasons have adopted a policy of only employing men as pilots'. That set the cat among the pigeons. Ansett's left (legal) hand didn't know what the right (management) hand was doing and the author of the letter obviously hadn't run it past anybody in authority.

Other witnesses spoke of the US Airline Pilots Association, which had a very short conference on the problems associated with hiring women pilots. There were no problems. Everybody went back to work.

The court case went down a rabbit hole, testing the legalities of whether being pregnant would render a pilot unfit to fly, because it was an offence to fly while unfit. If so, pregnancy could technically be classified as a disease under the Air Navigation Orders.

When they couldn't pin her on the strength test, they expressed concern about her likely lengthy early-career absences for childbearing and raising. They also indicated it was a pilot selection panel that had rejected her based on this assumption; that it was not a management decision. Given that the question of childbirth was apparently so important in their decision, it was surprising to find that only one of the interviewing panel made a note of it in their files. As the pregnancy debate continued, it shifted towards premenstrual tension and mood swings. Ansett sought a medical opinion from a gynaecologist, but the one they chose was Deb's own doctor. He refused to side with the airline.

On Deb's twenty-sixth birthday, in May 1979, she received a $2000 cheque from a group calling themselves the Wardley Fighting Fund. It was almost half the cost of her current fees. The motivation for the group was to see Deb's case through and establish a legal precedent for others to follow. Their supporters were of all ages and occupations, including some anonymous Ansett employees. There were people and organisations who took a firm stand, opposing this outright discrimination. Some of the leading groups were the Women's Electoral Lobby, the Victorian branch of the Australian Labor Party, and the Australian Federation of Business and Professional Women. Passenger growth dropped by about 70 per cent during the financial year to June 1979, so the boycott was definitely having an effect on Ansett's bottom line.

The hearing dragged out until the middle of June 1979, with continued cost estimates tabled about lost time and productivity when women have children. Deb regularly, though hesitantly, granted media interviews and in one interview told the ABC she believed Reg Ansett was personally blocking her employment. He was certainly living up to his statement to *The Age* in 1964 in which he admitted a grim determination and the ability to fight long and hard.

Ansett's final argument to the Equal Opportunity Commission Board was that Deborah's rejection was due not to her being female but to the circumstances of being female – of actual or probable pregnancy. If she'd already had her children and stated she intended to have no more, they said, it might have been different.

In an interview after the whole event was over, Captain Theunissen said, 'the panel said we would be quite happy to employ her ... and word came back from Head Office ... "no further processing and we cannot employ her".' In that selection panel's recollection, it was the only time that Reg Ansett had handed down such a direct edict. The panel knew it was a matter of time until a woman was hired to fly with the airlines in Australia, but they had to adhere to the boss's wishes and reject her application.

As the hearings came to an end on 6 June, Deborah was acutely aware of the media presence that surrounded her as she sat in the front row waiting for the Board members to arrive and present their findings. A photographer from *The Age* captured her mood perfectly when he lined up a shot of Deborah with her chin on her hand, her elbow on her crossed knee and eyes cast to her shoe hanging precariously from her toes. She would have barely heard the shutter click among the hushed conversations that rose and fell around her, reinforcing the gravity of the moment. She was steeling herself.

Soon, the cameras were turned to the front of the room to capture Dr Sharp, of the Equal Opportunity Commission Board, direct Ansett to include Deb in their next pilot intake on the seniority that she should have had. In the meantime, he said, they were to pay her $40 per day. They also had a fortnight to stump up $14 500 in legal costs.

The message was loud and clear: 'anatomy should not be destiny'. Women's child-bearing potential could not be used as an excuse to limit their role in Australian society. And that sentiment, backed by the historic ruling, set the tone for women in the workforce in Australia from that day forward.

It had been ten months in the courts and Deborah was now $10 000 poorer for her trouble, though greatly relieved that it was over. Except that it wasn't.

The following day Reg Ansett was stopped on the way to his helicopter by Channel 7 reporter Pamela Graham, who had taken a particular interest in this story. In trying to shake his shirtsleeve free from her firm grasp, he told her the court battles hadn't even started yet.

Deborah went back to work at Moorabbin and tried to distance herself from the drama. The standoff only lasted two weeks. Ansett appealed to the Supreme Court of Victoria to have all the recommendations rejected.

Personally, Deb was feeling the pressure. She was overwhelmed by the task of fighting such a big force and feeling that so many people were against her. She was so tired and angry that just hearing Reg Ansett's name made her feel physically ill. She was incredibly thin and exhausted, and craved a semblance of normality. Her mother, Dorothy, worried about the effect of it all, asking, 'Deb, do you really have to do this? You have a science degree and you are a fantastic student. Do you really have to put yourself through this?' But her daughter, though down, was not defeated.

'It was cruel,' Dorothy told me in 2019. 'She got to the stage where she had to go on. My other daughter Robyn went to a lot of court cases. I was working full time and I'm even amazed now that I didn't go. I'd been there for every step of the way with my children. Maybe this was too stressful. I used to get really upset about what was going on. I thought it was ruining her life.'

DEBORAH LAWRIE (WARDLEY)

Dorothy continued to reel at the ignorance displayed by some of the general public with whom she came into contact. Sometimes those misinformed and bigoted individuals frightened her, but mostly they angered her. In direct contrast to them, Margaret Geddes, president of the Australian Federation of Business and Professional Women, published a letter in the *Canberra Times* of 28 June 1979 calling for professional groups to boycott Ansett: 'The company is making a mockery of all our efforts to obtain a fair go for all Australians. The Commonwealth Government has a firm commitment to the introduction of anti-discrimination legislation. So I call on people in government departments also to boycott Ansett.' They were firmly supported by the National Council of Women of Victoria, which covered about 145 affiliated women's groups.

Ansett Airlines copped the flak but the Australian government airline, Trans Australian Airlines (TAA), were actually no better. Deb had been to see them and got a noncommittal brush-off. TAA were awaiting the outcome of the Ansett mess and in the meantime enjoyed a disproportionate share of business growth.

DOWN AT THE LOWER END OF TOWN, VICTORIA'S SUPREME Court in William Street is as sombre as the southern weather. On a mid-winter's day, Deb ascended the court's eight stone steps, which have worn but not softened over a hundred years of receiving judge and juror, plaintiff and defendant. Under the double-sized bronze figure of Lady Justice that sits high above double arched columns, she crossed the verandah, pushed the brass plate on the front door and entered the same building where Ned Kelly had been tried 90 years beforehand.

Ansett went into the Supreme Court challenging the orders of the Equal Opportunity Commission Board and the authority that empowered them.

Publicly, Deb said it was like water off a duck's back. That was putting a brave face on it. Having to sit in court and have her character picked to pieces, listen to grown men tell lies about her, and read the negative statements in the newspapers was crippling. And when the Ansett Queen's Counsel turned to Deb in the courtroom, reiterating why the company did not want to employ her, she felt it was personal.

The legalities became more and more obscure and technical, and arguments went to and fro about overlapping legislation in various states and governments. And then in a blow from behind, a private pilot who had had a close encounter with Deborah's aeroplane at Moorabbin, bought into the debate. Failing to identify himself as the cause of the problem, or the fact that he had burst into her office and verbally abused her, he wrongly claimed that Deborah had cut him off in the circuit back when she was instructing. What should have been a minor incident was now a fly in the ointment, but her barrister John Dwyer set the matter straight with great haste.

The Supreme Court judge, Justice Gray, reinstated the orders of the Equal Opportunity Commission Board and Deb waited for the next pilot intake at Ansett. Meanwhile, because of the legal technicalities associated with the *Equal Opportunity Act* nationally, her case was referred to the High Court of Australia. If the High Court deemed the Equal Opportunity Board unable to enforce her employment, then Ansett would win and she would be back flying circuits at Moorabbin.

While all this argy-bargy was going on, Ansett was running critically short of pilots and had to begin another round of training. Until the High Court hearing in Sydney, the Equal Opportunity Board's decision held and Deb readied herself for the next pilot intake. But the build-up was anything but friendly.

Ansett Captain Alan Lane stated that Ansett would only take Deborah on because they had to and would get rid of her 'forthwith'. It was within their rights under the Australian Pilots Agreement.

DEBORAH LAWRIE (WARDLEY)

WITH THAT NEGATIVITY RINGING IN HER EARS, ON 29 OCTOBER 1979 Deb sat in the High Court in Sydney with a new solicitor. Pilot and advocate Trish Roberts was unable to get to Sydney. Deb's other main support, her husband, couldn't make it either. If she was feeling lonely, she felt a whole lot more so when the courtroom assembled and her barrister, John Dwyer, didn't arrive. It was an eternal ten minutes before he came flying in, skidding to a halt like a harassed cartoon character.

Six of a potential seven judges sat on the all-male bench. Two of them were clearly in favour of Ansett, two were clearly in favour of Wardley and the other two were undecided. There was a multitude of legal representatives from the various states, who were present with their own counsel to protect the state laws. Deb had just Dwyer.

Justice Anthony Mason, in discussing the Pilots Award, noted the provision for 'wives of pilots' and said that this indicated the award considered that no woman has a wife. He translated that to mean that a pilot's spouse is necessarily female, meaning pilots need to be male and the argument was used to try and support the legality of disallowing competent women from becoming pilots.

After a long two-day hearing, the group dispersed for a two-month wait until an outcome was to be announced. Later that day Reg Ansett stood down as chief of Ansett Transport Industries. He was now 70 years old and the combination of the stress of the legal battle, ill health and some smart investor manoeuvring meant he was about to move aside and let Robert Holmes à Court take the reins. As a bonus, Holmes à Court's wife Janet let it be known that her husband would welcome Deborah into the Ansett fold.

A week after the High Court hearing Deb received her telegram of offer to begin as a trainee pilot on Monday 5 November 1979. She asked the company if they would sack her straight away. They replied, 'No Comment.'

A PILOT NEIGHBOUR CHAPERONED DEB TO THE ANSETT training school and led her in the back way. She didn't care about all the eyes that turned to check her out. For all she knew, she might only be there for a day! But the course went well. Until Friday afternoon.

When she arrived home, Deb found a letter from Ansett management informing that they would investigate the near-miss incident that the court had already thrown out. She rang the head of the Pilots Union, who was furious. He informed her to take no action. They would handle it.

A week later, under instruction to say nothing at all, Deborah sat stock still in a meeting room, while the union reps and the management reps almost came to fisticuffs about how many people were allowed to be at the meeting. Was it two or was it three union reps? Harsh insults were thrown from both sides and the meeting ended abruptly when a union official told the flight department they could all get f*****!

Within ten minutes, they were back outside and Deb was told with a grin to forget it ever happened. It was the end of the matter, but it was another unnerving incident for an already nervous new pilot. It is a credit to her that she was able to maintain her motivation and focus, while her inner dialogue must have been battling with all this negativity.

Now that she had joined the ranks, the company had to provide her with a uniform. In the absence of a better plan, they issued her with men's trousers and shirt and a weirdly fitting hat. She felt silly getting around in men's clothes but put it aside to enjoy the course. She got on well with her classmates and beat them all in the theory exam. She flew well too, but the lingering sense of an imminent dismissal was hard to shake. Her unease grew when the class went to Launceston, Tasmania, for the last part of their training.

Along with two other pilots, Deb was held back from completing the course. The three trainees were stood aside with some lame excuses and she finished the year on shifting sands: her marriage was under strain but she was also nominated as Australian of the Year by *The Australian* newspaper, and she was buoyed by the news that newspaper magnate Rupert Murdoch was about to take over where Holmes à Court had faltered in his bid to control Ansett.

The discrimination continued when Deb started ground training. In an infuriating and disconcerting episode, she was told that even though Ansett had put her through ground school under sufferance, she would never be allowed to step foot in an aeroplane as pilot. Desperate by then, she rang one of her past students, John Calvert-Jones, whose brother-in-law happened to be her new boss, Rupert Murdoch. 'Oh well', he said, 'Rupert's here enjoying the barbecue. I might have a word to him.' If ever there was a ray of hope, that was it. Hopefully now, somebody could stop this circus.

Under Reg Ansett's hand, the case would surely have dragged on for years. Murdoch, then almost 50, came in without the prejudices of his predecessor and instructed that Deb be treated as fairly as any other pilot.

Ansett Captain Ron Neve was Deb's instructor on the Fokker. It was the first aircraft that she trained and worked on when she joined Ansett. 'She was tall and self-assured but not over-confident,' he said. 'She would just tell it like it is. She had been through a lot. She had to have a lot of guts to take that whole court case on.' He was impressed by her abilities. 'She was very skilful. Some of the other guys you'd have to repeat an exercise, or their tolerances would be a bit out, but she was different. And the same later in the DC-9 simulator, she was bang on. She flew it beautifully and I never had any problems there.'

Deb told Ron she was only too aware of the pressure on her to do well, but he didn't think her struggle to fly for Ansett was about paving the way for other women pilots. As he said, 'She just wanted to succeed for herself, but she did say she hoped the next lot got a better reception than she was afforded'.

Ron said that Deb 'loved aeroplanes, always knew the answers and put a lot of work in'. He was in awe of her ability to control an airliner, even in her training period. He noted:

> The training was very hard on the aeroplanes because we gave them a pounding. The asymmetric swing was quite enormous when we practised engine failures. Debbie, with her long legs and strong frame, she could just feed in the rudder and the aeroplane wouldn't swing at all. She had to be plus or minus 20 degrees to recover in the beginning and then be able to recover with just plus or minus five degrees. She did it bang on.

With the Fokker training complete, Deb arrived at work early in the morning for her first training flight. She would passenger to Alice Springs and then operate the aircraft to Darwin. No sooner had she settled in the aircraft with her training captain than Captain 'Dusty' Lane thundered down the phone, 'Who said she can go?' He wouldn't talk to the training captain about it, but Deb was disembarked and sent home on an excuse that there was a paperwork hold-up.

The captain of the flight was furious, but astounded at how calmly she took it. He didn't see that when she got back out through the airport, through the carpark and into her car, she burst into tears.

The following day she returned to the airport. Ansett had arranged for a press conference. Deb was extremely nervous about her flight, about all eyes being on her and at the intensity of the scrutiny. It was intimidating at best and she was still waiting to be tripped up. Would she say the wrong thing? Would the television camera capture a shot of her in uniform but without her mandatory, though ill-fitting, cap? What excuses would they find to incriminate her?

Guarded by Ansett staff and the airport manager, she faced a multitude of microphones and cameras, was photographed and filmed walking to the aeroplane, then sitting at the controls. It did nothing to ease her nerves about this, her first flight.

She flew as a passenger to Alice Springs and then operated as first officer to Darwin, where the press continued to track her. The captain on the flight, Alan Reid, says in Deborah's memoir *Letting Fly* that he knew certain senior executives in the company were antagonistic towards her. He gave her their names and told her to watch her back because they would use any excuse to come down hard on her. Alan recalled then how everywhere they landed, there was media waiting for them and he, the captain, had to move to one side.

Though she was patient with the media in Alice Springs, she was conscious of not delaying the flight. When they finally got underway, she breathed a sigh of relief. With her hands on the controls, the aeroplane lifted off and so did her career.

After two months of training in the air – line training – Deb flew her last overnight trip. It was the check flight, with two check captains testing her. Because she had a severe case of nerves, day one was not her best flying and she berated herself for it. She had a sleepless night, exacerbated by the absence of her husband. Why wouldn't he answer the phone? Despite only two hours sleep, she flew much better the next day and was stunned to arrive to another media storm back at Tullamarine in Melbourne. As a couple of company executives rushed to the cockpit and whisked her away, the captains shouted after her that she'd passed her check flight. With that wonderful news echoing in her head, she arrived in the terminal to journalists and television cameras. Having just gained her place as a qualified pilot with Ansett, she then learnt that the High Court had handed down their ruling the same day. They ruled 4-2 in her favour and Ansett were unable to sack her based on her sex.

The Commissioner for Equal Opportunity, Fay Marles, was very pleased with the outcome of the case because she felt that if the Equal Opportunity Board couldn't win this case, it would be hard to picture one they could win.

While Deb was treading on eggshells as her career launched, she was doing the same at home as her marriage spiralled out of control. When Peter suggested a separation, she was devastated and on a car trip home alone from Sydney, sobbed uncontrollably.

RON NEVE, DEB'S FLIGHT TRAINING INSTRUCTOR AT ANSETT, had empathy for her and his views were reflected among many of her colleagues:

> She was a loner. If you are talking about someone handling themselves in an awkward situation, I think she did very well. In the beginning she would go down to the bar at the end of the day to socialise, but she didn't go down to drink and she was extremely polite and retired early so she was playing it safe.
>
> Management didn't regard women as a long-term proposition. I think basically – underneath it all – they thought here was someone who was competent and very good but that she'd get married and have a family and disappear. They wondered if they should spend all that money on her. A lot of management pilots I spoke to had that attitude.

Meanwhile, Deb kept flying for Ansett. She spent only a year flying F27s and then transferred to DC9s. These planes carried around 125 passengers and her working day now expanded from regional airports in Victoria to nationwide destinations. After 18 months flying DC9s, she transferred to the slightly bigger Boeing 737. On the bigger aircraft there were more turbulent moments as sexist attitudes prevailed among the older pilots, who were intent on protecting their patch.

In *Letting Fly*, Marg Clarke, who was an Ansett flight attendant and close friend of Deborah's, says, 'A lot of the guys were really supportive but there were a few that came up with all the old chauvinistic remarks. We used to have great brawls on overnights; there were a few of us who would take them on. Some pilots were very apprehensive and put her through a lot tougher time when they first flew with her than they would have done with a male'.

She goes on to say that Deb really had to prove herself and how she finally won over even some of the most hardened opponents. Gerry Carman wrote for *The Age* in March 1980 that some of the older pilots who saw her as a stirrer were now impressed with her endeavour.

Despite all of the setbacks, Deb finally began to settle in. Swapping her ugly company-issued trousers for some more flattering culottes was a small symbolic gesture, but it helped. As her career continued, she began to feel she had the support of many of her flying colleagues. Soon a second female pilot joined Ansett, so Deb stood out from the crowd a little less. Felicity Bush was young, English, and reasonably new to flying. She and Deb quickly became friends but soon after she started the job, Felicity moved out of Melbourne and was then based in Sydney. The two women did not cross paths again for many years, and then in very different circumstances.

She realised she'd finally been accepted by the group when she was invited to the men-only annual retirement dinner. Sitting in the room full of men in tuxedos, presenting pewter beer steins to their retiring colleagues, she knew she'd been granted a place. But this strong show of faith in her had taken five years.

In 1982 Deb attended the first of many International Society of Women Airline Pilots conferences, in Montego Bay, Jamaica. There she joined 12 other women, the group providing a much-needed boost to ease her sense of professional isolation. In an ironic twist, when Deb organised the eighth conference in Sydney it was sponsored by Ansett.

In 1986 she transferred to the three-engine Boeing 727, the second-largest aircraft in the Ansett fleet. Even though she'd been with the company for seven years by then, her check captain still had to establish his position with the management team as there were still men in senior management who wanted to see her fail. Bruce Dewar, a man who means what he says, let it be known to her opponents that he was assessing her standard and his assessment would be no different to anyone else's: 'If she was good, she'd be told she was good. If she was crap, she'd be told she was crap – end of story!'

Was there any pressure placed on Bruce? He reckons they knew better than to try to sway his judgment: 'I thought she put an awful lot of effort in [to get through the court cases and win her place at Ansett] and in my opinion, for that she deserved some form of recognition.'

Deb flew the B727 for three years and in that time a few changes occurred in the airline industry. In 1984 Qantas employed its first female pilots, Sharelle Quinn and Ann Bennett. The following year four women pilots entered the Royal Australian Air Force. But TAA waited a whole decade after Deb's court case to take on any women pilots.

IN 1989 THREE MAJOR EVENTS TOOK PLACE IN DEBORAH'S LIFE. First, she married for the second time. Second, she began command training. Third, the day she was about to sit her final exam to become a captain, she was stood down along with 80 per cent of domestic pilots who never returned to work during the 1989 Australian pilots' dispute.

The dispute began with a pay claim by the pilots that was refused point blank by Ansett's owner, Sir Peter Abeles, who was good friends with the prime minister, Bob Hawke. They tried to force pilots to return to work on individual contracts. Some did and some didn't. Ansett stood down the pilots and then sacked and served writs on individuals within the first week. This forced a mass resignation to enable pilots to protect their assets.

The pilots' dispute was a stressful and divisive time that resulted in protests in the streets, mortgages unmet, overseas contracts being sought by Australian pilots, and the career that Deborah loved and had fought so hard to attain being ridiculed and diminished by Prime Minister Hawke when he called the airline pilots 'glorified bus drivers'.

Families that were once firm friends found themselves on opposing sides and falling out as they weighed the cost of their careers, commitments, conscience and stamina. Marriages faltered and public debate raged as the country literally came to a standstill.

Security guards were employed to escort returning pilots from their homes to work at the airport. Some pilots poured their life savings into a futile fighting fund. Former Ansett pilot, Alex Paterson, says on his website that in the space of just over a week the pilots were manoeuvred into a hopeless industrial position: resigned, locked out and with no industrial award. The year-long dispute was deadlocked within the first week.

When Deborah received a letter from Prime Minister Hawke addressing her as 'Dear Mr Lawrie', she knew she was no more than a number.

There were many sleepless nights and it was unthinkable to everybody involved that this could be happening or that it could continue for such a protracted period. Some pilots found themselves working as gardeners or chicken pluckers, but Deb returned to teaching as a stop-gap until she could return to a flying job.

Aged 36, she fell pregnant. Having had to constantly defend her desire for children, she was thrilled to be pregnant and equally devastated when it ended in miscarriage. She fell pregnant again soon after, and in early 1991 gave birth to her only child, Tom.

Although Deb was teaching, she wanted to continue flying and so she and her husband, a flight engineer also out of work as a result of the strike, agreed that wherever the first good job presented, they would go. Thus, 13 years after winning the right to fly, Deborah found that the only place that hired women pilots and would accept an Australian was the Netherlands.

In 1992, the family moved to Holland and Deb began work with KLM Cityhopper. She flew from Holland to the UK and Europe. It wasn't long before Felicity Bush, on her UK passport, joined the same airline.

By 1995 Deb was single again and on the occasional night that she was away from home, her son was placed in day- and overnight care with registered family carers, or left in the charge of a live-in nanny. The Dutch attitude towards working mothers was refreshingly positive.

Owing to age and circumstance, Deb was forced to reconcile herself to the fact that there would be no much-desired second child and this galvanised her resolve to raise her son with love and respect. Once life settled down, she and her mother visited each other as often as possible. 'She had a really good life in Holland,' says Dorothy. 'She had some remarkable experiences and met wonderful people. It was such a necessary balance after all that she had been through.'

One night she had 16-year-old Tom on the flight deck with her as city lights twinkled far below. 'Look Tom! That's Baghdad down there,' Deb said. The boy was astonished. From the security of the lounge room at home in Den Haag, Baghdad and its troubles seemed a world away. And they were. But now they were just down below and suddenly his mother's job was very cool.

After 15 years abroad it was time to return to Australia. Not only did Deborah want Tom to complete his schooling in Australia, she was approaching 57 years of age and would soon be ineligible to fly internationally. In Australia pilots can fly domestically for as long as they are able to pass the medical. Some airline pilots are still flying at 70 (and a few beyond that).

Thirty years after her first airline interviews in Australia, the contrast couldn't have been greater. Jetstar was a welcoming and progressive workplace. Deborah came in as the flight safety investigator manager and later flew as a captain, based in Christchurch, New

Zealand. In 2012 she joined Tigerair Australia, based in Sydney, where she was still flying as a check and training captain until the Covid-19 crisis hit in 2020.

Now in her mid-60s, Deborah is looking at ways to give back to the industry that has given her so much. She sponsors an annual academic award with the Australian Women Pilots' Association and is currently working on an updated memoir. In 2019, after 50 years in aviation, she was appointed to be a member of the general division of the Order of Australia (AM) for her services to aviation, and in particular women in aviation. In November 2020, she will be inducted into the Australian Aviation Hall of Fame.

TIMES HAVE CHANGED DRAMATICALLY FOR WOMEN PILOTS. Rather than being shunned and ridiculed as Deborah was throughout her court case and early airline employment, women pilots are (or should be) treated on their merits rather than their gender.

Deborah's case was the first of a long line of reforms that over the following 40 years have made it illegal to discriminate against people with disabilities, or on the grounds of race, religion, political belief or de facto status. Sexual harassment was added to the list in 1984 and now the law encompasses issues around breastfeeding, sexual orientation, gender identity and carer responsibilities. It's a great time to be flying as a woman, with a regular supply of female co-pilots and contemporaries.

There's surely not a woman in an Australian airline who doesn't know and thank Deborah Lawrie for standing up for herself and making it possible and easier for those who followed. Many of them will pre-empt their flying stories with, 'I remember when Deborah Wardley was in court with Ansett'.

Deborah is just pleased she survived and persisted long enough to enjoy it all. 'It's been a wonderful career,' she says. 'Unbelievable, really.'

IN 2017, ON A ROUTINE FLIGHT OUT OF COFFS HARBOUR, A flight attendant politely asked if a little girl could visit the cockpit. To her astonishment, Deb was greeted by a small child, about six years old, dressed from head to toe in a pilot's uniform. She told Deb very matter-of-factly that she would also fly one day and until then she would continue to wear her uniform. The white shirt, tie and hat were complemented by a hand-made set of wings and name badge.

'It warmed my heart,' says Deb. 'She was just so adorable and I was thrilled that I was able to be there to see and speak to her. It was a privilege for me to have my photo taken with her, but we never got her surname. I'd love to know who she is.' With a 60-year age difference, by the time that child begins flying, Deborah will be retired. Needless to say, Deborah Lawrie continues to be a role model and an inspiration to many women pilots, particularly those who sought an airline career and pursued it.

8

GEORGIA MAXWELL
AERIAL APPLICATION AND FIREBOMBING

I ain't going to the airlines, Buddy!

(Georgia Maxwell, laughing about the day she discovered
the sheer exhilaration of flying in an ag plane)

Fluffy white cotton balls hang on their stalks like fairy floss on a stick. Woody rows stretch for two kilometres under a drought-blue sky with an endless and shimmering horizon. It is late 2009 and the cotton-spraying season is in full swing. Cotton is big business here in northern New South Wales, where it accounts for half of all agricultural income. Their cotton is among the world's best.

The production process includes pest control and defoliation prior to harvest. There are a couple of aerial application companies with pilots working in this area and 32-year old Georgia (Wall) Maxwell holds a hard-won place among them. She, too, has earned respect doing a job that would put the fear of god into most people.

As she spears along about ten feet off the ground in a Cessna AGwagon spray-plane she is focused on maintaining her height, heading and spray coverage, all the while avoiding the deathly single-slung powerline in the paddock ahead. She scans left to right and back again, monitoring the two power poles and her proximity to the wire strung between them. Alone in the single-seat aeroplane a short ditty she learnt from a colleague helps her focus and she mentally sings:

> Wire Wire Wire.
> Fly a little higher.
> The farmer was a liar.
> If I hit it, there'll be a fire.
> Wire Wire Wire.

She observes that she is running out of spray and will soon have to reload back at the strip and then pick up where she left off. Flying towards some trees at 220 km/h, she stops singing and switches to her standard checklist. She pulls the control stick back towards her stomach in a swift, well-rehearsed manoeuvre. The plane rears skyward and the treetops rush by mere metres below.

Clear the trees, push down the other side, get back to spray height, almost out of spray, won't make the end of the run, WIRE! Too late to pull out – Push forward – Go under – Lower! DUCK … She ducks her head. Her thoughts race: there was no bang. Everything's feeling all right. I've still got my head on. Return to the strip. Is the tail still on?

She shakily lands at the airport and finds a quiet corner. From shock and fear of what might have been, she puts her head in her hands to process what just happened. For a split-second, Georgia took her mind off the wire. It happens that quickly and she knows it happens to almost everyone. Some pilots are lucky enough to get away with it and some aren't. She's seen other pilots sit in a corner looking sick, having a moment to themselves too. She has just learnt one of her biggest lessons.

During aerial application flight training Georgia learnt the theory that an adult can store around half a dozen items in their short-term memory at once. When you throw in more, something has to move out to make way for that. It was the empty spray tank and the looming trees that had crowded her thoughts and pushed aside the powerline danger. This classic mistake is often fatal.

With a healthy 1300 hours flying experience, Georgia had been around the aerial application industry for about a decade and seen and heard of a lot of the mistakes made by industry peers. Understandably, some of them had walked away from ag flying after a fright such as this.

AERIAL APPLICATION, OR CROP DUSTING AS IT WAS ONCE known before the industry set some stringent standards and rebranded, seems like an unusual occupation, but it wasn't totally out of left field for Georgia, who had grown up on a cotton farm at Wee Waa, in northern New South Wales. The family farm, Athelstone, is one of the longest running Australian farms held in the same family. The Walls first settled the property in 1867 and Georgia and her brother grew up in the weatherboard homestead with its impressive 13-metre hallway and wrap around verandah. The 1500-hectare property was next door to the local aerial application operators, Pay's Pty Ltd, who had spray planes, support vehicles and engineers on the ground. Georgia was always intrigued by the aeroplanes flying overhead, spraying and sowing crops for her parents and others in the district.

After six years of boarding school at Sydney's Kincoppal-Rose Bay, Georgia waved her best mate Bernie off to begin her nursing degree, while others in their year went on to study agriculture, beauty therapy, business management and accounting. Georgia chose the four-year aviation degree at the University of Newcastle, with a natural assumption that she would aim for an airline career.

Even though her father, Philip Wall, had done some flying in his youth, aviation hadn't been part of the family's life. So it was a huge surprise when Georgia announced she wanted to be a pilot.

Her mother knew Georgia to be a problem solver and a practical person, someone who worked hard both physically and mentally. Her parents assumed she might choose a career based around agriculture. She was definitely an outdoor kind of person, so anything sedentary was going to be off the careers list.

Trish Wall ribbed her daughter about choosing the most expensive course going but agreed to fund it so Georgia would not have a huge student loan to pay back. The payoff, Trish dared to dream, might be first-class travel for the rest of her life. That plan was doomed shortly before the course began, when Trish's 'ticket to the world' met local cotton farmer Lee Maxwell. As Georgia and Lee's relationship developed, an airline career seemed increasingly less likely.

The turning point in this trajectory came during Georgia's first mid-year university break, on a trip with her dad to order chemical from Pay's. Probably nobody paid much attention to young Georgia as she hopped out of the ute at the aerodrome. While Phil went into the office to discuss the job at hand, Georgia got chatting to pilot Paul Knight, who took her for a short flight. Paul unwittingly opened her eyes to her future.

She had been for a few joy rides with friends, but this was something else. As they flew up and around, doing a few basic aerial manoeuvres, Georgia fell in love with the aeroplane and the thrill of it. First class to London suddenly looked more likely to be first class back to the bush. When she revealed her epiphany to the family, her mother's heart sank a little as her imaginary Seat 1A boarding pass fluttered off on a cotton cloud.

Georgia returned to university with clear ideas about her future, which was set to include Lee, life on the land and flying as an ag pilot. It was well removed from the careers her 40 classmates in Newcastle were contemplating, only half a dozen of which were girls. Definitely none of them planned to be ag pilots. In fact, 20 years later, the realities of the long and difficult road to becoming a pilot doused the initial appeal for many, and Georgia is the only woman she knows of from her university class who is still flying.

A university house-share with conscientious medicine and law students diversified Georgia's outlook and encouraged an atmosphere of studiousness. One of the most useful things she learnt from one housemate was how to build computer systems. He did this as a sideline and occasionally would say something like, 'OK, this weekend we have to build four computers.' By Sunday night they'd have completed the computers and loaded the operating program, ready for dispatch to the customers.

But she was at university to learn to fly and so a few times a week she drove the one-hour trip to Hunter Valley Aviation, near Cessnock, NSW, for her lessons. The flight training was self-paced, and she found the flight school excellent and nurturing. From her first solo flight, she knew beyond doubt that this was the most exhilarating thing anybody could ever do with their life and that she was committed to flying.

At the end of 2001 Georgia joined Lee at Gunnedah. She had her university degree and commercial theory subjects behind her, but though she was ready to move into the workforce there was no work locally. She returned to Pay's at their base in Moree – a town of around 8000 where there were seasonal non-flying jobs. She was desperate to get a foothold in the industry and could see this as a great way to get started. She spent the next three months, the cotton-spraying season, driving around in the dark putting pilot navigation lights around the edges of paddocks. Most ag pilots begin their career doing these sorts of jobs. It was a humble beginning, but there was no doubting the value of the apprenticeship. Her university education then got her into the office door at Pay's, where there were plenty of pilots but very few IT geeks.

If she harboured any concerns about her boyfriend of four years, he proved himself on New Year's Eve when her services were required at work. It was the height of the cotton season and she was busy working with the night pilots. While everybody else was at a party somewhere, Lee settled into the passenger seat of the ute where they talked about their future, the industry, the weather … there was no end of conversation. Then, after two hours or so, Georgia would collect the lights and move on to the next paddock where they'd settle in for another couple of hours talking.

At the end of the season Georgia stayed on, hoping to work her way up to an ag flying job. Proprietor Ross Pay took her on her merits. He could see how keen she was and that she had the right sort of background to work in agriculture. It was 2002 and the millennium drought, at that time Australia's worst recorded drought, was into its sixth year. The last couple of years had been particularly dry around Moree. Old timers had seen nothing like it and the young ones thought it would never end. Agriculture was extremely affected, and Trish says that though there was only one year that they didn't grow cotton due to lack of water, for much of that period there was no profit in the crop. It was a lot of hard work and worry that she's chosen to put out of her memory.

For the aerial agricultural operators, million-dollar ag planes sat idle in their hangars. Training of ag pilots was at an all-time low, with one organisation claiming they only trained three pilots over the decade to 2010. The average age of ag pilots was 50 and over, and these pilots began to retire or diversify, while younger potentials went to airlines or chose other occupations.

The small amount of cotton spraying required in the district was done in the ideal conditions at night. Georgia, together with her mate Harley, carted lights all over the NSW northwest slopes, getting a feel for the industry. This work gave her time to tick off other requirements such as completing a chemical mixing course, obtaining a truck and forklift licence, and dabbling in a welding program. Suddenly she found she was surprisingly useful and there was plenty to be gained by starting slowly.

As is the industry standard, she had worked for the first two summers on the ground in a support role. But it was in the office that her farming background and university degree came together nicely. She built and managed Pay's website and helped out with regulatory compliance issues, stocktake, managing work orders, answering the phones and generally picking up the slack. Annie Miguel, the office manager, loved having the extra pair of hands around, and when reordering the company's branded work shirts, suggested they cross out the standard 'blue' or 'green' on Georgia's form and instead get some in pink. It wasn't to make any grand feminist statement, or otherwise – it's just that Georgia looks good in pink.

The pink work shirt was unique, as women in aerial agriculture are invariably employed in management or administration.

Very few, if any, work as mixers or loader drivers and, in its 50-year history, only a few women have been fixed-wing ag pilots. Georgia has also stayed at the job for more than a decade longer than any other women pilots.

She only needed a few more flying hours to complete her commercial licence and then she could start on her ag rating, to work as a spray pilot. She built her hours by flying people and goods between the company's offices around north and central NSW. She also divulged her love of photography and flew the crop imagery camera operators as they completed surveys of clients' farms.

It was possibly the longest two-year wait in history but in 2004 the excitement started: she began to train for her ag rating in the six-seat Cessna 185, a larger and heavier aeroplane to fly than what she was used to, and with a more exacting tail-wheel configuration – tail-wheel aeroplanes are notoriously less stable on the ground than their nose-wheel counterparts.

Her boss, Ross Pay, began with the basics, teaching her how to use the global positioning system to fine-tune the runs as she laid down the spray rows across the paddocks. Then they moved on to basic aerial manoeuvres, including the standard P-turn used at the end of each spray run where the pilot pulls straight up a few hundred feet, looks right along the wing to get an aiming point, turns 70–90 degrees to the right while still pointing skywards and then rolls to the left, swinging the aeroplane back around to realign for the next run back, retracing beside the row they've just sprayed.

The challenge for such a small woman doing P-turns was having the physical strength to handle the limits of the machine. Ross told Georgia that if she couldn't manage an hour of P-turns in the Cessna 185 then they were going to be in trouble. Most pilots have trouble adjusting to this aeroplane and she embarked on the steep learning curve with gusto, starting with the flaps.

Flaps, used to slow the aircraft down while keeping it

airborne longer, are extended using a hand-operated lever like the old floor-mounted parking brakes between the seats of a small car. First you push a release button on the tip and then extend it up on its hinge until it clicks into place in a four-stage process. For a beginner, it takes a lot of strength and ability to manage the flaps with one hand and maintain direction and height, holding the control column with the other, and also coordinating with the feet in the turns. A driving equivalent would be the physical and mental dexterity of a rally driver intent on steering, accelerating and shifting gears around a mountainside. Georgia needed to put all of her strength into it. With the advent of GPS, P-turns have given way to a racetrack pattern; however, the procedure is still integral to the job.

Ross is a man of few words and quite averse to women swearing, but Miss Wall wasn't running for Miss World. She was there to be an ag pilot. So Ross wasn't sure which way to look when Georgia let fly with some particularly well-chosen words, ground out through gritted teeth, as she gave 110 per cent, exerting her utmost into reefing on the required stages of flap, holding onto the aeroplane and booting it around in the turns. Six years of maintaining her focus, fending off well-meaning concerns and of having to prove herself were riding on this training and, in rivers of sweat, she wrested control of the machine and the procedures.

At the end of the training, and pleased to escape her profanities, Ross told her she had begun at a C Grade standard and graduated with an A. Next it was his father Col Pay, and his colleague Dave Bergus, who took over the latter stage of training. Col was a well-respected pioneer in the aerial application industry, and he called a spade a shovel.

'We're gonna knock this over in a few days,' Col said and took her out to do more P-turns, flying out from the small agricultural airstrips wedged between hillsides, some of them with only one way in. Col pushed her to the extreme of her ability, to see how she dealt with it.

He was a straight-shooter and when Georgia wasn't performing well enough, he wasn't averse to letting fly with, 'What the **** do you call that?'

But Col knew all the tricks and traps and at one point, to simulate flying with a full load of chemical, he stacked the back seat with some self-loading freight – a couple of nervous 1.8 metre, 100 kilogram more junior pilots that Georgia worked with. Col had Georgia fly with reduced power to teach her that being slow and heavy is a quick lesson in fine-tuning.

'How's that working out for you?' he smiled.

Georgia held fast. She found the 70-year-old intimidating but she always knew exactly where she stood and by the end of the week she stood before Ross as a newly qualified ag pilot. Cheering silently in the background was Col's wife Dianne, who encouraged Georgia every step of the way into her career.

Everything continued as before, until one ordinary-seeming day when Georgia had been working around the place in the morning and in the afternoon helping Annie finish some reports in the office. She finished up a chemical stocktake around 4.30 pm and wandered over to see Ross, who was chatting to a cotton grower and about to open a cold beer. As she approached, Ross said, 'So Chris, conditions are looking good for now. Put that beer on ice. We might get Georgia on this one.'

Georgia couldn't believe her ears. This was the day she'd been waiting for – her first spray job. She couldn't move fast enough! As there was no time to nick home and get her flight suit, she grabbed a spare pair of overalls from the cupboard in the hangar. They were white and suitable for a bloke the size of Santa Claus. She didn't hear the quips about how attractive she looked in that get-up because in her head she was screaming to herself: 'This is finally happening!'

Ross met her at the paddock to supervise and she sprayed two neat, fat square blocks that were perfect for a beginner. It was the most exciting 70 minutes of her life. She landed back at the base looking all red-faced in her white suit and Ross shook her hand. 'Looks like our newest pilot deserves a beer and it's her shout.'

Oh my gosh, thought Georgia. Yes, yes, it's my shout!

Now as a pilot, her days began before daylight and the first job was to pull the plane up onto the concrete preparation pad, sort load sizes and maps, and manage the people who mixed chemicals and loaded the aeroplanes, ensuring the right chemicals were put into the hopper.

Starting out as a pilot was particularly stressful because – aside from concentrating on the low flying – she was also following the sat nav to stay on-line, coordinating with other pilots who could be working in the same paddock at the same time, and liaising with staff and clients. There was a lot going on, but when it became familiar, she was able to enjoy it. And she *really* enjoyed it. Her name went on the work board each day and she took her place among the flight team.

Four years later and with her career on track, right after the cotton harvest of 2008, Georgia and Lee were married in the chapel at a family friend's resort in Fiji. There were many jokes from friends such as, 'Georgia's from Wee Waa, Lee's from (nearby) Gunnedah; of course they have to get married in Fiji!', and the friends in Fiji joked, 'Georgia flies ag because she's scared of heights.'

It was ten years since the couple had first met. You might assume that marriage would mean living under the one roof but as Lee had his dream job managing a 1200-hectare cotton farm, he stayed put at Gunnedah and Georgia held tight to her job two hours north at Moree. When marriage and flying are mentioned in the same sentence, Lee stage-whispers, 'Don't ask which she loves more.'

With only a couple of cattle dogs for company in the few months following the wedding, Lee couldn't help but ponder that the main thing missing was his shiny new wife! Running beside the large manager's house was the property's immaculately maintained airstrip, so in order to bring the two of them together, a red and white four-seat Cessna 172 was delivered to Georgia at Moree with an invitation to visit her husband as often as she felt inclined.

For the next three years, Georgia would hop in the plane to fly 'home' for her days off. Lee was supportive of her career, though the realities of her high-speed office always worried him. One Christmas Eve early in the piece gave him good reason to be worried, when Georgia rang from Moree.

'What have you been doing?' he asked.

'Just a bit of fencing,' she replied. 'Not by choice.'

Georgia's mum was in Sydney when her phone rang and Ross's wife said, 'Georgia has had an accident but she's alright.' Trish vividly remembers that she physically went cold.

Lee arrived in Moree within a couple of hours to learn that the gusting wind had picked up the aircraft as it was about to take off from a very narrow strip. It threw her into a nearby fence. The young pilot was unhurt and after some colourful words was calm enough to ring her boss and then her husband.

Apart from this incident, Georgia had one other mishap early on in her ag piloting career. 'I had two crashes in less than 400 hours,' she says. 'In March 2003 after 4.2 hours of direct supervision I had a partial engine failure. It was only my third ever ag job. I didn't dump in time [dumping the chemical load is done if a pilot needs to lighten the load to manoeuvre quickly to avoid an accident] and didn't have the experience to handle the emergency properly. I had to make an emergency landing but it was into a wet paddock. We'd had storms the night before.'

The plane dug into the mud and a wheel was ripped off before pancaking (doing a belly flop landing) and bending the wings, fuselage, undercarriage and spray gear. 'My career was not off to a good start,' she sighs. 'I didn't get to fly ag again for 12 months and by then the drought had really set in. My profession was leaning towards a mixer/assistant secretary. Others had encountered mishaps early on and got put straight back in a seat, but it was months before I was allowed back in the saddle.'

Of Australia's 1500 cotton farms, some in northern NSW are as large as 10 000 hectares or more. The fields can be up to a kilometre long and three or four kilometres wide in the irrigation blocks. Pilots fly using the wind to best advantage so as not to get spray back onto the aircraft, and choose the longest run in the paddocks so they spend minimal time turning and doubling back. 'We are always looking for the most productive way to spray the blocks and even run as many of the blocks together as we can. Sometimes these runs could be 15 kilometres long.'

With one hand on the control column and the power set, the pilot then grips a handle to release the spray and can be flying in that position at three metres above the ground for a couple of kilometres. If the weather is difficult or the pilot considers there is a risk of getting into trouble, they will have their hand at the ready on the 'dump' handle, which allows them to dump the load in one go. Georgia never used it on the cotton, but she would soon use it in a bushfire.

The drought finally broke in 2010 and farmers were scrambling to sow and spray their crops. The pressure on aerial ag operators intensified as they tried to provide services that had been so severely depleted over the previous decade. There weren't enough pilots for the planes and barely enough planes for the work. Pilots were being brought out of retirement and others couldn't be trained quickly enough. Suddenly Georgia was flying at her maximum capacity and in the ensuing two years she gained as many hours as she'd flown in the previous eight. She had made it!

Out at Tibooburra in the state's far north-west, she worked on a locust campaign for the Australian Plague Locust Commission (APLC). There, for the first time, she met another female ag pilot in the making. The other young woman was working as a mixer but had her own Cessna 185 and was working with the APLC as a spotter pilot. In between loads, the two women got to know each other well. Sitting under a wing in the red dirt in the middle of nowhere, there was nothing for kilometres but the smell of dead locusts. Georgia was well along her career path by then and enjoyed the company of her new friend, who was just beginning.

When GPS coordinates pinpointing the locust swarms were radioed through, Georgia would load up with spray and head out to the area. With few landmarks, she would be out spraying for up to four hours at a time in a small piston Brave aeroplane, with just the sound of the engine to keep her company and a flashing light bar on her control panel to indicate the boundaries of the swarm area.

During evenings in the Tibooburra pub the pair devoured the standard schnitzel and salad, talked about the future and dreamed of working together as pilots. They parted as friends and met up again a few years later.

The Holy Grail of ag flying is to graduate to the AT-802 Air Tractor, the largest single-engine agricultural aeroplane in the world. As she'd become proficient in the smaller AT-502, Georgia took her turn to step up. She was the only woman in Australia, and possibly the world, endorsed on the AT-802 at that time.

Compared to a standard double-decker London bus, the AT-802 is a metre longer from nose to tail and just half a metre shorter from the ground to its roof. The enormous wingspan is 18 metres from one wingtip across to the other. This plane is colloquially called 'The Acre Eater' because it gets through so much work so quickly. A couple of years after her endorsement, a local newspaper published a story with their photographer Nicola Gibson's photograph of her during the fire campaign at Coonabarabran in central NSW. With her slight build, Georgia looked like a butterfly perched up on the long wingtip. If you flip back to the cover of this book, you'll see the shot.

Over the summer of 2010/11 there was abundant work spraying up at Krui Airstrip, 60 kilometres west of Moree, where Georgia became the fifth member of Pay's flight team. And along with the rains that had brought locusts came an increased risk of bushfires as winter growth dried off and became tinder-dry fuel.

Harley McKillop was in charge of the firebombing team training for the coming contract with the Rural Fire Service of NSW (RFS). First, the pilots needed 100 hours on their aircraft type and so on Christmas Eve, when the rest of the pilots had already finished for the holiday break, Georgia was still going at 3 pm, chasing the 100 hours required so she could start her fire training. She was as happy doing that as anything else on her thirty-first birthday. By summer's end, in early 2011, she had logged enough time.

When work slowed down after the cotton season, Harley organised a training day and each pilot would take off with a full load of water and practise a string drop, releasing water in a long line as though along a piece of string.

They'd fly along the runway with Harley on the radio relaying their performance and guiding them through the process of dumping 3000 litres of water. The danger in such a sudden dump is the immediate and drastic weight shift in the balance of the aircraft. It is a finely tuned manoeuvre to let go of the water and pole the aeroplane forward at the same time.

Georgia says, 'It's physically demanding. The boys don't seem to have any trouble with it, but if you're not ready for it, it can throw you about and you can find your legs are coming up and things are floating at eye level in the cockpit as the aeroplane suddenly drops its nose.'

The next training phase was target practice. Harley talked to the pilots on the radio, making sure the aircraft was configured properly with its siren wailing and strobe lights flashing to warn ground personnel of their approach and drop. As each aeroplane approached a burning tree, Harley called them in, 'three, two, one, drop-drop-drop'. By being guided to the target, the pilots could therefore see where the aircraft's nose needed to be as it approached and dropped on its target.

There had been some publicity around Georgia, being a woman in this job, and so Harley wanted to make sure she wasn't just any sort of pilot – she needed to be tip-top. And she pushed him to educate her in every aspect of the job. She was sometimes photographed and videoed at work and, directly or not, felt the attention on her.

In August 2011 the RFS held a day at Taree to profile women in their aviation division. As a female fixed-wing firebombing pilot, Georgia spoke alongside Viki Campbell, who was the RFS's first female air attack supervisor, and Susan Dibley, the service's second helicopter pilot.

The cotton crop that summer was the best ever and there were only a few small fires. Flying back to base one day after dealing with one of these small fires, with a bit of retardant left in the plane, Georgia came across a fire near her home. She called in the coordinates to the RFS air desk and they issued approval for her to use the last bit of retardant to put out the fire before it spread. She flew down, put the fire out and kept going.

The following year, the summer of 2012/13 was a whole different story. Heavy winter rains induced a couple of ferocious fire seasons and record heat, combined with the abundant dry summer vegetation, created a perfect storm.

The first fire she dealt with alone burnt over several days in August 2012, and Georgia's first callout was to fly 60 kilometres up to Armidale from the Scone base. It was only four degrees Celsius and there was a 70 km/h freezing wind. She flew to the fire with the heater on, which made little difference to her freezing hands and feet. She had to dump five or six loads on four spot fires with the air conditioner on then landed back at Scone with the heater on. Thinking about it later, she was not sure if the air conditioner was required because of the radiant heat from the fire, or because of the adrenaline and pressure of doing her first firebombing job.

On Christmas Eve 2012, Trish – now known widely as 'Georgia the pilot's mother' – arrived to provide a meal for 15 people. The birthday girl was fashionably late, bouncing the AT-802 up the runway beside the Gunnedah house right on dark. The usual birthday celebrations were cranking up as Georgia tied down the plane. She had just returned from a long 13-day tour.

For a woman who enjoys company and a cold beer after a long day, Georgia was unusually tired. She was on standby for the fires and even though the risk of getting called out was minimal because it was raining, she spent Christmas Day at home on the couch. She would value this rest, because all hell was about to break loose a few weeks later.

January 2013 was the hottest month since records began in 1910 and with 50 km/h winds gusting to 80 km/h, a fire started at Coonabarabran. By mid-afternoon the wind strengthened to 60 km/h with temperatures in the mid-40s. The fire raced away and burnt 90 per cent of the Warrumbungle National Park, 56 homes and hundreds of head of livestock. Twenty-eight firefighters were injured, and 100 local residents were evacuated as it came within a couple of kilometres of their town.

The firebombing aeroplanes were working long and hard and Georgia recalls the exhaustion of the other 20 or so pilots, some of them snatching sleep in between duties. She too would curl up under the lunch table. It was flat out or stop and she was focused on doing her best.

Later in the month she was moved to Cooma for ten days, where the conditions were rated as Catastrophic. The wind was too strong to take as a cross-wind on the local airstrip and operations were moved to Jindabyne, where there was a small dirt strip on top of a hill that was more aligned with the wind direction. Though it meant the aeroplanes could depart more readily with the wind blowing directly at them, the shorter strip on hilly terrain exacerbated the workload. When the end of the strip raced past all too quickly, the pilots were then staring down into a valley and used the advantage of suddenly being a few hundred feet airborne to steady themselves. The take-off was manageable, but not what any pilot would have ordered. These were the worst conditions she'd ever flown in. At times they flew off into 100 km/h wind and the resulting horrendous turbulence.

As the Cooma fires roared around the mountains, the nervous and grateful locals cared for the crews. There were five fixed-wing firebombers and at Cooma there were four or five helicopters. Georgia felt conspicuous as the only woman, in the only white aeroplane.

A typical flight at that time saw her in her flight suit and aviator gloves, sitting high in the cockpit of the Air Tractor, departing for the massive forest fire over the Kybeyan State Conservation Area south of Canberra. Once airborne and heading towards a fire, the air will change from clear to a general haze. It is a calm before the storm. Visibility deteriorates and the pilot is met with columns of smoke. Even though Georgia was in the large AT-802, the flying double-decker bus, she felt like a little buzz box up in the sky wondering how she could help against the might of Mother Nature. The fires and smoke columns emanating from the hotspots were reminiscent of a war zone, and flying towards the sheer terror of it, she knew that any minute the air support aircraft sitting high above the scene would look down and see her flashing light and call her in to the fire zone.

In the unbearable heat and turbulence, she was soaked in sweat and her heart was racing. Her anxiety dulled everything superfluous to the job at hand and she was sick with nerves. Her stress levels were at full throttle as her commitment to the task at hand took over.

She always hoped the air attack person guiding her in wouldn't make a mistake. The air attack's role was to guide firebombers upwind of the fire, away from the smoke so they could see what they were dropping onto. Many times during these fires, Georgia had to fly into the smoke. She could always see the ground, but she couldn't always see ahead. High above the flames and smoke, her thoughts whirled. What if they put her into a valley and she couldn't see out? What if the load didn't let go and she had to fly out burdened with the heavy water tanks? She would consider and reconsider the risks and refine her emergency procedures before making her inbound call, telling the air attack person she was five minutes out.

Then the reply would come back, telling her they'd guide her in to where they wanted her to drop her load. She would follow the plan, do a high-level survey of the scene and then descend, with the air attack guiding her in above the fire. And then finally she would release the load, hoping it would hit the target. All the time she thought about the effect a mistake would have on her reputation, and her relationship with the RFS and her employer and colleagues. With such a big fire and so many different firefighting teams in attendance there were many eyes watching her from the ground.

Firebombing is an exact science. The 3000 litres of water carried by the big AT-802 were to be dropped from 20 metres above the target. If the water is released too high, much of it will evaporate. If released too low, it will impact too hard and the fire can flare up against its force.

Soon after dropping a load of water, the heat and turbulence at the fire zone were so extreme that she had to pull out. There were times, fighting these fires, that she was forced to dump the load early and return to the strip before she was knocked from the sky. At one point, the conditions were declared unbearable and flying ceased.

It was a relief, when those fires were all over, to be endorsed by her colleagues and the air attack officers, who commented that she did well, taking her time and maintaining accuracy. They said she didn't seem flustered. You weren't in the cockpit with me! she wanted to say back, thinking also: They'll never know the conversations that weren't broadcast.

Jindabyne was the last of the big bushfires in NSW until nine months later, in October 2013, when a series of large fires burnt along the eastern seaboard. It wasn't just nerves that churned Georgia's stomach the previous summer. While nursing her eight-week-old son, Hunter, at home she learnt that a friend, David Black, with whom she flew at Cooma, had been killed due to a structural failure of his aircraft above a fire in the mountains. The tragic news spread as quickly as the fire at its centre and it rocked the close-knit aerial ag community. Eight hundred people attended Blackie's funeral.

The dangers in aerial agriculture have been greatly reduced over the past 20 years through regulated work practices and improvements in technology and equipment, but it's still a dangerous job.

By November, a wonderful nanny had settled in at Gunnedah to look after Hunter and Georgia was back at work, returning home between loads a couple of times a day to feed the baby. Unlike his mother, Hunter couldn't stand the smell of avgas, which had to be showered away before each feed. He was weaned by February 2014, in the midst of Georgia flying in another huge fire season.

When Georgia was five months pregnant with her second child, she was interviewed and flight-tested for the role of chief pilot at Pay's Pty Ltd, the spraying arm of the company. She was excited to become chief pilot and particularly to be shown consideration as she was pregnant. Both Ross and the Civil Aviation Safety Authority were very supportive.

Once again, the birth was perfectly timed. Phoebe, Georgia and Lee's August baby, fitted nicely into the four-month window between the finish of one and the start of another cotton season. Returning to work was a smooth transition for the family because the nanny was so efficient and reliable, Lee was running their own cotton contracting business from home and the flying was now second nature to Georgia.

Then came the busiest season the cotton industry had had for years, with several aircraft written off and a couple of fatalities. Lee was away a lot more, managing their expanding contracting business; and then the nanny, who was by now also Georgia's good friend, moved on after four years. The next nanny was a disaster. By the time Georgia had her pack her bags and loaded her onto the next train, she was exhausted. She'd come to a crossroads.

In considering her position, Georgia concluded that she'd achieved all her goals. She'd been successful as a spray pilot and graduated to the largest aircraft possible, firebombing and then becoming chief pilot. She had been flying ag planes longer than many of those around her. She had a good reputation, no longer needed to prove her capabilities and had nothing to be disappointed about. Most importantly, she could walk away in one piece.

She had been 'Georgia at Pay's' for so long that she didn't know another identity and it was a heartbreaking decision, but after 15 successful years together, she needed to rein it all in. The family business was expanding, and Georgia wanted to be there to help with it. She broke the news to Ross, and it was an emotional parting for both of them.

When I asked Georgia if she thought she would have stepped back if she'd been the farmer and Lee the pilot, she thought for a moment and said yes. The kids needed their mother. Hunter was four and Phoebe was 15 months old.

These days she works in their own ground contracting business three days a week. The company employs eight people and provides services for in-row cropping and tillage, and planting – anything that can be done with a tractor.

Also in her new role as an aviation contractor, she was commissioned by Pay's to establish some IT services for a conference and, soon after that, a couple of aerial ag companies asked her to step in and manage their businesses while their owners took a few weeks off over the winter.

Georgia still flies for Paul Knight, the pilot who took her for that very first flight in an ag plane. He now owns a business at Wee Waa.

There have been a few women entering the industry as pilots over the past few years and in 2015, Georgia did meet up again with her locust spraying friend. The future they dreamed of in Tibooburra had arrived. Paul called them his 'pilettes' and says he wouldn't have gotten through the busy season without them.

The two women became great mates and loved working together. They laughed about how they managed to 'have it all' as they each flew an Air Tractor, had as much work as they could handle and 'there we were, a pair of five foot nothing pilettes with our booster seats, carving it up'.

Georgia has fielded quite a number of calls in her time from young women wanting advice. Some of them considering aerial ag didn't want to start off on the mixer/loader route and so took charter jobs to keep flying. She was recently asked by a father to mentor his Year 12 daughter who was keen to fly ag planes. Georgia's advice was to try and get a mixing job for a couple of years to gain insight and to use her spare time then to get her basic pilot's licence. She sometimes feels uncomfortable speaking on behalf of women when she spent so long trying to fit in with men. But when asked, she is happy to speak about her unique experiences and believes that women deserve a spokesperson. She doesn't want to be seen to be pushing an agenda. However, women are clearly different to men and she says that while there are some fantastic male mentors, they can't always be expected to see things from the female perspective.

'A good pilot is a good pilot,' she says. 'And to make it as an ag pilot takes a lot more determination and hard work than most other aviation pathways.' She recommends that young women stick to their guns and not lower their personal standards to get where they want to go.

The Aerial Application Association of Australia – known as 'four As' – plays a critical role in the industry, delivering a wide range of programs, training, accreditation and lobbying with a strong focus on safety. The tagline 'Fly to come home' sits prominently on all of their training courses. They offer guidance to aspiring pilots and support to the industry. Their Spraysafe program is recognised nationally for the issuing of the mandatory chemical distribution licence.

AAAA CEO Phil Hurst says women play a critical role in the industry. All member companies are family-owned and run, some with up to third generation ag pilots. While there are about half a dozen female ag pilots, there are many more women running offices and working with their pilot partners managing successful businesses.

The Gunnedah spraying arm of Pay's closed when Georgia resigned, and they now run rotary and fixed-wing firebombing operations and helicopter spraying. Sadly, Col Pay was killed in 2007 while test-flying a new system for firebombing aircraft. The Four A's has an annual Col Pay scholarship of $10 000 to encourage new pilots into the industry. The scholarship honours his memory and encourages the skills and values that Col held dear. As a pilot, engineer and manager, he was also a firm believer in the need for a professional association to represent the interests of aerial agriculture. Col trained many ag pilots in his role as an instructor/tester.

The proof was in the pudding with Georgia, who brings a new perspective to this largely male-dominated industry. She has 4500 hours as an ag pilot and maintains a strong relationship, both with the company that gave her a go in 2001 and with Paul Knight, the pilot who, against the norm, encouraged and guided her over the next 15 years.

None of it would have happened though, had she not shown the guts and good grace required to make it in one of the most challenging, rewarding and heart-stopping jobs that aviation offers.

9

NICOLE FORRESTER
FROM AKUBRA TO FLIGHT HELMET

I thought I wouldn't be accepted to the RAAF due to their prohibitively high standards, a few knee surgeries, and my age.

(Nicole Forrester)

It is late Spring 2011 and 23-year-old Nicole Forrester guides her Honda Revere 650 cc motorbike around the undulating red soil country of Kingaroy in Queensland. She pulls up at the historic World War II aerodrome and greets Tony Pratt. The long-time aerial application pilot knows plenty about low-level flying and Nicole needs to know it too.

She is one of the first women to seek his help as an instructor. His students are usually men doing aerial application, station flying, airshows or Coast Guard training. Nicole has the manner and bearing of someone with purpose and it is quickly obvious to Tony that she has come to learn because, as she's just been told at her flying school graduation, she is Australia's newest unemployed pilot. On the promise of an outback station job, she needs some instruction in low-level flying.

Over the week that Tony helps her, he tries to impart his 50 years of knowledge and 30 000 hours of flying experience to someone with three years knowledge and only 150 hours in the air.

Tony raises his chalk to the blackboard and sets out the traps of flying well below normal minimum height. 'Other than take-off or landing,' he says, 'most pilots don't fly below about 3500 feet above the ground.'

He has to quickly condition her to fly by the seat of her pants. To be in tune with her machine and to react quickly, not be reliant on her instruments, and to anticipate the speed at which things happen. This stuff is not taught in basic training and Tony's course is inspired by a litany of industry disasters, like the near miss Georgia had with a powerline, mentioned in Chapter 8. There are 57 low-level fatalities from the previous decade in Australia to draw upon, if you search the Air Transport Safety Bureau reports.

Out of Kingaroy, Nicole and Tony skim the earth and fly up the Stuart River. Tony throttles back and instructs her to simulate an emergency landing. Of the ample landing spots along the river flats, there is always one deadly obstacle to consider: powerlines. Heavy multiple wires are visible for miles but the main conductor, the earth wire, is strung above them and it's invisible. 'Fly up and over the pylons, not just over the wires that you can see,' he says. Maybe it will save her life one day. Maybe it won't. She is astute and sharp and she impresses Tony the same way she has impressed Roger Simpson, her Brisbane ground instructor. She's not afraid of the aeroplane.

The young student shows confidence but Tony gives it a good shake-up on day three as they enter the circuit to land. He asks to take control, then dives straight down towards the ground, whizzes under three sets of power lines, then pulls up almost vertically in front of a stand of trees. Back up at 1000 feet, he hands back control for landing. When I interviewed Tony in 2017, he said, 'If you need to fly under a wire, it's nice to have been under a wire and to know that it's not the first time you've done it.'

Nicole will never forget this five-day baptism of fire. She rides out of Kingaroy with newfound knowledge and a new Akubra hat, ready to head bush.

The Akubra did fit well in the air-conditioned shop, but as the head swells slightly outside in the heat, the hat forever sits perched. The flight training however, stands her in good stead.

NICOLE CAN PINPOINT HER FLYING AMBITIONS TO A FORTnight's holiday in the Solomon Islands when she was about six years old. The family took nine flights around the islands, landing on grass strips and collecting their baggage from terminals that were little more than garden sheds. On relaxed island-time, among gaggles of giggling children and lazy summer days, it was flying at its romantic best.

Nicole grew up at Camp Hill, ten kilometres from the Brisbane CBD and more or less under the airport flight path. She was an adventurous kid and with three siblings and an abundance of cousins, was equally at home with dolls or soccer balls. Her sense of adventure was confirmed when, aged ten, she took a school exchange trip to Japan. She returned home to become school captain.

Her favourite teacher at Brisbane's Mayfield Primary School, Mrs Featherstone, saw what was coming and wrote on her farewell card to Nicole at the end of primary school, 'Set your sights high, the higher the better. Expect the most wonderful things to happen. Reach for the sky.'

Nicole's inquiring mind and adventurous spirit didn't come from nowhere though. In the 1980s, her father Jeff found the perfect woman in her mother, Betty, when his motorbike rumbled to a stop out the front of her share-house in Belmont on Brisbane's south-east fringe, and he moved in as the new housemate. Soon they were travelling through Europe on a motorbike and in London Jeff took time to photograph the British Airways Concorde, which appeared over their house at the same time each day.

Betty took her skills as an occupational therapist to Saudi Arabia before the couple returned to Brisbane to start a family. Their first child, Nicole, was followed by three siblings over ten years. If Betty thought she was going to raise a little poppet, she only had to look at the calibre of the man she married to figure the offspring they'd produce.

A practical man, Jeff understood aerodynamics and design. And true to his Kiwi roots, he understood anything that produced adrenaline, though nothing was quite so adrenaline-inducing as his final flight in an early prototype hang-glider. One day when Jeff was out soaring in it, he attempted a 360-degree turn. Unfortunately, the craft didn't have enough room to complete the manoeuvre. It ended hard up against a cliff, leaving Jeff with multiple broken bones. All that remains of his sterling effort is a foot that fits no shoe easily, the story that goes with it and a lasting love of aviation.

Apart from an adventurous spirit, Jeff and Betty instilled a love of other cultures and languages in their children. Nicole caught the travel bug from her parents but she was also a cautious and sensible eldest child who mentored her younger siblings and cousins with innovative games and activities to entertain them.

It was certainly entertaining when Jeff, still the driver of excitement, took the kids to the 1998 Riverfire Festival, an annual arts festival held in Brisbane. In the huge crowd, they waited for an RAAF F-111 fighter jet that, within a couple of minutes of departing the coast, would roar down the Brisbane River at a splintering 400 feet. With its afterburners on, the jet screamed over the three bridges and dumped fuel, which ignited on release. All of a sudden there was a huge noise as the jet thundered up the river around 550 km/h and then pulled straight up into a vertical climb, flames that were longer than the jet itself trailing behind it.

Down on the ground in the onslaught of music and fireworks, the crowd saw the flaming warplane approach and felt the blasting aftershock of the jet as it rocketed overhead. The impact was not lost on young Nicole, who vividly recalls the noise, the heat and the thrill of the night.

As a teenager, Nicole set high standards for herself and excelled. She was accepted into the Year 8-10 French immersion course at Mansfield High School in Brisbane, which took only the highest achieving students. All her French, maths, history, geography and science lessons, assignments and exams were conducted in French.

She inherited the gene that made her seek out the adrenaline rush, but it was tempered by a strong desire for self-preservation – something that was apparent to Jeff when he taught the 16-year-old to ride an adult-sized motorbike. As a last-minute intervention, Betty offered her $6000 for a car, but Nicole agreed to meet her halfway and to ride carefully, as was her nature.

Around this time Nicole enquired about flying schools and learnt she would have to cough up $60 000 for flying lessons that would see her through to a commercial licence and hopefully lead to a career. Even though she'd always held jobs coaching soccer, delivering papers and serving bread in a bakery, $60 000 seemed unattainable.

Option two was to join the RAAF, something her free-spirited father vehemently opposed. So, Nicole started a double degree in information technology and law, thinking a lawyer's wage could easily fund a pilot licence. Among the IT crowd, Nicole felt like a fish out of water and within the year she changed courses. Brisbane's Griffith University had introduced their three-year Bachelor of Aviation degree with the flying training funded under a government study loan. She was one of 110 students who signed up; only 28 of them women. It all fell into place.

'I felt as though I had found my people. Some of my classmates were skydiving instructors and we all went camping and scuba diving on weekends. It was a great time,' she says.

Nicole encountered different training instructors, including many junior ones who simply saw their job as a stepping-stone to a bigger career. There was also an older instructor, jaded with the job, who failed many of the students on their first flight tests, including Nicole, twice. Her theory instructor Roger Simpson, who was nearing retirement, was different. He delighted in Nicole's company. He liked her punctuality, commitment and the fact that she was serious about her studies but not about herself.

Failing was a huge blow to her confidence and she learnt to dig deep and try again. Her navigation flights took her as far as Chinchilla, around 300 kilometres north-west of Brisbane, and on an overnight flight out to Longreach, in the centre of Queensland, more than 1000 kilometres away from Brisbane. She was rather chuffed at finding her way there and back again and, with a new commercial licence upon completion of the training, thought hard about how to proceed. She asked Roger for careers advice, particularly about going bush.

From her parents' Stradbroke Island weekender, Nicole dialled a station manager. He was as busy as all hell but from his office a few hundred kilometres out from Mount Isa, he politely answered her queries about the role of a station pilot. He was impressed that she had a commercial pilot licence when the minimum requirement was for a private licence and he eventually said, 'I do need somebody. Can you come out next week? Make sure you bring a hat and swag. And before you arrive, go and do some low-level training.'

In that ten minutes she got her break, dependent on the character references. She packed her life into boxes under the staircase in her parents' house and departed for low-level training, whatever that was.

Roger wouldn't describe her as a 'girly girl'. No, she's not fussed about makeup or shopping and he knew she could drive because he saw her in her brother's car once. She prefers motorcycles. He had no doubt she would give it her best. As Roger answered the recruitment lady's questions, his young student and good friend rode off towards her future, starting in Kingaroy.

NICOLE HAD A WEEK TO GET HERSELF FROM HOME IN suburban Brisbane to a 1 600 000-hectare cattle station in the Northern Territory. With a list of requirements that started at the head and finished at the feet, she went looking for country clothing stores. She had no idea what was ahead of her but she wasn't about to question the uniform.

'I had to google what a swag was, then track one down. I also had to buy jeans, boots, a hat, long-sleeved shirts and a six-month supply of personal products, particularly sunscreen. I was told to bring a belt and a knife. I asked if that meant a normal pocket-knife but they said that cowboys have special belts with a stitched-on pocket to carry a special station-style knife.' She felt like she was playing dress-ups and when she finally disembarked from Qantaslink at Mount Isa the following week, she was yet to don the new clothes.

At Mount Isa she transferred to the smaller plane that would take her all the way to the cattle station. They flew across the Barkly Tablelands, where the station's 70 000 cattle roam across its rolling Mitchell grass plains and sand dunes. Once across the station's boundary, they descended to 300 feet. Although that was just under the legal height requirement for flying over land, it was the height she would have to get familiar with because that was the height at which the outback stations did most of their work, checking bores and fences and working stock. Stations can apply for a low-level dispensation for their pilots to fly down to ground level within their property's boundaries.

The pilot began pointing out things Nicole would need to know and she tried to follow their progress on her new flying maps but on the treeless earth that splayed out around them, as flat and as green as a football field, there was neither hill nor hole to navigate by. The earth was as big as the sky and the station's large dam that she'd marked as a good navigation point prior to departure turned out to be 160 kilometres west of where they were heading. In all her time there, she never saw the dam.

Boggled by the size of the property and its vast boundaries, she scanned the horizon, which was as straight as a stringline, until eventually the settlement appeared. The pilot dialled up the correct radio frequency and did a pass over the homestead to announce their arrival, then circled to land on the station's wide red dirt runway.

Nicole disembarked into the stifling midday sun and helped the admin lady load the ute. The inevitable first question was whether Nicole had a protective hat to wear. She took a deep breath. 'Yep,' she said. 'I've got a hat …' and gingerly placed the thing on her head. She felt ridiculous. When Nicole got out to shake the boss's hand, he pointed to her head and said, 'I'll bash that for you later.' She reeled and thought, OK! Woah. What's that all about?

'I was already confounded and I began to wonder why I'd done this to myself. What was I doing out here in the middle of nowhere?

I assumed I'd be living with the jillaroos in a dorm block. But the head stockman was actually a woman! And she was my age and she wanted a housemate so I was unbelievably lucky to get a room in her house. The other workers told me that as a lowly pilot it was most unusual. I was very impressed that there was a woman in a management role.'

The settlement was set around a lightly treed well-watered lawn that defied its stark surroundings. From the wraparound verandah of the manager's large house, the boss could keep an eye on the other few houses, kitchen, butcher shop, office, storerooms, clinic, and jackaroo and jillaroo quarters that housed everybody down to the most junior of the station's 50 workers. The nearest neighbours, and for that matter everybody in Nicole's address book, lived somewhere to the east, beyond the curvature of the earth.

The moment of truth came after crossing the timber floors, when she heaved her suitcases onto her single bed and stared blankly at her new shirts. One of them had to come out. Within a couple of hours, she was wearing it down at the stock camp, gagging at the sights, sounds and sensations of sweat, poo, blood and bulldust that surrounded her.

Her job as the station pilot would be interspersed with regular chores, and when she was not flying, she was expected to muck in with everybody else, which included working in the stockyards. As the heat and dust crusted her sweaty face, she shifted in her crisp clothes and peered out from under her stiff new hat, wondering how this would all pan out. Her new colleague and housemate looked back worriedly at her and wondered the same thing.

Her nerves did not ease the following morning at muster when 19 of her co-workers assembled in the courtyard for a staff briefing. Thankfully, nobody pointed out how overdressed she was. They didn't need to. They could see the glint of the fancy pearl shirt buttons and it was painfully obvious that she was looking more rodeo queen than station hand. She dropped her gaze to her stiff boots and reminded herself how lucky she was to have got this difficult first job.

DESPITE A WARM WELCOME, THE CULTURE SHOCK WAS greater than any on her travels to Japan, Europe or the Pacific. Considering she'd only gone half-way across her own country, it felt strangely as if she'd arrived in a world where everybody dressed, spoke and thought differently. She strained to understand their broad accents and mostly had no idea what was being said, literally or contextually.

And though she was in great shape for skydiving, hang gliding, touring on her bike and bushwalking, the city girl physically paled beside her tanned brawny colleagues. Nicole's real strength though, had always been her determination and motivation. Her mother was so proud of her initiative and courage in going off into the unknown world of the outback. To establish herself, she was almost entirely reliant on the people around her at work now so she had to make sure she fitted in with the crowd. It was an entirely new ball game and she tried to ensure she got off on the right foot.

Beside her sunglasses and flying cap on her dressing table sat the aeroplane keys. The little two-seater Cessna 150 was nicknamed Jazzy and Nicole's first solo trip in the plane, a 30-minute flight to the neighbouring property, started with the usual flight planning. She went to the office to access internet to find out the wind strength and direction, but was quickly told that those wind readings would be useless. They started at 2000 feet and she would be flying down at 300 feet, which would be a different reading.

So she headed off, not knowing how much the wind would blow her off course and when she should have been arriving over the neighbouring homestead. At the 30-minute mark, instead of reaching the neighbours' place, she found herself flying out into a great big nothing. It was a terrifying realisation that she was lost, with flat earth stretching in all directions.

She pushed in the power and climbed higher to get a better perspective and was greatly relieved when she spotted a settlement in the distance. She swung Jazzy around and headed for it. The occupants welcomed her and served up a calming cup of tea. She bit into the whipped cream on a warm scone and tried to stop trembling.

Getting home was no better and when it also failed to materialise, she headed for a plume of smoke, thinking that must be the homestead. She was right, but never again in her time there did they have another fire at the homestead, though many more plumes of smoke appeared in different locations.

Back in Brisbane, as torrential rains continued to fall, Jeff received a frantic message from his daughter, begging him to send her a hand-held GPS. She'd repay him quickly she said, because the paper map was useless and her air navigation training wasn't helping much either.

The GPS arrived and with it a new nickname for Nicole. Tradition at the station dictates that the pilots are named from the film *Top Gun*. Her predecessor was Ice Man and the guy before him was Hollywood. She was their first female pilot so Nicole got the only female nickname in the movie, Charlie. Any subsequent female pilots would be Charlie 2, Charlie 3 and so on.

There was a little bit of Top Gun–inspired flying required for some of her jobs, such as taking a jackaroo to check the boundary fences, which involved flying so low that it felt like the wheels were almost skimming the grass. It was scary at first and sometimes meant having to clean the remains of a stray bird from the struts at the end of the flight.

She knocked on the door of the big house one day to report on bore water levels and the boss called out, 'Charlie. Come on in!' He flicked the switch on the kettle and held her hat over the rising steam, kneading and shaping the damp felt. This is what he was alluding to when they first met and he said he'd bash that in for her. He was talking about her hat, not her head! He proudly returned the bashed-in hat and Nicole rolled the softened felt over in her hands, hoping for a miracle. The teasing of her friends had eased, but to her eyes and in her hands the hat was still a foreign object.

About six weeks after Nicole's arrival, some of the regular staff took summer leave and that first Christmas was a lonely affair, with only a handful of co-workers for company. The 5 am starts became normal and as she departed in the crisp mornings to check roads, paddocks and bores, she enjoyed the glorious sunrises and sunsets under that huge sky that at first had been so intimidating.

Wildlife popped up in surprising places and she promised herself that once she became useful, she'd stop long enough to photograph the dingoes, goannas, kangaroos, galahs and cockatoos, big frogs, wedge-tailed eagles, tawny frogmouths, frill-neck lizards and a random emu that was reportedly hanging around. For now though, she was still settling in, flying about four days per week doing fire spotting, mail runs and whatever else needed to be done, including – on a couple of occasions – search and rescue and medical evacuation.

Station pilots have to be a jack-of-all-trades and one day when the bore runner hadn't returned by sunset, her boss hurried into the bar and told Nicole to take off, get some altitude and try to raise him on the UHF radio, which would work far better from the air. They all knew that by now his radio battery would be running low.

She quickly switched from barmaid to pilot. The last rays of daylight were edging out as she sprinted to the plane, did a fleeting pre-flight inspection and zoomed up the runway in the near dark. The bore runner was out there somewhere. Hopefully he was bogged, not injured or snake-bit.

Circling at 500 feet above the airstrip, Nicole called repeatedly on the radio. 'Bore Runner. Request location and status. Over.' Eventually, through the static, she heard a faint reply that ended with … maybe a six? Then nothing.

She landed ten minutes later in the approaching darkness, looked at the map of bores on the station, and took an educated guess. The boss took off in a ute before the plane was even put away and returned four hours later with his tired worker. His ute had broken down at Bore no. 56. He was inconvenienced but not injured, but when one of the jillaroos suffered an electric shock and burns while working on some electrical wires, she was immediately dispatched to the clinic in town for assessment. Flying over impassable roads, Nicole nervously checked the woman beside her all the way to see if her patient was still conscious. There was little else she could do.

When she was not flying she was figuring out how to service the aeroplane or helping with all manner of station tasks: working in the yards dehorning, ear tagging, weighing and processing cattle; mustering on motorbikes across cracked and potholed ground; bookkeeping and admin; cleaning; running the bar; helping the mechanics service the bore motors and station vehicles; and clocking up an inordinate number of hours on the ride-on mower. Staff were given half a day off after 14 working days and a full day after 21. By the end of her first fortnight, her muscles ached, she had four big bruises, a blister from her unyielding boots, and cuts all over her hands. Her black belt in taekwondo didn't help much with mud-wrestling cattle to brand or castrate them and some days it was a fairly confronting initiation for the soft-hearted animal-loving young woman from the 'burbs.

Having settled in somewhat, Nicole drew up a chair one Saturday afternoon to write a letter to her sister, who seemed a long way away. Outside, rain pelted against the loungeroom window as lightning split the grey sky and rain stained the dust. It was sweet relief to have the temperature drop and to be able to pick up a pen and think. She wrote the following lines to her sister, back in suburban Brisbane, to fill her in on station life:

If we all left the station and it rained (as it is now) then the roads would be boggy and flooded and we wouldn't be able to get back. And if we couldn't get back, we couldn't muster the bulls next week. And if we couldn't muster the bulls then there would be no calves for 2013. And no calves means no money. And no money means no jobs. I'm sure you get the point.

'Just watching the storms on the horizon was awe-inspiring,' says Nicole. 'Sometimes you'd get a full 180 degrees of lightning and black cloud in the afternoon, then the wind would start to pick up on an otherwise really still day, then you'd get that first gust, the smell of rain on the wind and there'd be a huge hive of activity while everyone prepared for the incoming storm – getting washing in, putting vehicles under cover, putting the mower away. I loved it.'

A few weeks later, in mid-January, she was at a neighbouring property to do mustering training in preparation for the approaching season. Aerial mustering is unique to Australia. It allows livestock to be herded across vast areas, saving a great deal of time and expense, but the risks are hefty. There is little time to recover from any kind of unusual event and pilots can become fatigued from the intensity of operating so close to the ground. The mustering training is imperative to train pilots in safety, aeroplane handling and stock movements while undertaking this work.

Nicole had already done about 50 hours flying at low level and listened intently as one of the head stockmen explained the moods of cattle and their 'eye' on the ground. Where you stand in relation to their eye will bring about a different behavioural response. If you stand in one spot, the cattle will stop. If you stand further back behind a certain line of sight, they will move forward and if you're too far back, they'll turn around.

Up in the air, the aeroplane needs to be as invisible as possible once the cattle are moving. It's important to be aware of the position of the sun and to fly accordingly so that the aeroplane doesn't create a shadow that can scare them. Likewise, wind will carry the aeroplane's noise that can also scare them. The task of a good mustering pilot is to make the cattle walk, not run, and to definitely not miss any.

Nicole learnt to be careful, to stay high and start them moving gently in the cool morning. Cattle, like aeroplanes, prefer the cooler weather. Then she would radio the stockmen on their bikes or horses, telling them to move behind the cattle while she flew off to search for stragglers.

In Brisbane, rain was still falling. The city was experiencing horrendous floods and Nicole's possessions, so carefully packed under the stairs, were lost to the flood, along with anything else that was stored on the lower floor of her parents' house. All that she owned was now with her on the station. She got to know the Royal Flying Doctor Service (RFDS) staff who flew in three times while she was at the station, to collect victims of horse-riding accidents. While she enjoyed chatting to the pilots and dreaming about flying their aeroplanes, she had no desire to be a patient in one. She made some lasting friends, most of whom were great with horses, but Nicole was still a stranger in a strange land. She was working with mostly men, while in the outside world, Julia Gillard was Prime Minister and Queensland Premier Anna Bligh impressed the country with her handling of the state's flood crisis, so there was no shortage of female role models in public life.

In perfect timing, the RAAF approved an annual fund to the Australian Women Pilots' Association (AWPA) for an aerobatic or formation endorsement and another for navigation training. Aerobatics and formation flying are two skills taught in order to fly aerobatic manoeuvres (as Reg Annabel did with Nancy Bird on her second flight) or in close formation with other aircraft. These are mostly used for demonstrations or combat flights and are standard skills for military pilots. Nicole saw the advertisement in a flying magazine and applied. Soon afterwards she received a letter inviting her to attend the annual AWPA conference in Bunbury, Western Australia, in April.

She tentatively walked into the boss's office to seek a week's leave. It was right at the beginning of the mustering season and she knew it was a big ask. As the news of the invitation spilled from her lips, his wife gushed with excitement and the leave was granted. The conference was a brilliant networking opportunity, and with her new aerobatic scholarship in hand, Nicole promised to return for the following year's event.

At the end of winter she left the station and returned to Brisbane. She now had about 450 hours experience and had learnt about flying and aircraft conditions, being challenged in the plane and trusting her instincts. That maturity stood her in good stead to continue her career but she had no idea what would come next, other than her plan to go home and study for her Air Transport Pilot Licence (the highest level of commercial licence), fly upside down on her new scholarship, and take it from there.

ON 16 OCTOBER 2012, NICOLE BEGAN A WEEK'S TRAINING AT the Royal Newcastle Aero Club with Phil Unicomb, one of Australia's foremost aerobatic instructors and pilots. In the sporty little biplane he used for aerobatic training, they spent the first three days doing emergency manoeuvre practice: pushing the plane to the limits of its abilities, stalling, spinning and recovering again. It is a course that Phil developed and has been teaching for over 30 years. By day four, they were doing loops, rolls and basic aerobatic manoeuvres.

As the little white aircraft was tossed around in the sky with its trailing red and blue detail blurring in the rolls, Nicole discovered that she loved flying upside-down a lot more than she'd expected to.

Seven weeks later she was back out in the Northern Territory at the invitation of the pilot who did her mustering training. She was to stand in over Christmas on a neighbouring cattle station but when she rejected the invitation to stay on as their permanent station pilot, the pilot recommended her for the next step up the ladder, flying a swish six-seat Beechcraft Baron for a private company. She moved to Cloncurry, near Mount Isa in north-west Queensland.

The trade-off for this cushy job was that it didn't help at all with building up those all-important flying hours, so a year later she downgraded aeroplanes to a job that afforded many more flying hours. She had finally acclimatised to the heat and the ways of the Territory.

THE FOLLOWING YEAR AT THE AWPA 2013 HERVEY BAY conference, Nicole returned as promised for the four-day event. Among the highly motivated group, she reacquainted herself with a couple of female RAAF pilots and marvelled at how down-to-earth they were and what brilliant flying experiences they'd had. It was not at all what she had expected from the Defence Force. As she listened to Group Captain Dee Gibbon discuss her PhD on women pilots, she was engrossed. Then as Squadron Leader Samantha Freebairn spoke about the women who are most likely to perform highly on the RAAF pilot course, Nicole sat there mentally ticking off every single box. Her father's concerns were weighed against what she was hearing and seeing and eventually Nicole's opinion was influenced by the women she met.

These women were only a little older than she was, and had a degree, flying experience, aerobatic experience and a strong support network. Finally, she decided to apply for the RAAF, though she says, 'I thought I wouldn't be accepted due to the prohibitively high standards, a few knee surgeries and my age.'

In an interview with the RAAF, she was asked if she'd ever failed at anything and how she dealt with that. Many high achievers are used to succeeding. Nicole recounted the experience of picking herself up after failing her first flying test twice. They looked on that as character building.

A year later she arrived at RAAF Base East Sale in eastern Victoria to begin officer training. For 18 weeks, the 25-year-old learnt how to iron her bed and measure out the 30-centimetre fold at the top for inspections; she saluted, marched, carried packs and set up tents in the bush, dug pits, filled sandbags and fired at her 'enemies' using blank bullets from a Steyr rifle. Not everybody gets a nickname in the military, but most seem to. Her new friends called her Forry, a derivative of Forrester.

At the graduation parade after completion of her RAAF training, her former university lecturer, Roger, stood proudly with the family as Nicole marched out with her squadron and stood stock still on the freezing parade ground in a short-sleeved shirt. What a turnaround for the outback pilot.

At Basic Flying Training School in Tamworth, NSW, Nicole, with around 1200 flying hours, went back to the basics to be taught how to fly by the military. The aircraft wasn't much different in size and speed to the one she flew out on the station, but now instead of a peaked hat and a water bottle, she had a helmet and a parachute.

The real test came at her next level of flight training in Perth, where her nickname mutated from Forry to Fozza. How could she ever have thought she wouldn't love the Air Force? The Pilatus PC-9 had two ejection seats, three times the speed and 60 times the power of a Cessna 150 like she flew on the station. The graduation flight displays the pilots' formation skills, where they fly just metres apart and then split to do eight to ten aerobatic manoeuvres, pulling up at 4G, which is two to three times the force of a roller-coaster ride. On re-entry to the display area, the group descends to 250 feet and flies a bombing simulation. Nothing can prepare you for flying the PC-9 at 400 kilometres an hour, within a metre of your nearest colleague.

With her wings firmly in place on her green fire-resistant flight suit, Nicole's new home was RAAF Base Amberley, south-west of Brisbane. There, she learnt to fly the KC-30, a modified 270-seat Airbus that is used to refuel other jets mid-air.

The excitement of the RAAF suits the active woman who loves nothing more than to pull on her uniform each day and ride her motorbike to work, or to get away on her holidays for more exploring and adventure. Sometimes the two combine, and in early 2017 she was on exercise with the US Air Force F-16 fighter fleet in Japan. Flying around snow-capped peaks with eight F-16s in close formation off her wings was something to behold.

From flying at 300 feet to muster cattle, when low-level was considered just a foot or two off the ground and she had to check the condition of potholed roads before putting down, Nicole now gets around at 41 000 feet and lands on large, sealed runways. From the front seat of the KC-30 the forward view is bright. She can remain in the fast-paced flying environment of the RAAF, seek overseas postings, or perhaps use her endorsement to become an airline pilot.

In the beginning, even when the future didn't reveal itself easily, it was by being open to opportunity that Nicole presented her RAAF application with low-level, mustering, aerobatic, skydiving, gliding, hang-gliding and shooting experience.

These days her bush flying is a wonderful memory and Flying Officer Nicole Forrester is sporting a very different hat.

10

ESTHER VELDSTRA

PILOT FOR THE ROYAL FLYING DOCTOR SERVICE

'I'm not flying with a girl.'

(Statement made by a distressed and wounded stockman before the painkillers kicked in)

ESTHER VELDSTRA

Darwin was literally the end, and the beginning, of the road. Just north of Alice Springs, at the Tanami Track turnoff, Esther had to make a decision: go left to Kununurra or continue on. She asked a passing truck driver for advice. He looked at the young Dutch woman driving alone in her little Datsun Sunny and drawled, 'Darlin', the wet season is going to be a bad one. Go straight to Darwin.' Esther took him at his word and pushed on up the Stuart Highway before the road was cut by floodwaters.

As a fresh pilot with only 250 hours flying time, Esther had set out from Sydney to find work. Over the Blue Mountains, she drove as far as Dubbo. She couldn't plan any further than that, but when she got to Dubbo, the age-old technique of knocking on hangar doors didn't yield any results. So, she kept driving, west towards the Flinders Ranges, north to Alice and beyond, making enquiries all the way.

The Top End in 1996 was experiencing a severe wet season that pushed Esther to keep driving, from fear of getting stuck somewhere without work. The 26-year-old had her eyes on flying for the Royal Flying Doctor Service. It was a big dream, but it had to start somewhere and right now it was starting in the Territory capital at the friendly and relaxed youth hostel on Mitchell Street.

With seven dollars to her name, money was tight – desperate in fact. Outside, her little car was packed with her worldly goods: clothes, books, camera, but most importantly her nav bag and logbook – none of which would pay the rent.

She'd get her jewellery back when she came up with some cash, but for now it was security against her rent. First, she undid the gold necklace and put it on the counter. Then she handed over her watch. Gold, without a chain and clasp, keeping perfect Swiss time. It had been her mother's. She had only passed away six months earlier and Esther missed her terribly.

ON THURSDAY 11 JUNE 1970, IN FOGBOUND LONDON, ANDRE Veldstra received the news that back home in Rotterdam, his wife Johanna had safely delivered their second child, a daughter. He was sad to have inadvertently missed the birth and as a consolation, Johanna allowed him to name the child. He chose the name Esther and his wife chose Yvette as the baby's middle name.

Over the next five years, the family moved many times, following Andre's work as a dredging professional. First to Sydney and then to Mackay, Queensland, back to Holland and then to Abu Dhabi, where Esther started school. When she was eight, they returned to Holland, while Andre took a job in Nigeria.

During her time at high school in the Netherlands, the Dutch airline KLM had an open day for prospective pilots and they informed the young hopeful that she was two centimetres too short to be a pilot with them. It killed her dreams because for airline flying in Holland it's KLM or nothing.

With no desire to be stuck at school, in 1988 Esther struck a deal with her parents. She could drop out of school if she studied something else. She worked as a groom at a horse stud, while completing 12 months of computer training. When she was 19, Andre took a job on the Sydney Harbour Tunnel and the family returned to Sydney, but Esther only lasted six months, after completing her secretarial studies. She returned to Holland and worked as a secretary by day and studied the Dutch equivalent of the Higher School Certificate by night.

An honours degree in international management then took her to Seoul in 1993 on an exchange program and she followed that with practical experience in Sydney. It was in Sydney over Friday night drinks that one of her colleagues from the office told Esther he couldn't imagine her continuing in this line of work. 'I want to be a pilot,' she replied without thinking. And right then she realised it was time to make that happen.

'I had a work colleague who used to be an air traffic controller,' she says. 'He took me out to Bankstown and I met Bill Whitworth at Whitworth Aviation. Mum and Dad supported me through all my flight training through to Commercial and Instrument rating. Then they returned to Holland again. Between university and flying, there had been an awful lot of study!'

In early 1996, Esther returned to Holland to spend time with her mother, who passed away shortly after her return. Back in Australia, alone, she packed the Datsun Sunny and headed off to look for flying work.

Once she settled in at Darwin, she met Nick Belfield. He was an engineer and had his own Cessna 210, a six-seat, high performance aircraft with a retractable undercarriage. He introduced her to his colleagues, also engineers, and that's how she came to work with Mick, Mick and Nick.

In January she did her first flight, a familiarisation flight to Batchelor, about 100 kilometres south of Darwin. The following month she took tourists to Jabiru in Kakadu National Park, and also flew out to Newcastle Waters Station, between Darwin and Alice Springs, but mostly she spent her time flying as the engineers' personal taxi driver. They became good friends and excellent colleagues.

After that first wet season, Esther went back to Holland to sort her mum's possessions and returned to Australia as a permanent resident. Now she could make firm plans and she went straight back to Darwin for the next wet season.

She got her first job with businesswoman Kathy Meyering at Gulf Air (Gulf of Carpentaria that is). The East Alligator River had flooded and so road access to Arnhem Land was cut. Esther's first job was five weeks of flying the six minutes from Jabiru across the river to Oenpelli.

In a steep learning curve, Esther also flew alone to isolated stations and communities. Airstrips that were clearly marked on a map would disappear when the sun was directly overhead, reappearing when the sun fell low and threw a shadow across the graded strip. Locals with years of experience in the Territory offered their advice and instructions on landmarks and on customs and procedures, born of many hours of bush flying. There were harsh lessons and some near misses.

One of Esther's flights was from Oenpelli out to a tiny, remote outstation. There had been several cases of women being severely assaulted out there at that time, but the lone pilot would only be making a quick stop to deliver some freight and one passenger. She would also be gone before the forecast adverse weather closed in.

As she came in to land on the rough red dirt strip, there was a bang. When she rolled to a stop and inspected the aeroplane, Esther could see that she'd blown a tyre. She needed an engineer. And she needed to get out of there. Looking around nervously, she phoned the company and spoke to the chief pilot. They both knew of the recent violence against women, and knew that it was essential to get an engineer out there as soon as possible.

To her horror, the chief pilot said, 'We can't get there until the weather clears in the morning,' and further instructed, 'Go to the building next to the airstrip. Take the scissors from the first aid kit and lock yourself in the room.' This was bad news. In the prickling humidity of a 30-degree day, with growing cumulus clouds swirling and breeding above her, fear turned her blood to ice. Surely this wasn't really happening.

Many miles from nowhere, she acquainted herself with the rudimentary building and dared not to think too much. Would they come? Would the door hold? Would they turn the scissors on her? Would she survive this night?

Inside the room, with only spiders and dust for comfort, Esther stared at the pitted grey concrete blocks and assessed her options. She didn't have any. She was a sitting duck. As the shadows began to lengthen, a phone rang outside. She ventured out of the building and answered it nervously, hoping for a miracle. It was Speedy, another of the pilots. 'I'm not leaving you out there alone,' he said. 'I'm coming to get you.'

GPS navigation was reasonably new then, but Speedy had entered the coordinates of the runway thresholds of every airstrip they flew to. He gave his estimated time of arrival and instructed Esther to sit in her aeroplane with the radio on. 'I don't care if the battery goes flat,' he said.

Esther had relayed the wind direction and velocity to him and Speedy was able to come down out of the deteriorating weather right on point and collect his relieved and grateful passenger. It had been an extremely long few hours.

IN 1998 ESTHER WAS FLYING TOURISTS AROUND THE BUNGLE Bungles in Kununurra. Through word of mouth, at the end of the dry season, she got a job back in Darwin with Air Manymak, owned by Michael Bourke. The job was based out of Ramingining, an Aboriginal community of 800 people. It is 500 kilometres east of Darwin on the edge of the Arafura Swamp. She vividly recalls her welcome:

> The first day at Ramingining was amazing because it was customary for every new pilot to receive an initiation, or welcome ceremony, by the Aboriginal people of the community. I was told to be ready for collection at 1 pm. When the ute-load of guys arrived, they took one look and were flabbergasted that their new pilot was a woman. They swiftly turned around and shouted that they'd be back. Ten minutes later they returned with a big sofa chair in the back because a woman couldn't just 'ride in back of a ute'. I felt like a queen.

They couldn't do the normal ceremony because they couldn't take me hunting. That was only for men. However, they did show me their weapons, spears, and how to hide and then chase animals. They went through the motions, but actually killing the animals can only be done by men. It was a fascinating afternoon.

On the way back to town, we got stuck in the middle of a crocodile-infested river. I was instructed to stay in the sofa chair in the back of the ute in the middle of the river, while they waded to shore and went for help. One guy stood on the side of the river to keep guard. The others returned with another ute and we were towed out, with me still sitting in the sofa chair.

That night they barbecued fish. It was an amazing welcome and unlike anything I'd experienced before.

On 31 October 1998, after a scheduled flight had been cancelled due to the aircraft being unserviceable, Esther was chartered in a Cessna 210 to deliver any passengers who elected to go on to Darwin. Five passengers had boarded and they were up at 4500 feet, heading towards Darwin when the engine began to run rough. As the engine cylinder head temperature soared, the aircraft was unable to sustain altitude. The only option was to get the aeroplane to the ground.

She knew there was a narrow strip close by but, with high trees all across the countryside, it was hidden by the surrounding bush. Without a GPS she had no quick way of finding it and so she radioed Flight Services in Adelaide with a mayday, stating her intention to force land in the only clear bit of ground around: a disused gravel pit/quarry. She brought the aeroplane down safely; however, on the roll out, it hit some large mounds of gravel that hadn't been obvious from above. Esther says:

I never doubted that the forced landing would work out OK. If you haven't been through it, you don't doubt it. I was quite determined to pull it off. As soon as I touched down though, the undercarriage broke off and so there were no brakes. Immediately, I had a flash of recognition of the trouble we were in.

The aeroplane careened towards a stand of high trees then hit a mound of gravel, which brought them to a dead stop. The pilot's seat sheared off with the force and slammed her head into the dashboard.

The aeroplane came to rest on its right wingtip, with the separated engine flung out in front. The shocked passengers evacuated and helped their semi-conscious pilot out of the cabin. Esther lay in the gravel trying to direct the passengers to the emergency location transmitter, which was held in the aircraft. They were unable to find it. Fortunately, Adelaide Flight Service contacted another overflying aircraft and asked them to locate the accident. They then arranged for a rescue team to be sent out from Darwin.

Down on the ground, to the astonishment of those around her, Esther ripped off her shorts. Her legs were burning and stinging because she was covered in fuel. Most of the passengers were reasonably unharmed, or at least, they were in better shape than she was. Somebody wanted a light to have a cigarette and she screamed at them because there was fuel everywhere. 'And flies!' she says. 'The flies were really annoying and clinging to the blood coming from my head. I wasn't in any pain but the passengers kept telling me to rest. They were more shocked than me because I wasn't aware of how much I was hurt. Somebody was discussing that they wanted to walk off to find water, but I knew that rescue would come soon because I could hear an aeroplane circling overhead. The biggest chopper I'd ever seen, maybe it was a Chinook, arrived to medevac me to Darwin

Hospital. I struggled to sit up but I so desperately wanted to watch this huge thing land.'

The subsequent Air Transport Safety Bureau report stated that the engine baffles, used to direct cooling airflow over the engine cylinders, were in a generally poor condition, with several cracks, broken mounting rings and worn areas. In one place, a baffle had been worn through by contact with an engine hose.

The engine had been overhauled on 18 August 1997 and fitted with six overhauled cylinders. On 11 August 1998, the number four cylinder head had failed because of cracking and was replaced. On 28 August 1998, the number six cylinder head had similarly failed because of cracking and was replaced. On 14 October 1998, 16.4 flying hours before the accident, the engine had passed a cylinder pressure leak check during routine maintenance. There had been 60 other reported occurrences of this problem, including a number of forced landings, with only one other injury.

Back in Darwin, Esther continues the story:

> They fixed my head with concrete and titanium and wired my jaw, which was broken in three places. I could only taste extreme flavours like laksa soup or sweet chocolate milkshakes. I was extremely lucky because my eyesight wasn't affected and the only visible scar now is just above my nose. I've never seen what I looked like [straight after the accident] but everybody who walked into the hospital room burst into tears ...
>
> My jaw was wired for a few months and it took me almost six months to get back onto my shaky feet. It's amazing what the brain is responsible for and I was walking like a doddery old lady at the time. I got back to work and did an endorsement on the twin-engine Beechcraft Baron. One day when I was flying in to Darwin, the left engine failed on it and the aeroplane wouldn't maintain height. I had to glide down into Darwin

airport. I decided then to drive back to Sydney. I was done with Darwin.

With everything that had happened, Esther reassessed her options once she got back to Sydney. She worked at a pet shop, a supermarket, waitressed and did all the 'usual stuff' that unemployed pilots do to keep life moving forward. She was worried about having her medical validated and as part of her recovery from a second operation to correct the plates in her head, had counselling with a psychologist at the invitation of WorkCover. The psychologist recommended that Esther hop back in an aeroplane and do ten hours training.

'I needed to prove that I could still fly and not be shit-scared,' she says. 'It was the right thing to do. In small aeroplanes I began flying parachutists and traffic reporters. Then I did an endorsement in a ten-seater Queen Air with pilot Ray Clamback [who features in Lyn Gray's story (chapter 6)] and used that for night freight and bank runs up and down the east coast, delivering newspapers and overnight bank documents.'

On New Year's Eve 1999, when everybody claimed the clocks would stop, computers would die and the Y2K bug would get us all, Esther departed Mascot Airport at one minute past midnight. She wanted to be the first pilot to see in the new decade. 'All the way from Sydney to Newcastle the fireworks appeared below us during breaks in the cloud. I flew across the top of them all and it was the most magnificent and beautiful flight I have ever done,' she says.

Two years after her near-tragedy in the Northern Territory, Esther had one last challenge in her career. She was flying into Sydney with nine passengers, on board a Chieftain. Coming over the Hunter region, the electric trim cable broke and the aeroplane could not be balanced. She requested that all the passengers move to the front of the aeroplane, including someone to sit in the co-pilot's seat. She landed safely at Bankstown, but the Civil Aviation Authority was quick to ground the airline. The ensuing media storm pointed to pilot error. Esther went into hiding for two months to avoid the media attention. She could not believe that, with all the bad luck she'd already had, this event was going to bring her undone. It looked like it would, though. She figured her career was over and doubted she'd ever fly again.

Then she had a phone call telling her that she was not to blame. The Chieftain that Esther had been flying was sold and the new owner had asked Jake Jansen, the avionics service manager at Adelaide's main airport, to rewire the plane and to complete or coordinate any other work that needed to be done.

When the Chieftain arrived, Jake found the cause of Esther's problem was the elevator trim system. Like many other things in the plane, it needed to be overhauled. The motors needed rewinding and the trim system, including the indicators, had to be reworked to operate as the Piper Aircraft Company had designed them to work. He was aghast that this aircraft had been flying charters.

'Esther appeared ecstatic', says Jake, 'because she'd finally found someone who believed and supported her story and knew the engineering facts about it. I reassured her that it was most definitely not her fault.'

When I interviewed her, Esther admitted that if she hadn't been given this feedback from Jake, she would probably never have got back into an aeroplane. It took six months before she was able to return to work and over the next three years she went back to bank runs and night freight, carted mine and railway workers around NSW, and opened a base for a bank run company in Queensland.

Occasionally she would hear a German woman over the radio, flying a NSW Air Ambulance King Air plane. It was reassuring to know that women were being employed in other parts of the industry (well one was, at least), and this strengthened Esther's resolve to continue her career with a move to the Royal Flying Doctor Service

(RFDS), a non-profit aeromedical organisation that provides primary health care and 24/7 emergency services to remote and regional parts of Australia.

As well as first aid training, the RFDS's minimum flying requirements were a whopping (for a young pilot) 2500 hours flying experience, with 500 of those hours to be at night. This was far more than was required even to be an airline pilot (500 hours in command and 300 hours twin engine flying). Most RFDS pilots, however, have far more experience than their organisation's minimum requirements.

In 2005 Esther decided that if she didn't get a job flying with the Flying Doctors, she would go back to university and become a vet. It's always good to have a backup plan. She received a rejection letter from RFDS Western Australia and was put on the hold file for the South Eastern Section. But when the new chief pilot at RFDS Central Operations (South Australia and Northern Territory) went through all the pilot applications on file, Esther, who was 'on a charter out in woop-woop' got a call:

> I was still living on a tight budget and so I had to borrow money from a friend to buy the air ticket to Adelaide for the interview. In Adelaide, I faced two men and a woman for a casual interview. They liked that I had 5000 hours in my logbook and particularly liked that 2000 of them were at night. RFDS does a lot of night flying. I got the job. And for the first time in my flying life I had a full-time wage.

Esther arrived in Adelaide and stayed at a city hotel on company expense. She stood in the elevator next to a well-dressed man in a suit. In her excitement, she wanted to talk to someone; anyone! He told her he was in Adelaide on 'business'. It turned out it was the same business as Esther, and she and Greg became firm friends, beginning with the initial two-week training course. Esther says, 'That first course was focused entirely on flying the RFDS Pilatus PC-12 aircraft. I studied until midnight and was back into it by 6 am.'

From Adelaide the class moved to Port Augusta, 300 kilometres north, for practical training. The first thing she noticed was the huge amount of right rudder required on departure to keep the aeroplane straight. The single engine turbine has a strong corkscrew effect that needs plenty of oomph to keep it on track.

Their training took them to a few different airstrips on short trips so that by the end of the time, she was well used to the procedures and all the radio calls. On her first day of flying as an RFDS pilot, she flew to Whyalla, Adelaide, Port Lincoln, Cleve, Whyalla, Port Pirie, Adelaide and back to Port Augusta. She did four flights under supervision to learn the stretcher loading system, how to ensure passengers and patients are secured and to really get a good handle on the aeroplane.

The new job did not disappoint. 'The first time you take off alone is like doing your first solo again,' says Esther. 'There is a great feeling of excitement, pride and freedom. I couldn't believe I was really doing this!'

She stayed on in Port Augusta for about 14 years, where for the first few years she flew a couple of hundred hours per year (about six or seven hours per week). This had increased four-fold by the time she left. She was the first woman pilot to be employed by Central Operations and she was always proud to pull on her uniform and be part of the team. In January 2006 she bought her first house and Port Augusta became home.

As her first year unfolded, Esther rolled with the surprises and learnt lessons that are unique to flying with the RFDS. In 14 years, there was never a baby born on her flight, but she will never forget two consecutive nights when she was new and impressionable.

During a short stint based in Adelaide a nurse and doctor boarded along with a Mansell unit. The Mansell Infant Retrieval System was designed in Queensland and is used to transport premature or critically ill babies in ambulances, helicopters or aeroplanes. Esther was told they were collecting a newborn baby whose vital signs had gone 'flat' after birth.

At the destination, they faced the distressing sight of devastated parents and their perfect tiny intubated infant. After eight hours trying to stabilise the baby in the hospital where it was born, they transferred to Adelaide. With blind faith, Esther never doubted the little baby would survive. She was extremely upset to learn the next day that it hadn't.

Before Esther had time to process the event, the aeroplane was out again the next night to collect another mother and baby. Esther says, 'The mother was in no fit state for parenting and didn't even want to accompany the baby. Amazingly, the child survived and the balance of life was brought into sharp focus for me that night. It really woke me up. I was so upset by the whole series of events; both for the children and for their parents.'

Esther's medical initiation came shortly afterwards, when she was called to a car accident out bush. She and the flight nurse were met at the airstrip where they landed and were driven to the accident scene. As the nurse took stock of the situation, she tasked Esther to get hands-on and cut the patient's trousers up his leg from the bottom hem so she could assess his injuries. 'It was the first real bush job I'd had and I felt useful then. We put the guy on a stretcher and loaded him into the back of a ute and drove the ten or fifteen minutes back to the aeroplane.'

One of the tasks required of the RFDS pilots is to be able to land on remote properties at day and especially at night. At one-and-half-million-hectares, Clifton Hills Station in the far north-east corner of South Australia is one of the largest rural properties in the world. It is 200 kilometres south of Birdsville in spinifex and saltbush country. On an ink-black night, it was easy to find using the aircraft's advanced flight navigation program; however, the night was so dark that landing by flares Esther couldn't see the actual strip until she was almost on top of it.

Recalling that night, she says, 'I was up at 24 000 feet and it was pitch black. At the top of descent there was no cloud and no lights as far as I could see. No horizon either. All I could see was a line of lights on my instrument panel.'

With no visual cues, she followed her instruments down to 1500 feet and at four kilometres out she spotted the parallel rows of flares. As she approached the airstrip, guided by her instruments and the flares, all her senses were alive:

> Your adrenaline is going flat out and you are really on alert during this type of flight because there's so much that can go wrong. It was the best short-field landing I've ever done because there was so much riding on it and everything had to be 100 per cent accurate. There is no room for a mistake. I don't know what the retrieval was about but I'll never forget that landing. If you don't do it perfectly, it will not have a perfect outcome.

The next night landing etched in her mind was at a small settlement near the Flinders Ranges in South Australia. A tradesman had been badly burned and required immediate evacuation, which in turn required a night landing on a bitumen strip, lit with flares. Being so close to the hills in a massive cross-wind made her draw on all her skills to bring the aeroplane in and out safely.

But her admiration was reserved for the bush people on-site who managed to put the patient into a bath with water to cool the burning, call the RFDS and then organise to have lights at the airstrip.

> After landing, I opened the door and got the stretcher out. Out of the darkness, all I could see was this poor man with burns

to about 70 per cent of his body, walking towards me in his underpants. The pain was so intense that he'd stop every few steps and throw up. I couldn't imagine how much pain he must have been in. We covered him in Glad Wrap, which is your best friend [in burns situations like this] because it prevents infection from entering through the open wounds.

Due to his condition, it wasn't feasible to strap the patient down and so Esther allowed him to fly partly unrestrained. These decisions have to be made thinking on your feet and calculating the risks. Pilots tread a fine line sometimes by knowing about the patient's condition because it can then play into their operational decisions, while their job is to focus on the safety and efficiency of the aeroplane. There have been many occasions though, when Esther has requested air traffic control to divert her around the Adelaide Hills to avoid their turbulence for the sake of patient comfort or care.

In 2010 Esther had moved 40 kilometres north of Port Augusta to live with her then partner in the small town of Quorn. When she fell pregnant, she was surprised to find that she was having twins. The girls arrived safely and the all-encompassing love she felt for them took her by surprise. 'I was totally unprepared for how much I would adore being at home with my babies!' she says. 'I just l-o-v-e-d it.' The relationship with their father was short-lived. The best thing he did for her though was urge her to return to flying because it was her first love.

The following year she was back at work and living back in Port Augusta. With no family support nearby, she relied on child care, babysitters and, in an emergency, a few good friends. It was tough and the level of commitment that the RFDS work demands, with night shifts and call-outs, didn't do much to ease her work–life balance. However, there was no more worthy job to be had, not that she could see anyway. She fully expected to be in that role until she retired.

Soon after returning from maternity leave, Esther had to fly out bush again to collect a heavily pregnant mother. The nurse pulled Esther aside and confided, 'I just want to warn you not to say you have twins. This lady has just heard that hers have not survived.'

The doctor was unable to detect a heartbeat and diagnosed the disaster; however, both Esther and the nurse listened through the monitor and reckoned they could hear at least one beating heart. On the way to Adelaide they excitedly shared the hopeful news with each other through the security of their headsets. A month or so later, a letter from the parents shared the happy news: healthy twins.

Flying with the RFDS wasn't all night flights to bush emergencies though. Esther enjoyed the routine of piloting doctors on their rotating roster of clinic rounds. One week it would be a general practitioner, the next the podiatrist and the following week could be speech pathology or any other service from the allied health network going to small and remote hospitals.

ESTHER ENJOYED RAISING HER GIRLS TO BE PART OF THE RFDS family. When she flew the medical team to do general health checks one year at the Oodnadatta races, the girls came too. They enjoyed sharing their knowledge and one became rather adept at demonstrating blood sugar level testing, which requires the patient to monitor their own levels using a pin-prick test at home. Her daughter's technique improved as time went on. Luckily enough, the 'patients' were tough bushies, well able to handle the young student's early learnings.

The girls had long been making bracelets for their mum to give to any young patients who might appreciate them. When she collected a little girl who was in a critical condition, Esther comforted her by allowing her mother to nurse her on the flight and passing on a special bracelet when she was being loaded onto the aeroplane. It was a small gesture that had a small result, but it was good for the twins to know that they could do small things to help.

IN 2016 CENTRAL OPERATIONS BOUGHT A NEW PILATUS PC-12, the type of aircraft used for RFDS flights, and it was Esther's exciting task to fly it back to Australia from the Pilatus factory at Buochs airstrip, near Lucerne in Switzerland. The Swiss Alps are majestic and the mountains around Lucerne rise to over 1800 metres. 'Seeing the Pilatus factory was amazing. It is immaculate and runs like Swiss clockwork,' she says.

The first task was to take an 'acceptance flight' with a Pilatus test pilot, who would demonstrate the new aircraft, and another Pilatus company pilot, Gary, who was to accompany her back to Australia in the plane. For the acceptance flight, Esther sat in the third seat. Then the next day she and Gary departed on the first short leg of their trip, stopping in Crete: 'We had to take off over the lake towards the mountains. We aren't used to that type of terrain. They are impressive mountains! I flew the first, short leg, which took us along the magnificent Yugoslavian coast and into Crete. I couldn't get over how busy the European skies are!'

On the way, they stopped at Hurguada on the Sinai Peninsula to refuel. The previous year there had been a number of bombing attacks on the local resort, with 88 people killed and 200 more injured. Security was tight and when Esther asked to use the bathroom, she was escorted by half a dozen guards into the bombed-out disused old terminal, passed through a metal detector, then went through the same steps in reverse to get back to her aeroplane.

'It was a whole new experience again!' says Esther, who then debriefed over dinner with her father in Dubai the following evening. The flight continued through to New Delhi, which was memorable for the amount of smoke in the air and required the use of an instrument approach into the airport.

The next day they flew out of the city, this time in beautiful flying weather. Though Gary had done this trip many times before, he had never seen Mount Everest so clearly. Flying at 29 000 feet, they looked out at the Himalayas splayed out across the horizon, with Everest just poking up its head at around the same altitude that they were flying. In Chiang Mai in Thailand, they spent a fantastic day at an elephant sanctuary, a dream come true for the animal-loving pilot; and from there they flew through Kuala Lumpur in Malaysia and Lombok in Indonesia.

The first stop on Australian soil was at the RFDS hangar in Broome on the northern part of the West Australian coast, and welcome drinks with the other pilots. And finally, to Adelaide where, 'When I arrived, it was amazing to see my girls there to welcome me home.'

'I ALWAYS SAID I'D NEVER LEAVE THE RFDS UNTIL THERE WAS a baby born onboard; I wanted to add to the number of POB (people on board) en route. The nurses said to me, "That is the worst thing you could hope for," and they were right.'

The challenges of childbirth were again brought into the spotlight when a birthing mother was transferred to Adelaide. On the stretcher, the patient's condition became critical and the situation was dire.

> There was so much blood and I called out that we needed help now! When we got to the hospital, they ran in with the trolley and the baby was born soon after. We called the next day to see how they fared and unfortunately the baby didn't make it. That's the thing with this job. You never really know how the

shift will end and after living and working out here for so long, you will inevitably know and love people who may become your patients.

I loved the variety of the work and one night when I set off on a route check I expected to be home by 11 pm. At 9.30 pm we got a Priority 1 (life and death) call and had to transport a patient to Sydney. I got home at 5.00 the next morning.

Esther has faced a few hurdles as a woman pilot; some related to physical strength and some related to chauvinistic attitudes. And some people just hadn't had enough exposure to flying with women. Esther was the first female pilot in RFDS Central Operations. Another was there for six months in 2008 but she went on to work for the airlines. In 2018 they hired another woman in Alice Springs and one in Adelaide. Sometimes the patients are just troublesome:

Dementia patients can be challenging, but I noticed an increase in the amount of patients with drug-related psychosis. I'm a bit too old-fashioned for that sort of activity and the results of it were dangerous and frightening. There were times that I refused to carry someone who was abusive or out of control because they only sit a few feet behind me in the plane.

One guy was high on ice and smashing up the whole airport room. Seven police officers could not control him. Mental Health patients need a specially trained ambulance officer to accompany the flight nurse and if they are a real threat, they travel enclosed within a net so as not to disrupt aeroplane operations, such as trying to open the emergency exit.

I've had some pretty intense moments: I've had people have a heart attack and nurses call from the back of the aeroplane, 'Get us on the ground as soon as possible,' while I'm negotiating turbulence and flight traffic issues.

But working for the RFDS brings an enormous amount of respect and admiration from those who rely on it. Esther was and still is exceptionally proud of her position within the team, even though it came with some occasional misdirected abuse.

> I flew to a remote airstrip up in the Riverland [the region of South Australia along the Murray River, near the NSW and Victorian borders]. When we landed, we found a middle-aged farmer who had been mauled by a bull. His pain was overwhelming and he was extremely distressed. His eyes flicked around and he said, 'Where's the pilot?' I said, 'I'm here.' Well … then he let fly with, 'You look too young! I'm not flying with a girl!'

The nurse tended to the farmer's wounds and dispensed morphine. As the pain settled, so did the farmer, who saw the world in a new and rather rosy light. 'By the time we landed in Adelaide', says Esther, laughing, 'he wanted to marry me!'

EVENTUALLY THE GUILT ABOUT LEAVING HER CHILDREN, who were then eight-year-olds, won out. She was just away from home too much. Esther took long service leave and spent a couple of months on time-out: touring Europe, visiting family and showing her girls another side of life.

She returned to work at the RFDS and was based in Adelaide, thinking this would suit the family life better. After a year though, it became clear that while the job was still interesting, the kids still spent unpredictable and extended periods in the care of child minders. 'All I felt was guilt,' she says.

When a job came up with charter operator Alliance Airways, flying out of Adelaide, a friend encouraged her to apply for it. She was offered the job and now, for the first time in 25 years, she has another pilot for company in the cockpit. The new life suits her and aligns with family time and responsibilities. She flies regular runs with almost no weekend or on-call work. It is the most balanced her family life has ever been.

Andy Killcross, one of the doctors who has flown with Esther, has always been struck by what a determined, impressive and strong woman she is.

'She came to Port Augusta on her own,' he says. 'Into quite a male-dominated world. She's almost single-handedly raised the beautiful girls while working crazy shifts in unusual places. It's good to see her enjoying the simplicity of life now. I always enjoyed flying with her. There were never any worries.'

Esther believes that once you've got aviation flowing through your veins, it's important to follow that dream. 'It has to be your first love,' she says. 'It's not something to be taken on lightly.'

Even though her life is at a much slower pace now than during those exciting times with the RFDS, she still loves going to work every day and claims that the view out the cockpit window is the best office view going.

SOURCES

1 NANCY BIRD WALTON

AWPA Newsletter, various issues.
Huxley, John, 2009, 'Soaring words celebrate Nancy-Bird's life', *Sydney Morning Herald*, 22 Jan.
Mackersey, Ian, 1998, *Smithy: The life of Sir Charles Kingsford-Smith*, London: Little, Brown & Co.
Mascarenhas, Carla, 2019, 'Locals rejoice at Sydney's second airport to be named after Nancy-Bird Walton from Kew', *Port Macquarie News*, 8 March.
Walton, Nancy Bird, 1961, *Born to Fly*, Sydney: Angus and Robertson.
Walton, Nancy Bird, 2002, *My God! it's a Woman: The inspiring story of one woman's courage and determination to fly*, Sydney: HarperCollins.
Watson, Janine, 2018, 'Nancy Bird-Walton: What's in a name', *Camden Courier*, 28 March, <www.camdencourier.com.au/story/4557110/brave-pioneer-leaves-lasting-legacy/>.
Ian Debenham, interview with author 2016.
Anna Holman, interview with author 2016.
Jenny Houghton, interview with author 2016.
Senja Robey, interview with author 2016.
Dick Smith, interview with author 2016.
Margy Sullivan, interview with author 2016.
John Walton, interview with author 2016.

2 MARDI GETHING

Air Transport Auxiliary, website, <www.airtransportaux.com>.
Air Transport Auxiliary, Royal Air Force Museum website, <www.rafmuseum.org.uk/research/online-exhibitions/air-transport-auxiliary.aspx>. Ellis, Mary, 2016 (reprint edition), *A Spitfire Girl: One of the World's Greatest Female ATA Ferry Pilots Tells Her Story*, UK: Frontline Books.
BBC4 Documentary, *Spitfire Sisters*, <www.youtube.com/watch?v=M-xjUqiqVq0>.
Forces TV, 2017, 'The Extraordinary Woman Who Flew Spitfires in WW2', <www.youtube.com/watch?v=7I8o0C2EYu8>.
'A Special Correspondent', 1945, 'G for George Signs Off', *The Argus*, 28 April, <https://trove.nla.gov.au/newspaper/article/1105767?browse=ndp%3Abrowse%2Ftitle%2FA%2Ftitle%2F13%2F1945%2F04%2F28%2Fpage%2F30668%2Farticle%2F1105767>.
Australian National Maritime Museum, 'A comparison of vessels and journey times to Australia between 1788 and 1900', <www.anmm.gov.au/Learn/Library-and-Research/Research-Guides/Passenger-Ships-to-Australia-A-Comparison-of-Vessels-and-Journey-Time>.

SOURCES

Flight Global, 2011, *Women in Aviation: Molly Rose ATA ferry pilot of Spitfire aircraft*, <www.youtube.com/watch?v=UkBnHri8oHE>.
Gething, Mardi, 1944, 'A Ferry Pilot's Story', *The West Australian*, 26 December.
Gething, Mary-Jane, 2018, 'Mardi Gething – WWII ferry pilot', *Airnews*, No. 261, March, pp. 7–10.
Moggridge, Jackie, 1957, *Woman Pilot*, London: Michael Joseph.
Rush, Elva, 2000, *Up Above Down Under: Stories of Australian women in aviation*, Mansfield, Vic: E. Rush.
Shock, James R, 2012, *The U.S. Army Barrage Balloon Program*, Createspace Independent Publishing Platform.
Whittell, Giles, 2007, *Spitfire Women of World War II*, UK: HarperCollins Publishers.
The London Gazette, 1939, 'Air Force Medal', *The London Gazette,* 28 April, <www.thegazette.co.uk/London/issue/34620/page/2830>.
Mary-Jane Gething, interviews with author 2017–20.
Elva Rush, interviews with author 2017–20.

3 PATRICIA TOOLE

'Bobby Gibbes', 1980, *This is your Life* TV program.
Inscription by Bobby Gibbes in *You Live But Once* by Bobby Gibbes.
Gibbes, Bobby, 1994, *You Live But Once,* Wing Commander Robert H Gibbes DSO DFC & Bar.
Patricia Toole's diary.
Author unknown, 1999, 'Three Musketeers Reunite', *Newcastle Post*, February.
Burns Glen, Joyce, 1954, 'Piloting planes in New Guinea brings adventure to youthful housewife', *The Christian Science Monitor*, February 2.
Smith, Phil, 1999, 'Pilot Pat', *Paradise* (Air Niugini inflight magazine), no. 133, May–June.
Walton, Nancy Bird, 2002, *My God! It's a Woman: The inspiring story of one woman's courage and determination to fly*, Sydney: HarperCollins.
White, Osmar, 1953, 'She's a Bush Pilot', *The Courier Mail*, 5 September (Trove).
Angela Stevenson, Cathy Salvair, Annie Haynes, interviews with author 2016–20.
Patricia Toole, interview with author 2016.
John, Danny and Kathryn Toole, Ann Munro, interviews with author 2016–20.

4 GABY KENNARD

AAP, 1989, 'Pilot Stranded by Cyclone', *Canberra Times*, 17 September.
Earthrounders.com, Flights by single-engine aircraft, <www.earthrounders.com/singles.php>.
Gaby Kennard Solo Flight, <www.youtube.com/watch?v=z4_XbtW8OEo>.
Gregory, Denis, 2014, *The Hazelton Story: From an Auster to an Airline*, Saso Content & Design Pty Ltd.
Kennard, Gaby, 1990, *Solo Woman: Gaby Kennard's world flight*, Bantam Books.
Long, Elgen M and Long, Marie K, 2009, *Amelia Earhart: The Mystery Solved*, Simon & Schuster.
The Arab News, 14 May 2016.
Unnamed author, 1989, 'Flight was something special, on reflection', *Canberra Times*, 22 November.

Unnamed author, 1989, 'Gaby a "wreck" as she flies home', *Canberra Times*, 5 November.
Evelaine Berry, interview with author 2017.
Ryan Campbell, interview with author 2017.
Les Haywood (ret. Qantas captain), interview with author 2017.
Gaby Kennard, interviews with author 2017–20.
Mimi Heman, interview with author 2017.

5   MARION McCALL
Story on Marion McCall, 1993, *60 Minutes*.
Bishop's Pilot: Marion McCall, <www.youtube.com/watch?v=FQsRZ-y1fr4>.
Rev. Trevor Briggs, interview with author 2017.
Brian Condon, Interview with author 2017.
Elizabeth McCall, interview with author 2017.
Marion McCall, interviews with author 2017–20.
Barb Parish, interview with author 2017.
Thelma Pye, interview with author 2017.
Susan Ward, interview with author 2017.

6   LYN GRAY
Clamback and Hennessy at learntofly.com.au (no longer available).
Fly Oz, Flight training specialists, Cowra NSW, website, <www.flyoz.com.au>.
Lyn Gray, Personal Diary.
Jopson, Debra, 2006, 'Flying lesson, faulty planes can't swim', *Sydney Morning Herald*, 12 June.Jopson, Debra, 2006, 'Plucky pair survive after ditching plane', *The Age*, 13 June.
Leone, Diana, 2006 'Planes safe ditching was team effort', *The Star Bulletin* (Hawaii), 11 June 11, <archives.starbulletin.com/2006/06/11/news/story01.html>.
Niles, Russ, 2006, 'Two survive Pacific ditching', Pacific Avweb, 11 June, <www.flash.avweb.com/briefs/two-survive-pacific-ditching/>.
Lagan, Bernard, 2006, 'Pacific pilots plucked from sea as their plane sinks', *The Times* (UK), 13 June, <www.thetimes.co.uk/article/pacific-pilots-plucked-from-sea-as-their-plane-sinks-hp0d0brw8xm>.
Tom Caska, interview with author 2018.
Ray Clamback, interview with author, 2018.
Lyn Gray, interviews with author 2017–20.
Ray Gray, interview with author 2017.
Aminta Hennessy, interview with author 2020.
Kristian Kauter, interview with author 2018.
Margy Sullivan, interview with author 2017.

7   DEBORAH LAWRIE (WARDLEY)
Dahn, Susanne, 1987, 'Wardley vs Ansett: An examination and analysis of a leading and influential equal opportunity case', Masters Thesis, University of Melbourne, <minerva-access.unimelb.edu.au/bitstream/handle/11343/35884/268400_Dahn%2c%20Susanne_Masters%20thesis.pdf?sequence=1&isAllowed=y>.
Kelsey-Sugg, Anna and Zajac, Bec, 2019, 'Ansett told Deborah Lawrie that women couldn't

be pilots. She fought them to make legal history', ABC News website, 19 June, <www.abc.net.au/news/2019-06-19/ansett-discrimination-history-australias-first-female-pilot/11207292>.
McKenna, Elaine and Lawrie, Deborah, 1992, *Letting Fly: Deborah Wardley, Australia's trail-blazing pilot*, Sydney: Allen & Unwin.
Paterson, Alex, 2008, 'A pilot's perspective of the Australian Pilots' Dispute of 1989' <www.vision.net.au/~apaterson/aviation/pd89_document.htm>.
Scutt, Jocelynne A, 2003, 'Without precedent: Sex/gender discrimination in the High Court', *Austlii (Australasian Legal Scholarship Library Journals)*, vol. 28, no. 2, April, <www.austlii.edu.au/au/journals/AltLawJl/2003/25.pdf>.
Smith, Belinda, 2008, 'From Wardley to Purvis: How far has Australian anti-discrimination law come in 30 years?' *Australian Journal of Labour Law*, vol. 21, p. 3.
Summers, Anne, 2007, 'Putting Equality Back On the Agenda, Seventh Victorian Human Rights Oration Zinc, Federation Square Melbourne', speech, 10 December, <www.legacy.annesummers.com.au/speeches/putting-equality-back-on-the-agenda/>.
Dorothy Barnes, interview with author 2018.
Bruce Dewar, interview with author 2018.
Deborah Lawrie, interviews with author 2018–20.
Ron Neve, interviews with author 2018–20.

8 GEORGIA MAXWELL
Budd, Henry, 2013, 'Georgia, an angel of the skies' *Daily Telegraph*, 20 January 20.
Cotton Research and Development Corporation (CRDC), 2014, Australian Grown Cotton Sustainability Report <www.crdc.com.au/publications/australian-grown-cotton-sustainability-report>.
NSW RFS, 2012, *Bush Fire Bulletin*, vol. 33, no. 03.
McLeod, SA, 2009, 'Short Term Memory', *Simply Psychology*, <www.simplypsychology.org/short-term-memory.html>.
Rolland, Derrick, 1996, *Aerial Agriculture in Australia*, Aerial Agricultural Association of Australia Ltd.
Georgia Maxwell, interviews with author 2017–20.
Phil Hurst, Aerial Application Association of Australia, interview with author 2020.
Paul Knight, interview with author 2020.
Lee Maxwell, interview with author 2015.
Ross Pay, interviews with author 2015, 2020.
Patricia Wall, interview with author 2017.

9 NICOLE FORRESTER
Morley, Peter, 2008, 'High flying females to fill gap in pilot market', *Herald Sun*, 11 March 11.
Hurren, Clarice, 2020, 'Women take charge', *Defence News*, 10 March.
Civil Aviation Safety Authority, 2015, *Sector Risk Profile for the Aerial Mustering Sector*, <www.casa.gov.au/sites/g/files/net351/f/Sector_Risk_Profile_%20aerial_mustering_sector.pdf>.
Australian Transport Safety Bureau, 2013, *Aviation Occurrence Statistics 2003 to 2012*, <www.atsb.gov.au/media/4355945/ar-2013-067_final.pdf>.

Central Station Blog, <www.centralstation.net.au>.
Youtube video, F111 River Fire Dump and Burn Runs over Brisbane, <www.youtube.com/watch?v=gF5CMjVeTUI>.
Outback Publishing, 2011, *Outback,* issue 77, 26 May.
Neva Cavenagh, interview with author 2017.
Betty Kenny, interview with author 2017.
Nicole Forrester, interviews with author 2017–20.
Tony Pratt, interview with author 2017.
Roger Simpson, interview with author 2017.
Phil Unicomb, interview with author 2017.

10 ESTHER VELDSTRA

ABC Radio, 'Yanda grounded', *PM* (transcript of program), <www.abc.net.au/pm/stories/s241568.htm>.
Australian Transport Safety Bureau, Investigation no. 199804715, <www.atsb.gov.au/publications/investigation_reports/1998/aair/aair199804715/>.
James, Matthew, 2006, Parliament of Australia, Aviation Safety Regulation Chronology 1982–2004, August, <www.aph.gov.au/About_Parliament/Parliamentary_Departments/Parliamentary_Library/Publications_Archive/online/Aviation>.
Thomas, Ian, 1994, 'CAA Grounds Another NSW Airline', *Australian Financial Review,* 2 November.
Esther Veldstra, interview with author 2020.
Michael Bourke, interview with author 2020.
Andy Killcross, interview with author 2020.
Jake Jansen, interview with author 2020.
Anna Wakelin, interview with author 2020.

A NOTE ON THE ILLUSTRATIONS

NANCY BIRD WALTON – DE HAVILLAND GIPSY MOTH

The de Havilland DH-60 Gipsy Moth was the precursor to the legendary de Havilland Tiger Moth. It first flew in 1925 in England and the affordable aircraft finally brought flying within reach for the general public. It became a staple at flying schools and was used by early pioneers such as Amy Johnson and Francis Chichester. The RAAF used them for training before and during World War II. The oldest airworthy aircraft on the Australian register, VH-UAE, is a Gipsy Moth owned by David and Carolyn Salter from Walcha, New South Wales. It first flew in Australia in November 1925 and is one of about half a dozen still flying here today.

MARDI GETHING – SPITFIRE

The Supermarine Spitfire was designed in England as a fighter during World War II. Its elliptical (rounded) wings were able to carry (in one configuration) four 20 mm cannon or two 20 mm cannon and four machine guns. It's thought that 240 remain around the world. Only 60 are airworthy with a few more than that on static displays. There are currently three flying Spitfires in Australia, two at Temora Aviation Museum and one based privately at Archerfield in Brisbane.

PAT TOOLE – AUSTER

The Taylorcraft Auster was used during World War II as a military liaison and observation aircraft. The Auster has two front seats and a single bench seat in the rear. Its low wing loading makes it suitable for short field operations. The back seat can be removed to make room for extra freight-carrying capacity. There are currently 133 Austers registered in Australia.

GABY KENNARD – SARATOGA

The Piper Saratoga is a six-seat aeroplane with one engine. It is all metal and was made at the Piper Aircraft factory at Vero Beach, Florida. It has a retractable undercarriage, adding to its aerodynamics. It was mostly used as a personal aeroplane, or for freight runs. For Gaby's flight, she had the rear seats removed to store fuel tanks.

MARION McCALL – CESSNA 172

The Cessna 172 has stood the test of time. It was first built in 1955 and is still made by the Cessna Aircraft Company in America. The 172 is deemed by some to be the most successful aircraft ever designed due its popularity. It is cheap to operate, has a comfortable cabin, is nice to fly and has the stability required of a basic training aeroplane. It is the flying equivalent of a family sedan. There are currently 1110 C172s registered in Australia.

LYN GRAY – SEMINOLE
The Seminole was made as a four-seat twin-engine training aircraft by Piper. It was produced between 1979–82, then 1989–90 and again since 1995. The Seminole is not quite as big as Gaby Kennard's Saratoga, but with the smaller frame and extra engine, cruises about 10 km/h faster. Around 67 Seminoles are currently registered in Australia.

DEBORAH LAWRIE (WARDLEY) – BOEING 727
The Boeing 727 was designed for shorter field lengths than its B-707 predecessor. First launched in 1960, it had three early model jet engines and rear retractable stairs as it was designed to fly to airports where ground services were not available. Ansett and TAA both operated the B-727. After Ansett's final passenger flight in 1997, they continued using them for a time as freighters. The B-727, when it was introduced, brought about a new era of speed and comfort for Australian domestic travellers.

GEORGIA MAXWELL – AT-802
The Air Tractor AT-802 is an agricultural aircraft made in Onley, Texas. It is used mainly for agricultural works and doubles as a firebomber. It has been flying since 1990 and carries a chemical hopper between the engine firewall and the cockpit. It can be fitted with amphibious floats, and can scoop water from lakes, rivers and reservoirs.

NICOLE FORRESTER – A330
Airbus A-330s are converted to a KC-30 for use by the RAAF to refuel fighter jets mid-air so they can fly longer and with a greater load. It requires both aircraft to travel at high speed in close proximity to each other. The RAAF operates five KC-30 from RAAF Base Amberley in South East Queensland.

ESTHER VELDSTRA – PC-12
Made by Swiss company Pilatus, the PC-12 can fly as high as 30,000 feet (domestic airliners fly 30 000–40 000 feet). It only requires one pilot at any time and has state-of-the-art navigation and flight aids. The cabin accommodates a flight nurse and sometimes a doctor or other necessary passengers. There are two stretcher beds that can be configured various ways. The pilot can access the cockpit via a front door without disturbing operations in the back.

ACKNOWLEDGEMENTS

Thanks to the people who have brought me to this point of publishing my first book. Firstly, to Matt Hall and Janet English who so generously lent their names and endorsements to this project. It is not taken lightly and I thank you for it. To my husband Denis, who by his own admission generally only reads textbooks. His technical knowledge and broad interest in aviation have enabled me access to a much more rounded engagement with my subjects. From the Gipsy Moth to the GA aircraft to an A330 he had or knew how to find the answers. Likewise from plotting flight plans to human factors, radios and survival gear, he either had or sought answers and was calm when I woke him to ask some obscure technical questions that were keeping me awake. Thanks also for allowing me the space to finish this book. It has coincided with lockdown, standown, redundancy and home-schooling, through which he stoked the crackling fires while I rewrote and proofread; physically present but annoyingly absent. Thanks to our children, Harrison, Amelia and Kate, none of whom ever asked me to write a book. I hope you all like it though. The girls have only ever known me as a writer and photographer. While I wrote this book, Amelia excelled with baking cookies and making the occasional meal. She willingly engaged with Lyn Gray's story. I did see her sneakily snap a photo of the Cactus story and send it to her friend with a giggle. And Kate, my great wing(wo)man. Thanks for being a wonderful travel companion when we visited Esther in Adelaide for three days.

To my three writing champions: Annabelle Brayley, Kristen Alexander and Helene Young. Through *Outback* magazine I made a friend in Annabelle Brayley who set me on the road to publication. It seemed like a good idea at the time, but we never imagined it would take seven years and an inordinate amount of words. She has weathered the storms and sunshine with me the whole way and I thank her for that.

Kristen Alexander, whose work and work ethic I admire greatly. She is always quick to offer support, guidance, a cool head and a warm heart. Her research skills and retention of detail constantly astonish me, as does her ability to bring her subjects to life so vividly.

Helene Young, a pilot and aviation novelist, like Annabelle and Kristen, has been a wonderful moral and practical support. She generously shared experiences and offered advice and introductions. There have been many laughs and a few tears over artistic struggles.

To Patsy and Gary Mexted for welcoming me into the family 28 years ago and continuing to support us in all that we do; particularly if it involves aeroplanes, escaping for a holiday or grandchildren. And to my sister-in-law Emily Mexted, and my sister and brother Fran and Brendan Whitty for being great sounding boards and enthusiastic followers of my progress. I regret that Mum and Dad aren't here to share this. Mum was an avid letter writer and for the two years I lived in Singapore, we wrote at least once a week. While Dad rarely put pen to the same paper, he was a great storyteller and that is something that I have come to appreciate: a good story, well told. It's harder than you think (I'm still working on it). They were both supportive of my flying endeavours and I think Mum would be happy to see that I've finally 'settled' on something I love so much in writing and photography.

With writing and photography there are the two Bruces to thank. The first writer I ever met was in Singapore. Australian Bruce Dover, the South-East Asian correspondent for the Melbourne *Herald*,

ACKNOWLEDGEMENTS

introduced me to the idea that you could write for a living. I was so jealous of his job. When I had my first story published locally, Bruce Hedge rang to talk about it and unwittingly became my photography mentor. In Finley I briefly knew Ian Day, the editor of the *Southern Riverina News* before his untimely death, and I enjoyed our chats about news and photography.

It's important to know that words can have an effect to somebody starting out. Victoria Carey, editor of *Australian Country Style* magazine kindly chatted and said 'Go and do a course.' Susanna Bryceson, on my first day of the Professional Writing & Editing course I took said, 'Writing is a skill to be valued as it's not something that everybody can do.' People in the arts world were encouraging and so I gravitated towards them, beginning with Carolyn Salter, who advised me to contact *Outback* magazine.

Mark Muller, the editor at *Outback* magazine, was generous in welcoming me as a newbie and I thoroughly enjoy writing and photographing stories for them. Mark's associate editor, Terri Cowley, has been a great professional role model. It was only natural that I would begin writing about aviation. Brian Bigg as editor of *Australian Pilot* magazine said, 'You can write, you can fly and you can take photos. You're perfect for the job.' It seemed I was making a simple thing hard. Kreisha Ballantyne and designer Melinda Vassallo came after him and we had great fun as the all-girl team. There was plenty of encouragement as I wrote and rewrote seemingly endless drafts of various versions of this book, and at the same time Mel finally published her second book on street art and Kree got started on a memoir.

Shelley Ross, Steve Hitchen, James Kightly and Rob Fox were also supportive and approachable in the aviation magazine world. James's wife Bev Laing has also provided sound advice, including a line I often recall: 'If you're going to be a writer, it's a good idea to be married to someone who thinks it's a good idea that you're a writer.' Never a truer sentence was spoken.

Back in the beginning, there was also Sue Peacock, who I met at a cocktail party. When she said she was a journalist, I grabbed her with both hands and she guided me through those early days. Her best advice? Don't be too precious and don't be scared. She also breezily shared the basics of a magazine article: Active introduction, back story, current story, conclusion. You will see the extended version of that formula throughout much of this book.

Now, to the book. Thank you to: Andrea McNamara who helped pioneer the project. To my publisher Phillipa McGuinness who I met at a literary event. Even as I signed the NewSouth Books contract on Christmas Day 2019, I couldn't quite believe it would happen. To the team at NewSouth Books for their patience, professionalism and cheering: editor Fiona Sim, project editor Sophia Oravecz, designer Jo Pajor-Markus, publicist Caitlin Lawless and publisher Elspeth Menzies.

To the people who helped me with the stories and research: Anna Holman; Dick Smith; John Walton; Senja Robey; Margy Sullivan; Jenny Houghton; Judy Rainsford for her eagle eye in proofing Nancy's story; to David and Carolyn Salter for sending photos and dimensions of the Gipsy Moth luggage compartment and checking facts; the State Library of NSW; Mary-Jane Gething who I thank for sharing unpublished and published information about her mother's life with me and reviewing drafts of her story; Elva Rush for her peptalks; Frank Deeth for his general aviation knowledge and WWII Spitfire knowledge in particular, and his continued good humour in offering to read the same story in many rewritten forms. Huge thanks also to Andy Wright of Aircrew Book Review for jumping in with a technical read through at the last minute. To the ATA Museum in London; to *Airnews* editors Delia Jones and Bronni Bowen; and to John and Danny Toole (Pat's sons), and Danny's wife Kathy and their sister Margaret, who generously shared their mother's papers with me and reviewed her story. To John Stokes and Ann Munro;

ACKNOWLEDGEMENTS

to Jock MacGregor's children Will and Catriona, it was so lovely to find you. I was in love with the idea of Jock MacGregor emerging, rain-sodden, from the deep jungle with a swinging hurricane lamp. From the second I heard Pat utter the words 'Jock, would you like a rum?' I instantly saw a film.

To Jan Goodhew who I found at the last minute and who, together with her husband Peter, shared Wewak flying knowledge and pulled out their PNG WAC charts, found important landmarks such as the Keang River, the Torricelli Mountains and explained why it was always called 'gloomy' Lumi. To Gaby Kennard for generously sharing her story with yet another journalist. It is a privilege to know you. To David Warburton who paid for dinner the night we all jumped onboard in Sydney. To Gaby's daughter Mimi. To Ron and Evelaine Berry for sharing their memories and photos. To Marion and David McCall for hosting me in Adelaide and for their diligence in checking over my words and interpretations. To Kreisha Ballantyne who said, 'Why don't you interview Lyn Gray?' What a gift that was, because hers is one of my favourite stories in the book. A special thanks to Lyn's husband Ray Gray and to co-pilot Kristian Kauter and to Tom Caska, Ray Clamback and Aminta Hennessy for generously diving back into their experiences, thus enabling a well-rounded version of events.

To Deborah Lawrie who willingly agreed to speak to someone she'd never heard of. I was so nervous going to meet this legend and yet she greeted me warmly, with a bright smile and a glass of red wine. The next time we met, she was clutching the manuscript and said with a twinkle in her eye, 'I don't want to give it back!' Deb's mother Dorothy was a great source of information and a delight. Thanks for having me for such a lovely afternoon, Dorothy. I will definitely speak at your bowling club if Melbourne ever comes out of lockdown! And to ex-Ansett Captain Ron Neve who enthusiastically provided a review and showed me his whole shelf of books on women pilots.

To our long-time neighbour and good friend Ansett Captain Bruce Dewar who sadly passed away before the book was finished. Thanks to my mate, Julie Black, who is always up for an adventure and takes on a project like there's nothing to it. You nut out problems and help with solutions. Thanks for introducing me to Georgia Maxwell. I profiled Georgia for *Outback* magazine and when I approached her about the book, she thought for a minute and replied with, 'I'm happy to be a part of something that you are a part of.' We never imagined that she would end up on the cover, but as soon as I saw that photo by Nicola Gibson, I fell in love with it. Thanks to Nicola for allowing us to use it, and to Lee Maxwell, Trish Wall, Phil Hurst, Paul Knight and Ross Pay for helping with this story. When I told Georgia who else was in the book, she responded by saying nervously, 'Are you sure I belong in this book?' My best mate Suzi Wyatt read the manuscript and couldn't stop talking about Georgia, the way I couldn't stop talking about Pat Toole.

Nicole Forrester gave a funny speech at the Australian Women Pilots Conference in Bendigo and agreed to be included in the book. We did the interview with me sitting on a hotel bed with a laptop on my knee, while she balanced on the edge of a couch, carefully choosing her words. When I told her who else was in the book, she also said, 'Are you sure I belong in this book?' Yes, Nicole. You do! It was so refreshing to hear your self-deprecating story of trying to fit into outback life. A place that startled and then endeared you. I also thank her mother Betty Kenny for offering some valuable insights into Nicole's childhood that gave depth to the story. The same for her flying instructor Roger Simpson, low-level instructor ag pilot Tony Pratt, and aerobatics instructor Phil Unicomb. Thanks also to Neva Cavanagh for proofing an early draft. The fondness that the younger AWPA members have for Nicole was evident in Perth when she walked into the cocktail bar at the Perth conference and a cheer went up throughout the room. Everybody was smiling.

ACKNOWLEDGEMENTS

To Anna Wakelin for putting me in touch with Esther Veldstra, with whom I spent a few days in Adelaide. It took all of that and more to record and unravel her extreme story of survival. As soon as I heard it, I knew I had to start her story with the necklace and the watch sliding across the counter in Darwin. It's so General Aviation! Thanks to Michael Bourke and Andy Killross and to Alliance Airlines and the Royal Flying Doctor Service for supporting publication of this story. Also to Jake Jansen who so vividly recalls the details contained therein.

Other people who proofread, encouraged and cheered have been (in no particular order): some of the family – Geoff Whitty, Shauna Whitty, Madeleine Whitty, and particularly my youngest brother Damian Whitty with whom I enjoy sharing storytelling and writing ideas. Others to thank are Beth Stewart for generally being excited when 'book' is mentioned. Keith Rodger who so enthusiastically took time to read and discuss some of the stories. It meant an awful lot to me to be taken seriously as a story-teller. Owen Zupp, Jacqui Wood, John and Joy Williams, Haidee Wong, Dee White, Pete and Geri Walsh, Cate and Jon Thomas, Nola Pinnuck, Sue McLean, Fleur McDonald, Claire MacTaggart, Sarah Mexted, Sue Macklin, Therese Lynch, Linda Weeks, Abbie Place, Alice Martin, Kirsty Manning, Leongatha Lynne, Kristen Lowe, Sarah-Jane Leech, Jennifer Laird, Barb Jansen, Lisa James, Sarah Hope, Nadine Hartnett, Dr Alice Gorman, Kellie Flanagan, Michelle Fink, Mary Grimes, Carol Dehn, Mary Drendel, Jennifer Clarke, Ryan Campbell, Paul Carter, John and Josie Sanderson, Julie Skinner, Catherine Spencer, Col Patching, Evelyn Leckie, Elizabeth Kennedy, Nadine Hartnett, Michelle Day, Mia Cowling, Virginia Coster, Jenny Congdon, Cathie Cocker, David Bonnici, Joanne Bey, Linda Beilharz, Genevieve Barlow, Jennifer Bailey, Chery Austen, Bill Armstrong, Suki Allen. You've all encouraged, assisted or supported me in some important way. I'm sorry if I've possibly left anybody out!

Also important to mention are the local bookshops: New Leaves at Woodend, Red Door Books at Lancefield and Aesop's Attic in Kyneton.

Special thanks to the Finley bush telegraph – Ashley Haynes, Jenny Philpott and Bella Jackson – who managed to find me a computer charger when mine inadvertently went home to Victoria and I had two days to send in the edits of this book. A very special thanks to CC, who set my screensaver early on while I wasn't looking with, IGNORE EVERYBODY AND WRITE YOUR BOOK. And Judy McNamara, who continually asked, 'Have you finished the book?'

Hey Jude. I finished the book.

Thank you all.

www.ingramcontent.com/pod-product-compliance
Lightning Source LLC
Chambersburg PA
CBHW042224250426
43661CB00081BA/2898